EDUCATION IN ANCIENT ISRAEL

THE ANCHOR BIBLE REFERENCE LIBRARY is designed to be a third major component of the Anchor Bible group, which includes the Anchor Bible commentaries on the books of the Old Testament, the New Testament, and the Apocrypha, and the Anchor Bible Dictionary. While the Anchor Bible commentaries and the Anchor Bible Dictionary are structurally defined by their subject matter, the Anchor Bible Reference Library will serve as a supplement on the cutting edge of the most recent scholarship. The series is open-ended; its scope and reach are nothing less than the biblical world in its totality, and its methods and techniques the most up-to-date available or devisable. Separate volumes will deal with one or more of the following topics relating to the Bible: anthropology, archaeology, ecology, economy, geography, history, languages and literatures, philosophy, religion(s), theology.

As with the Anchor Bible commentaries and the Anchor Bible Dictionary, the philosophy underlying the Anchor Bible Reference Library finds expression in the following: the approach is scholarly, the perspective is balanced and fair-minded, the methods are scientific, and the goal is to inform and enlighten. Contributors are chosen on the basis of their scholarly skills and achievements, and they come from a variety of religious backgrounds and communities. The books in the Anchor Bible Reference Library are intended for the broadest possible readership, ranging from world-class scholars, whose qualifications match those of the authors, to general readers, who may not have special training or skill in studying the Bible but are as enthusiastic as any dedicated professional in expanding their knowledge of the Bible and its world.

David Noel Freedman
GENERAL EDITOR

THE ANCHOR BIBLE REFERENCE LIBRARY

EDUCATION IN ANCIENT ISRAEL:

Across the Deadening Silence

James L. Crenshaw

DOUBLEDAY

New York   London   Toronto   Sydney   Auckland

THE ANCHOR BIBLE REFERENCE LIBRARY
PUBLISHED BY DOUBLEDAY
a division of Bantam Doubleday Dell Publishing Group, Inc.
1540 Broadway, New York, New York 10036

THE ANCHOR BIBLE REFERENCE LIBRARY, DOUBLEDAY,
and the portrayal of an anchor with the letters ABRL
are trademarks of Doubleday,
a division of Bantam Doubleday Dell Publishing Group, Inc.

Book design by Oksana Kushnir

Library of Congress Cataloging-in-Publication Data

Crenshaw, James L.
Education in Ancient Israel: Across the Deadening Silence / James
L. Crenshaw. — 1st ed.
p.   cm. — (The Anchor Bible reference library)
Includes bibliographical references and index.
1. Jews—Education—History.   2. Jews—History—To 70 A.D.
I. Title.   II. Series.
LA47.C74   1998
370'.95694—dc21   97-33440
CIP

ISBN 0-385-46891-1
Copyright © 1998 by Doubleday, a division of
Bantam Doubleday Dell Publishing Group, Inc.

First Edition

1 3 5 7 9 10 8 6 4 2

To
Elizabeth and Emily

PREFACE

Communicating across generations, transmitting parental teaching to successive generations—that is what this book explores. It recognizes the gulf that frequently exists between representatives of the past—often, but not always, fathers and mothers who value the tried and true—and of the future—sons and daughters whose efforts to break free from all restraints lead them to question traditional claims. It seeks to understand the dynamics of this struggle for the mind and heart, asking such elementary questions as Where did instruction take place? Who did the teaching? How did these nameless individuals capture the minds of students? What written aids did the teachers assign? What kind of resistance did the youth offer? Why is a student's voice never heard?

The primary focus of the present study is the nature of knowledge being transmitted from one generation to the next, not the degree of literacy in Israel or the specific locations of educational institutions. Although I touch on these matters, I address other issues in more depth and seek answers of an entirely different kind. What interests me most is the epistemological problem: the manner in which learning took place, and the horizon of knowledge. To throw light on this significant issue, I examine the vocabulary for educational achievement in ancient Israel and the limits to knowledge as expressed in biblical and extrabiblical literature. In this investigation I concentrate on a group of texts identified by modern interpreters as wisdom literature.

Not all instruction in ancient Israel aimed at moral formation; much of it was purely vocational. Members of various guilds (potters, smiths, artisans, clothiers, jewelsmiths, metal workers, arrow makers, barbers, priests, diviners, magicians) passed along vital skills and well-guarded information to a younger generation. In this way scribes, among others, acquired the skills essential to their profession. Such education usually took place within the narrow confines of the family; the royal court was a notable exception. In this rarified atmosphere specialized scribes probably taught privileged young men the art of writing in the requisite languages and introduced them to the literary style appropriate for high office.

The evidence for education in ancient Israel is largely inferential. Not until the early second century B.C.E. does an extant text refer to a school, and at least one interpreter has understood that allusion in Sir. 51:23 to "my house of instruction" as a metaphor for the Book of Sirach. We are left therefore to speculation, largely through analogy with neighboring cultures, but also through surviving examples of writing, both official and otherwise, from biblical times.

This book is the product of more than thirty years of research in Israelite wisdom. It represents my attempt to understand the driving force that produced the Books of Proverbs, Job, Ecclesiastes, Sirach, and the Wisdom of Solomon. In that endeavor, I have learned much from others—teachers, colleagues, and students—in whose debt I shall always remain. Their views have challenged me to rethink many formulations of the problem and have often pointed the way to new insights. Like parents' and teachers' instructions long ago, words of these colleagues have reached me across the deadening silence of ideological differences.

A short version of Chapter Two was published in *Word & World* 7 (1987) 245–52; Chapter Four appeared in *Civilizations of the Ancient Near East*, vol. IV, 2445–2457; and Chapter Six appeared in a Festschrift for George Coats, entitled *A Biblical Itinerary*, Eugene E. Carpenter ed. JSOTSS 240 (Sheffield: Sheffield Academic Press, 1997), 133–43. Two other chapters were presented at professional meetings as plenary addresses: "Resistance to Learning," to the Catholic Biblical Association at a meeting in Los Angeles; "Probing the Unknown: Knowledge and the Sacred," at the AAR/SBL Upper Midwest meeting in St. Paul, Minnesota. Several others were presented at the Colloquium for Biblical Research; these include "Schools in Ancient Israel," "The Missing Voice," and "Language for Intellectual Achievement." "The Acquisition of Knowledge" was read to colleagues in Old Testament both in Cambridge and in Oxford during a sabbatical year. I thank the publishers of chapters two and four for permission to include these studies in the present work, and I am grateful for the many helpful suggestions that colleagues have made after hearing my formulation of various issues and answers.

Several specialists in wisdom literature have kindly shared offprints with me, especially Claudia Camp, Michael Fox, Avi Hurwitz, Norbert Lohfink, Roland Murphy, Carol Newsom, Leo Perdue, Antoon Schoors, Choon-Leong Seow, R. J. Williams, and Norman Whybray. In addition, Peter Machinist and Alan Millard generously supplied me with several offprints dealing with fate in Qoheleth and evidence for writing in the ancient Near East respectively. I am grateful to all of these individuals for their help in shaping the views expressed in this book.

Once again, I wish to thank David Noel Freedman for his extraordinary editing. From him I have learned more than I can express here. Again, too, Gail Chappell deserves the credit for turning my handwritten manuscript into an attractive form for submission to the publisher. I also thank David A. Mills for preparing the indices.

This book is dedicated to our granddaughters, Elizabeth and Emily, twins who at three years old bring more happiness into our lives than any of us deserves. At the same time, they remind us of the urgent need to communicate across the deadening silence.

CONTENTS

Preface   vii

Introduction   1

Chapter One: Literacy   29

Chapter Two: The Contemplative Life   51

Chapter Three: Schools in Ancient Israel   85

Chapter Four: The Acquisition of Knowledge   115

Chapter Five: Resistance to Learning   139

Chapter Six: The Missing Voice   187

Chapter Seven: Language for Intellectual Achievement   205

Chapter Eight: A Literary Canon   221

Chapter Nine: Knowledge as Human Discovery and
    as Divine Gift   239

Chapter Ten: Probing the Unknown: Knowledge
    and the Sacred   255

Conclusion   279

Abbreviations   285

Selected Bibliography   287

Index   291

EDUCATION IN ANCIENT ISRAEL

INTRODUCTION

~

"When the dead are quoted, their lips move."
BABYLONIAN TALMUD

In the Bible, education originated with the desire for order and continuity. To combat the powerful and seductive
lure of chaos in various forms, societal or personal, older
and more experienced individuals tried their best to prevent
the younger generation from falling into the pitfalls confronting them in the nooks and crannies of daily life. Parents personalized this struggle for survival, heightening
both the intimacy and passion. Whereas leaders within a
community raised their voices as a means of protecting the
general well-being, mothers and fathers sought to ensure
the integrity of the family.

The aim of this instruction was moral formation, the
building of character.[1] Having embodied the teachings

---

[1] William P. Brown, *Character in Crisis: A Fresh Approach to the Wisdom Literature of
the Old Testament* (Grand Rapids: William B. Eerdmans Publishing Company, 1996),
studies the community's role in shaping character and examines the depiction of character in Proverbs, Job, and Ecclesiastes. He also recognizes the importance of
worldview in determining moral values; to some readers, his assessment of the sages'
view of the world may be somewhat less skeptical than the texts warrant.

themselves, elders praised the virtues of self-control, restraint, eloquence, and honesty. The first of these acknowledged the enormous power of passion, whether expressing itself as fear, anxiety, anger, or lust. The second virtue, restraint, provided a necessary balance in a culture characterized by rhetorical excess. It lifted up modesty and reticence as timely conduct when the crowd was in danger of losing its perspective. The third, eloquence, indicated an awareness of the persuasive capacity of speech for good and evil. The fourth virtue guaranteed integrity, the tongue being used as a power for good in the communication of truth, especially in judicial settings.

Undergirding these virtues was religious devotion, a sense of awe and obligation directed toward the creator, who was thought to sustain the universe and to assure that good conduct was rewarded and that misdeeds were punished. Over time this conviction gave rise to serious soul-searching as obvious exceptions piled up, leading to skepticism and even outright attacks against the belief in divine justice.[2]

A cursory glance at the literature produced by the educative impulse in ancient Israel reveals a missing voice, that of the young people to whom the instruction is addressed. By their very nature, moral lessons are tedious, for they state the obvious. In addition, they intrude on the inner life,

---

[2] These two themes, theodicy and skepticism, lie at the center of my own research over three decades, as Walter Brueggemann discerned in his analysis of my contribution to the study of the Hebrew Bible ("James L. Crenshaw: Faith Lingering at the Edges," *RSR* 20 [1994] 103–10). Pertinent essays are reprinted in James L. Crenshaw, *Urgent Advice and Probing Questions: Collected Writings on Old Testament Wisdom* (Macon, GA: Mercer University Press, 1995).

where self-doubt lurks in dark corners, ready to pounce at the mere hint of uncertainty. The individuals who desire to discover for themselves what is good resist being told the things a previous generation considered right and proper. The overt appeal to paternal authority alienates teachers from students, encouraging resentment and silence. This atmosphere forces parents to raise their voices, increasing volume in the hope of reaching children across the abyss. Exhortations and warnings abound, alternatively pleading and threatening.

A comparison with ethical wills illumines the resulting situation.[3] In these late Jewish documents a father conveyed to his children the values he wished them to embody in their daily lives. He hoped to communicate with them beyond the grave, to achieve in death what he was unable to accomplish in life. No one likes to be silenced, and this reaching out to those left behind amounted to a bid for immortality. These documents reproduced only one side of the dialogue, that of the aged teacher. How youthful readers responded to these wills can only be conjectured.

It has been said that "The task of schools then, as now, was not so much to work out of human nature 'the ape and the tiger' as to expel the donkey."[4] That attitude, if present among Israel's teachers, would undoubtedly have exacer-

---

[3] Judah Goldin, *Studies in Midrash and Related Literature*, eds. Barry L. Eichler and Jeffrey H. Tigay (Philadelphia, New York, Jerusalem: The Jewish Publication Society, 1988) 187–97. The subtitle of the present book is borrowed from Goldin's comment that the writers of ethical wills "want to be heard across the deadening silence" (197), as is the caption at the head of the Introduction.

[4] John Paterson, *The Book That Is Alive* (New York: Scribners, 1954) 55, 63. This reference is taken from William Barclay, *Train Up a Child* (Philadelphia: Westminster, 1959).

bated any ill-will between representatives of the two generations, past and present. The harsh punishment associated
with formal instruction did not ease the situation.

From the resulting one-sided conversation, modern interpreters learn about the silent partner only indirectly, de-
ducing the facts relating to students from what the teacher
says. This procedure may easily skew the facts, primarily as
a result of oft-repeated warnings that do not necessarily indicate the true situation. The frequent description of the
wiles of wicked women, for instance, may relate to a specific
period when foreign women threatened those who held title
to the land. Through intermarriage with these foreigners,
citizens of Judah risked losing their inheritance to children
of mixed parentage. Fear of such consequences may well explain the animosity behind warnings in the Book of Proverbs about the foreign woman.[5]

What do we really know about education in ancient Israel?[6] Not very much. The preceding observations are

[5] Joe Blenkinsopp, "The Social Context of the 'Outsider Woman' in Proverbs 1–9,"
Bib 72 (1991) 457–73.

[6] In 1908 August Klostermann emphasized the father's role in education on the
basis of Isa. 1:2 and Prov. 1–9, called attention to prophetic disciples (Isa. 8:3), and
viewed Isa. 28:9ff. as evidence for elementary education. He stressed the joint effort
of schoolteachers and parents ("Schulwesen im alten Israel," *Th. Zahn Festschrift* [Leip-
zig: A. Deichert (Georg Böhme), 1908] 193–232). Eleven years later Fletcher H. Swift
issued a word of caution about drawing too many conclusions from meager evidence
such as the Siloam inscription; he rejected the hypothesis that schools existed during
the monarchy (*Education in Ancient Israel from the Earliest Times to 70 A.D.* [Chicago:
Open Court Publishing Company, 1919]). Both Nathan Morris and Nathan Drazin
concurred in Swift's negative assessment (*The Jewish School from the Earliest Times to the
Year 500 of the Present Era* [London: Eyre and Spottiswoode, 1937], expanded in He-
brew to two volumes, *History of Jewish Education from the Earliest Times to the Rise of the
State of Israel* [Tel Aviv: 1960], and *A History of Jewish Education* [The Johns Hopkins
University Studies in Education, No. 29; Baltimore: The Johns Hopkins Press, 1940]).
In 1932 Lorenz Dürr published an important monograph entitled *Das Erziehungswesen*
(Mitteilungen der Vorasiatesägyptischen Gesellschaft 36/2; Leipzig: J. C. Hinrich).
This study marked a significant advance, the attempt to understand Israelite education
by reference to the ancient Near Eastern culture, particularly the practice in Egypt

largely conjecture; whether or not they accord with reality can be debated, and undoubtedly will be. For Jews in later times, specifically the two centuries before Jesus and the longer period of Rabbinic Judaism generally, tradition ascribes the beginnings of compulsory education to the high priest Joshua ben Gamala (63–65 c.e.) or to Simeon ben Shetah (second century b.c.e.).[7] To be sure, some sort of mass education is envisioned in the time of Ezra (fifth cen-

and in Mesopotamia. Dürr treated philosophical questions such as principles, motives, and science of education, insisting that instruction took place in a number of settings: among priests, seers, prophets, the wise, and expert scribes. Hellmut Brunner's classic study of education in ancient Egypt followed (*Altägyptische Erziehung* [Wiesbaden: Otto Harrassowitz], 1957). Hans-Jürgen Hermisson, *Studien zur israelitischen Spruchweisheit* (WMANT 28; Neukirchen-Vluyn: Neukirchener, 1968) 192, posited a theory of an Israelite school at the center of wisdom, and Bernhard Lang sought to demonstrate the correctness of such a reading of wisdom literature ("Schule und Unterricht im Alten Israel," *La Sagesse de l'Ancien Testament*, ed. Maurice Gilbert [BETL 51 (Gembloux: Duculot, 1979)] 186–201), particularly through archaeological, philological, and comparative evidence. In 1981, André Lemaire concentrated on epigraphic data in formulating a lavish hypothesis of educational institutions throughout ancient Palestine (*Les écoles et la formation de la Bible dans l'ancien Israël* [OBO 39; Fribourg: Editions Universitaires; Göttingen: Vandenhoeck & Ruprecht]). For Lemaire, schools played a central role in shaping the Bible. Four years later came the publication of an assessment of the evidence (James L. Crenshaw, "Education in Ancient Israel," *JBL* 104 [1985] 601–15). Graham I. Davies, "Were there schools in ancient Israel," *Wisdom in Ancient Israel*, eds. John Day, Robert P. Gordon, and H.G.M. Williamson (Cambridge: Cambridge University Press, 1995) 199–211, continues that task. Other important monographs include R. Norman Whybray, *The Intellectual Tradition in the Old Testament* (BZAW 135; Berlin and New York: Walter de Gruyter, 1974), which denies the existence of schools in Israel, and Stuart Weeks, *Early Israelite Wisdom* (Oxford: Clarendon Press, 1994), who concurs in this judgment (132–56). The opposite opinion is assumed by E. W. Heaton, *The School Tradition of the Old Testament* (Oxford: Clarendon Press, 1994), with dubious results (similarly, his book entitled *Solomon's New Men* [New York: Pica, 1974]). David W. Jamieson-Drake, *Scribes and Schools in Monarchic-Judah: A Socio-Archaeological Approach* (Sheffield: JSOT Press, 1991), doubts that schools existed prior to the eighth or seventh centuries, and Friedemann W. Golka goes much farther, denying their very existence ("Die israelitische Weisheitschule oder 'Des Kaisers neue Kleider,'" *VTS* 33 [1983] 257–70, ET in *The Leopard's Spots* [Edinburgh: T. & T. Clark, 1993, 4–15]).

[7] A. Demsky, "Education," *Encyclopedia Judaica*, VI (Jerusalem: Keter Publishing House, 1972) 385, and Max Arzt, "The Teacher in Talmud and Midrash," *Mordecai M. Kaplan: Jubilee Volume on the Occasion of his Seventieth Birthday* (New York: Jewish Theological Seminary of America, 1953), 35–47.

tury B.C.E.), when the oral reading of the Torah was followed by learned interpretation (Neh. 8:7–8). Similar attempts to familiarize the populace with the demands of the Mosaic legislation are referred to in Deut. 31:12–13, and the Chronicler reports that in King Jehoshaphat's third regnal year he commissioned a group of princes, Levites, and priests, deploying them throughout Judah to teach the Torah to the people. The same written source mentions formal education of the children of royalty (e.g., David [1 Chron. 27:32]; cf. the similar observation in 2 Kg. 10:1–6 with reference to the seventy sons of the northern ruler, Ahab).

Much uncertainty exists, however, about this important bit of legislation. According to the Jewish historian Josephus (*Against Apion*), every Jewish man, woman, and child knew the law completely, but this claim can be discounted as exaggerated apologetic. Moreover, it may refer to knowledge acquired from hearing the Torah recited in the synagogue rather than from studying a written text. The New Testament attests readings in synagogues, for in one story Jesus goes forward and reads from the Book of Isaiah. Jerome, a Christian theologian four centuries later, went one step further than Josephus, stating that Palestinian Jews of his day were able to cite both the law and the prophets from memory. Jewish devotional legends make similar claims even about imprisoned youth.

In chapter five of Aboth (*Sayings of Fathers*), we find the following observation: at five, children are ready for Scripture; at ten, for Mishnah; at thirteen, for the Commandments; at fifteen, for the teachings that gave rise to the Talmud; at eighteen, for marriage; at twenty, for the pursuit *of righteousness;* at thirty, for full strength; at forty, for discernment; at fifty, for counsel; at sixty, for old age; at seventy, for gray hairs; at eighty, for labor and sorrow; at ninety, for decrepitude; at one hundred, death.

Such pre-Ericksonian efforts to describe the stages of life occur in Egyptian literature from roughly the same time. "He [man] spends ten [years] as a child before he understands death and life. He spends another ten years acquiring the work of instruction by which he will be able to live. He spends another ten years gaining and earning possessions by which to live. He spends another ten years up to old age before his heart takes counsel. There remain sixty years of the whole life which Thoth has assigned to the man of God."[8] In this connection the unknown author of *Papyrus Insinger*, named after the Dutchman who acquired it for the Leiden museum, observes that anyone who approaches the peak (sixty) has already lost two thirds of life.

The seventeenth-century Jesuit Baltasar Gracian continues the tradition of dividing life into segments; the choices combine realism with humor. "At twenty years desire rules us, at thirty, expediency, at forty, judgment."[9] Again, "At twenty man is a peacock; at thirty, a lion; at forty, a camel; at fifty, a snake; at sixty, a dog; at seventy, an ape; at eighty, nothing."[10] Somewhat differently, "Spend the first period of your life in conversation with the dead [books], the second with the living, and the third with your own mind."[11]

The rabbinic source that reported on the stages of life

[8] *Papyrus Insinger* 17/22–18/3. See Miriam Lichtheim, *Late Egyptian Wisdom Literature in the International Context: A Study of Demotic Instructions* (OBO 52; Freiburg & Göttingen: Universitätsverlag & Vandenhoeck & Ruprecht, 1983).

[9] Gracian, *The Art of Worldly Wisdom* (New York: Barnes & Noble, 1993) 173.

[10] *Ibid.*, 161.

[11] *Ibid.*, 134–35. (The actual observation is much longer than this summary.)

from five to one hundred also characterizes students. It mentions four types of disciples: (1) quick to learn and quick to lose; (2) slow to learn and slow to lose; (3) quick to learn and slow to lose; and (4) slow to learn and quick to lose (Pirke Aboth 5:13). Differently, four characters sit before the wise: (1) a sponge, which soaks up everything; (2) a funnel, which lets out what it takes in; (3) a strainer, which lets out wine and retains the dregs; and (4) a sieve, which lets out coarse meal and keeps the fine (Pirke Aboth 5:18). Eliezer ben Hyrqanos was described as a plastered cistern that did not lose a drop of water. Gamaliel the Elder classified students as unclean fish (persons with no understanding), clean fish (rich people with understanding), fish from the Jordan (scholars without talent for give and take), and fish from the Great Sea (those who have such talent). Similarly, the Stoic philosopher Zeno remarked that his successor Cleanthes was like hard waxen tablets, which are difficult to write on but retain the characters written on them.

The issue of the best age at which to begin study prompted the following comments in Aboth de Rabbi Nathan II. Whoever studies the Torah in youth is like lime spread on stones, which rains don't injure. The one who studies during old age resembles lime on bricks, which disappears as a result of frequent rains. Version I of Aboth de Rabbi Nathan uses a different and much more powerful simile. In its view, whoever studies the Torah as a child absorbs the words in his blood and articulates them distinctly, but one who acquires knowledge of the Torah in old age does not absorb the words into the bloodstream nor speak them clearly.

Considerable debate took place about suitable students for instruction. Should the doors be open to everyone, or should strict limits be imposed? The school of Shammai restricted education to the talented, the meek, persons of distinguished ancestry, and the rich. Hillel's followers insisted that all boys should have access to instruction. Simeon ben Yohai stated that the Torah was for a wide spectrum on the economic scale, manna eaters and the wealthy. The expense of getting an education naturally reduced the number of those embarking on a lifetime of study. A comment in Aboth de Rabbi Nathan implies that fees were required. "When a scholar comes to you saying, 'Teach me,' if it is in your power to teach, teach him. Otherwise, send him away at once and do not take his money from him."

According to Judah Goldin, in elementary education apparently one first studied the Shema (Deut. 6:4–9) and Tefillah, Scripture and prayer (Amidah, *Shemone Esreh*, or Eighteen Benedictions), together with the blessings spoken as grace at meals.[12] Students learned to write the alphabet backward and forward like the Greeks, who moved from the first letter to the last, alpha to omega, then both ways at once, then to syllables in order and every combination. Formal education of boys began at five, six, or seven and was functional. Students memorized prayers, Scripture, and the Torah. They may have spent five years on the Bible, ideally turning to Mishnah at age ten. They were taught aphorisms and exempla; above all, they studied the lives of their teachers. For slackers, punishment was harsh. One reads in this

---

[12] *Studies in Midrash and Related Literature*, 205.

regard: "Smack him down at once or hold your peace and say nothing."[13] A Mishnaic observation implies that at fifteen boys began the study of the teachings that gave rise to the Talmud (Pirke Aboth 5:21). Study was oral, consisting of Midrash, Halakot, and Haggadot, that is, exegetical interpretation of Scripture, legal texts, and homiletic narratives. The goal was to preserve the teachings of the past, not to discover original insights. In Haggadah, one was free to be original. No heavenly interference as proof was allowed in the Academy, not even a revelatory message, a *bath qol.*

The status of teachers is a subject of debate. On the one hand, Mishnah states that one should recover what a teacher has lost before something lost by one's father. In the same vein, it observes that one should ransom a teacher before one's father, and that one ought to feel the same awe toward a teacher as toward heaven. In the Talmud and Midrash, God is described as a teacher, and guardians of children are promised a place at God's right hand. On the other hand, teachers earned such meager wages that they were exempt from taxes. Although a certain Samuel ben Shelat accumulated a great deal of wealth, the authorities did not tax him because they could not imagine that a teacher had sufficient funds to be taxed. Teachers were the objects of scorn by some, who remarked that only a schoolteacher would ask such a question, meaning that the question was not very learned. Unmarried men were not permitted to teach because of the daily contact with mothers who brought children to school. Instruction seems to have lasted all day, but

---

[13] Goldin, *Studies in Midrash and Related Literature,* 208.

class was suspended under certain circumstances, particularly excessive heat.

Some specialization took place, with a Bible teacher (*sôpēr*) being the lowest level and a *ḥākām*, or Talmudic scholar, occupying a higher rung on the ladder. According to Max Arzt, the normal number of students was twenty-five, and a curtain divided rooms into two compartments. Supervision of teachers was exacting, especially to alleviate suspicion of sexual impropriety. Salaries of teachers came from fees and taxes levied on the general populace.[14]

JEWISH EDUCATION IN ALEXANDRIA

Whereas Jewish education revolved around the study of Scripture, instruction in the Greek world covered language, music, and athletics. In a sense, the Greeks endeavored to train individuals in the service of culture.[15] Alexandrian Jews felt the impact of the Greek educational system most notably. Philo's debt to secular education is remarkable, as Alan Mendelson has shown in great detail.[16]

The encyclia, or standard curriculum in liberal arts and sciences, consisted of the study of arithmetic, geometry, as-

---

[14] "The Teacher in Talmud and Midrash," 45–46.

[15] Barclay, *Train Up a Child*, thinks education in Sparta sought, in his words, "to obliterate" individuality in the service of the state, whereas Athenians trained students in the service of culture.

[16] *Secular Education in Philo of Alexandria* (MHUC; Cincinnati: Hebrew Union College Press, 1982). The discussion that follows is taken from this informative study.

tronomy, and music (the *quadrivium*), together with that of grammar, rhetoric, and dialectic (the *trivium*). Philo attributed inherent spiritual value to the encyclia. For him, grammar included both reading and writing, while rhetoric protected one from sophistry and ensured that speech interpreted thought accurately. Thought was primary, speech being its instrument rather than a substitute for reasoning. Dialectic was a structured discipline by which one discovered the truth by asking a series of questions. Philosophy was the overriding constraint for both geometry and grammar. Music included both theory and practice, but the emphasis fell on theory. Astronomy, the queen of the sciences, transcended mundane science and embraced magic. However, Philo did not ascribe to the stars any governing power over human lives.

Only upper-class Jews studied the encyclia. Women did not, but learned domestic arts in seclusion. Philo disparaged women's nature as such. Jews studied in the gymnasia as a means to greater social mobility. Philo approved secular study during the week but insisted on a shift to the Torah on the Sabbath. The highest level of knowledge was philosophy and wisdom, a stage beyond the encyclia, itself a step above technical knowledge. Whereas the various disciplines in the encyclia yield only probability and conjecture, since they rely on sense perception, philosophy and wisdom produce truth. Philo recognized a dynamic interplay between God and humans, an irresistible impulse toward education, with spiritual progress depending on natural endowment.

Students experienced four stages of development: (1) childhood, when one's soul was like smooth wax; (2) adolescence, an apprehending of virtue and vice; (3) a borderline period; and (4) maturity. Instruction in arts and sciences began at seventeen and lasted twenty years. The passions persisted through the third stage, and not until stage four did one attain victory over them. Certain dangers lurked within the encyclia. Grammar and music seduced students through the sounds of words; rhetoric could be distorted into sophistry; astronomy could lead to pantheism or superstition. Philo did not consider the intellect capable of achieving ultimate truth; only God was its guarantor. Ignorance was both involuntary and moral (thinking too highly of one's intellectual abilities).

According to Philo, humankind fell into three types: sages, progressives, and ordinary people. In other words, some were unbodied souls or angels, others had a mixed nature, and still others were evil, not trying to rise beyond their present level. Persons of mixed nature sought to become better but frequently fell back. Philo also believed there were three moral spheres: the God-born (Abraham and Bezalel), sages by birth (Isaac and Moses), and men of heaven who become sages (priests and prophets). These persons ascend by two paths, knowledge of God's existence and knowledge of the harmony of the world and its parts. Earth-born people prefer onions and garlic; they are the Nimrods of the earth. Philo believed in free will, but thought that God's activity included human response. Although Moses and Isaac were perfect from the beginning, Abraham rose to the level of a sage. Philo thus considered him a model for emulation. Like him, students should study the encyclia, for heaven-borns can ascend to knowledge by means of the encyclia.

In this way, through studying the encyclia, students master the senses, arriving at speechlessness on the ascendancy to the heights. One ascends spiritually by way of "skepticism (or speechlessness), growing out of the encyclia, realization of the nothingness of created being, self-knowledge, self-despair (a sense of personal nothingness growing out of introspection), and finally knowledge of God."[17]

To sum up, Philo was an elitist who understood the *encyclia* as a first stage, subordinate to *sophia*. Nevertheless, he introduced theology into the equation: one can arrive at knowledge of God only through a study of creation.

The unknown author of the Wisdom of Solomon, equally enamored of Greek education, actually alludes to the branches of knowledge in his day, probably the first century B.C.E. This author attributes such knowledge to God. He writes:

> For it is he who gave me unerring knowledge of what
>   exists,
> to know the structure of the world and the activity of the
>   elements;
> the beginning and end and middle of times,
> the alternations of the solstices and the changes of the
>   seasons,
> the cycles of the years and the constellations of the stars,
> the natures of animals and the tempers of wild beasts,
> the power of spirits and the reasonings of men,
> the varieties of plants and the virtues of roots;

[17] *Secular Education in Philo of Alexandria*, 76.

I learned both what is secret and what is manifest, for
wisdom, the fashioner of all things, taught me.
(7:17–22)

EDUCATION IN ANCIENT
MESOPOTAMIA

Schools in ancient Sumer originated soon after someone
impressed a whittled reed on soft clay and discovered that
the imprinted symbol would dry and harden in the sun, or
the clay could be baked into terra-cotta. They existed from
2500 B.C.E. on. An abundance of texts written in clay has
survived, richly documenting Mesopotamian culture. The
tablet houses were modeled on guilds, a master craftsman
gathering around himself a number of sons. Together they
formed a skilled class. From him the young apprentices
learned the trade. Similarly, a master of literature had a
group of students, figuratively called "sons," who studied
with him and acquired the essentials of the scribal profession through long practice and diligent effort.[18]

The head of the schoolhouse was assisted by preceptors,
whose responsibility ranged from supervision of writing to
maintaining discipline in the classroom. A senior teacher

---

[18] C. J. Gadd, *Teachers and Students in the Oldest Schools* (London: University of Lon-
don, 1956), Samuel Noah Kramer, *The Sumerians* (Chicago & London: University of
Chicago Press, 1963) 229–48; *City Invincible: A Symposium on Urbanization and Cultural
Development in the Ancient Near East*, eds. Carl H. Kraeling and Robert M. Adams
(Chicago: University of Chicago Press, 1960) 94–123 (dealing with both Egypt and
Mesopotamia), and Laurie E. Pearce, "The Scribes and Scholars of Ancient Mesopo-
tamia," 2265–2278 in *Civilizations of the Ancient Near East*, vol. IV, ed. Jack M. Sasson
(New York: Charles Scribner's Sons, 1995).

(father) of the tablet house instructed students, adminis-
tered examinations, and provided adult leadership. He
would write about twenty-five lines of text on one side of a
clay tablet and a student would write the text on the other
side from memory. A senior clerk, or overseer, was responsible for administration, regulating the lives of students. Specialists in various subjects assisted in the task of instruction,
particularly mathematics, music, languages, public service,
magic, and the like. The primary responsibility for teaching
fell on a group of subordinates known as "big brothers." This
arrangement led to considerable unrest, with conflict between students and instructors occupying much of their
time and energy. Insults were the inevitable result.

Presumably, students came from the elite households in
society, those with affluence and power. Exceptions to this
did occur and are alluded to in the texts, which refer to a
student who had been cast out at birth and to one who was
adopted by a hierodule who became the wife of a divorced
citizen. Only boys attended schools, although a few female
scribes are known, most likely the daughters of royalty or
wealthy individuals who could provide private tutoring for
their girls.

Rivkah Harris found some evidence to indicate that occasionally a woman managed to acquire an education in Mesopotamia.[19] A slave girl received rations in a scribal text
from the Ur III dynasty (c. 2000 B.C.E.), and *naditu* women
(a special group of holy women) of a cloister at Sippar
served as scribes to women only. At least ten women, all

[19] "The Female 'Sage' in Mesopotamian Literature (With an Appendix on Egypt),"
3–17 in *The Sage in Israel and the Ancient Near East*, eds. John G. Gammie and Leo G.
Perdue (Winona Lake: Eisenbrauns, 1990).

slaves or persons of lowly status, functioned as scribes at Mari, mainly to limit access to women of the harem by males. Dandamayev's study of more than three thousand scribes from the Neo-Babylonian period did not turn up a single female name.

Women poets also existed. Enheduanna, a high priestess of Nanna and daughter to Sargon the Great of Akkad (c. 2300 B.C.E.), used the image of giving birth when composing hymns to the temple. Ninshatapada, daughter of Sin-Kashib, the founder of the Old Babylonian dynasty of Uruk, composed a letter prayer, possibly by dictation. A request for an oracle from Lahar indicates the low self-esteem of women: "Disregard that it is a [mere] woman who has written and submitted [this] to you." Samsi-Adad advised his son to send grown daughters to Shubat-Enlil to learn the art of singing, and Kassite letters refer to illnesses of young women in a music academy attended by princes and princesses.

Women also became physicians. At Larsa during the Old Babylonian period, a female physician is mentioned, and at Mari a secondary wife has responsibility for a female physician remiss in caring for women of the harem. Women were excluded from divination, "the leading Mesopotamian science and intellectual endeavor," according to Benjamin Foster, although some exceptions are known. Women were involved in the interpretation of dreams, and in the late Assyrian period, they were thought to have had a greater propensity for sorcery. Women also offered counsel now and again. The female ale servant Siduri advised Gilgamesh, and the princess Kiru of Mari gave her father political advice. Here, too, one finds an indication that such counsel was exceptional, for it adds the words: "even if she is only a woman."

John Baines has concluded that in Egypt a similar situation existed, women occasionally acquiring an education.[20] The New Kingdom witnessed the flourishing of a remarkable group of women—Hatshepsut, Tiy, and Nefertiti. Five tombs covering three hundred years provide visual proof of nonroyal female literacy. A female physician, Peseshet, is mentioned in the Old Kingdom, and a text refers to a "knowing woman." Still, Eighteenth Dynasty graffiti compare earlier graffiti to "the work of a woman who has no mind."

This minimal evidence of learned females is offset in large measure by the extraordinary achievements of women in society. Tikvah Frymer-Kensky sums things up beautifully.[21] In her view, women mediated between nature and culture, transforming the raw into the edible, grass into baskets, fleece and flax into yarn and clothes, and babies into social beings. Such activity must surely lie behind Ben Sira's concession that those who work with their hands "keep stable the fabric of the world," adding a spiritual dimension as well ("and their prayer is in the practice of their trade," 38:34). Furthermore, through their intelligence and persuasive power, women have always influenced events, as it were, behind the scenes, even when excluded from the ranks of the educated members of society.

---

[20] "Literacy and Ancient Egyptian Society," *Man* 18 (1983) 572–99; further evidence occurs in Edward F. Wente, "The Scribes of Ancient Egypt," 2211–2221 in *Civilizations of the Ancient Near East*, vol. IV.

[21] "The Sage in the Pentateuch: Soundings," *The Sage in Israel and the Ancient Near East*, 276.

Schools were not associated with temples, but seem to have been part of the headmaster's living quarters. Instruction may have taken place in open courtyards, although buildings with writing tables were required for formal work. (Benches, running along brick walls, have been discovered centuries later at Qumran). Mastering the complex system of cuneiform signs required years, so students began their education at a very early age and continued it into late maturity.

A romantic account of school days in a text that runs for ninety lines tells of a boy returning home and informing his father as to what had transpired at school. Then the lad bathes, eats, and goes to bed asking to be awakened early lest he arrive at school late. The next day he eats bread under his mother's watchful eye, hurries to school, and encounters all kinds of trouble. The boy endures whippings at the hands of several supervisors, eventually receiving one from the headmaster. At wits' end, the student implores his father to try bribery, an approach that works. The father invites the headmaster to his home, giving him wine and oil, a fine garment, and a ring. The headmaster then praises the student. Other texts about school days have survived, reflecting a scribal self-image.

Such descriptions have been compared with burlesque. C. J. Gadd writes: "The absurdly complacent professor, the obsequious assistants, the bullying of students who, in turn, ape but too faithfully the conceit of their superiors, the hoodwinking of parents, the venality of teachers, the undiscipline and rowdyism of the schoolrooms—all these might be the creations of a satirist, even a reformer, rather than the writings of men themselves engaged in the activities thereby so invidiously described, even caricatured."[22]

In later times, the scribes assumed an added burden, the preservation of Sumerian culture in an Akkadian environment. They translated the Sumerian stories into Akkadian, transforming stories into tragedies, episodic texts into a continuous story and even an ethical norm for life. A single theme, death's inevitability, animated these stories. These scribes drew up compendia of legal phrases, omens, prayers, hymns, laments, and incantations. Primarily concerned with grammar, they compiled lists of personal names and cuneiform signs, a kind of bilingual dictionary. They surrounded their profession with protective myths of the patron deity Enki, the supremely knowing one; Adapa and the antediluvian Seven Sages of divine revelation, one of whom, Onanes, was thought to have taught culture to humanity, and the fundamentals of civilization, called *ME*. These scribes also developed a dialogic approach to education, elevating debate to a high level, but attributing such altercations to animals and inanimate objects as well as to human beings. They copied literary works dealing with the creation of the world and the quest for eternal life.

For whom did these scribes compose their texts? Certainly not for ordinary citizens, who could neither read nor write. For the government? Not likely, because priests, kings, judges, and governors were illiterate. In the entire history of Mesopotamia only three kings claimed to be literate—Ashurbanipal, Lipit Ishtar, and Shulgi—and the evidence does not support the boast. Court scribes for Ashur-

---

[22] *Teachers and Students in the Oldest Schools*, 36.

banipal had to explain simple Sumerian logograms for him, and Shulgi's claim appears in a context of other things equally unlikely, like running from Nippur to Ur. Did scribes write for themselves? It seems probable that the vast majority of scribal texts were art for art's sake, hence read only as writing exercises. Exceptions did occur, such as hymns and laments for use in the temples. An exclusivism among the scribes prompted them to guard writing zealously and even make it more complicated. For example, the person who inscribed the statue of Idrimi showed off his knowledge by seldom writing the same sign twice in the identical form. Nevertheless, popular proverbs were collected by the scribes, thus infusing the elite culture with elements from the masses.

Who read the essays and disputes? Did scribes copy the epic texts like Gilgamesh and the creation narrative just for practice? How much instruction actually took place? The answer is debated, but one can scarcely imagine that scribes read such texts dispassionately. Popular proverbs taught morals, often in a humorous vein. A by-product of such instruction was training in rhetoric, regardless of whether or not scribes ever argued cases in court. Still, it is improbable that libraries just for reading existed. For the most part texts were functional, not expressions of originality. If this is correct, most scribes probably worked as administrative assistants in government, while only a few found private employment handling business documents, legal transactions, and the like. Some even became specialists in diagnosing illness, interpreting charms, and in magic.

Despite occupying subordinate positions in society, these scribes believed that they alone attained "humanity." They fell into the category of poor aristocrats, but they had a high self-image and considered themselves special objects of patronage by the goddess Nisaba.

EDUCATION IN ANCIENT EGYPT[23]

Papyrus, the preferred medium for writing in Egypt, was less durable by far than the tablets of clay used by scribes in Mesopotamia. The vast majority of inscribed papyri perished over the centuries, leaving modern interpreters with huge gaps in knowledge that can be filled only by informed guesses. Moreover, the poor quality of many texts has led Egyptologists to conclude that scribes frequently could not understand what they were copying. The shift from hieroglyphs to hieratics over the years, and finally to demotic, gave rise to numerous mistakes.

Beginning in the third millennium, schools for priests were connected with temples. Much writing fell into the category of magic, particularly incantations directed at securing life after death. Classic literature includes *Pyramid Texts*, the *Coffin Texts*, and the *Book of the Dead*. Sacred writings were deposited in the House of Life, but these texts were never considered inviolate with respect to a rigid form. A great deal of variation in content occurred from time to

[23] H. Te Velde, "Scribes and Literacy in Ancient Egypt," in *Scripta Signa Vocis: Studies about Scripts, Scriptures, Scribes, and Languages in the Near East, Presented to J. H. Hospers*, eds. H.L.J. Vanstiphout, K. Jongeling, F. Leemhuis, & G. T. Reinick (Groningen: E. Forsten, 1986); Ronald J. Williams, "Scribal Training in Ancient Egypt," *JAOS* 92 (1972) 214–21; Brunner, *Altägyptische Erziehung*, and Eberhard Otto, "Bildung und Ausbildung im alten Ägypten," *ZÄS* 8 (1956) 41–48.

time. Besides these texts there were wisdom writings, in which a superior instructed an inferior. Occasionally a king taught his son, but more often a high official in the royal court instructed his son to succeed him. These texts aim at building character, equipping young men to occupy positions of authority. The superior either admonishes or warns the inferior; alternatively, he uses maxims to communicate moral guidance.

In addition, the royal administration sponsored a school to train the numerous employees necessary for a smooth-running government—secretaries, clerks, paymasters, letter writers, and so forth. During the New Kingdom (1567–1085 B.C.E.), scribal schools proliferated in the palace and temple. Whereas education during the Old Kingdom had been restricted to children of bureaucrats, the need for a huge workforce opened the schools to all qualified children. The texts from this period indicate that a new emphasis on personal piety had swept over the land. As for scribes, they developed a powerful sense of self-importance. *The Satire of the Trades* (also known as *Khety*), a text comparing various occupations such as soldier, barber, fowler, farmer, leather worker, weaver, potter, and smith with that of the scribe, who unlike all the others is his own boss, was copied over and over in this period.

These Egyptian scribes copied a wide variety of texts. Besides the classic mortuary texts and Instructions, there were narratives of extraordinary descriptive power. These include an account of an envoy on a mission to acquire wood for the Pharaoh's funeral bark; stories about shipwrecked sailors; a tale about a corrupt governmental official and an eloquent peasant; myths of creation, and various conflicts among the gods; hymns and prayers; noun lists classifying all known rivers, plants, flowers, animals, and the like; admonitions and prophecies; love songs, and much more. Several scribal texts deal directly with problems associated with going to school, which were possibly exacerbated by cruel punishment at the hands of demanding teachers.

This rich legacy from ancient Egypt is not sufficient to clarify education there. Precious little is known about priestly education, and scholars are left to speculate about the real nature of administrative schools of later times. Paintings frequently depict scribes at work, and fortunate discoveries such as that at Deir-el-Medinah, where a huge contingent of scribes worked and left copious records, assist in filling out the lacunae. In this elite community of scribes a single family persisted in office for six generations. One man, Kenhikhopshef, occupied a position as scribe for either forty-six or fifty-four years. Still, considerable mobility existed in Deir-el-Medinah, the better qualified individual often making it to the top of his profession.[24]

In the Egyptian setting teachers contrasted the passionate, or hotheaded, individual with the person in control of his passions, the silent one.[25] Early texts emphasize a pragmatic self-mastery of one's destiny, but this confidence gives way during the Middle Kingdom to a kind of disillusionment, and in the New Kingdom to servile piety, in later times drifting off into skepticism. The journey from confident trust in order, symbolized by the goddess *Ma'at*, in the

---

[24] Harold C. Washington, *Wealth and Poverty in the Instruction of Amenemope and the Hebrew Proverbs* (SBLDS 142; Atlanta: Scholars Press, 1994) 25–83.

[25] Nili Shupak, *Where can Wisdom be found? The Sage's Language in the Bible and in Ancient Egyptian Literature* (OBO 130; Fribourg & Göttingen: University Press and Vandenhoeck & Ruprecht, 1993).

Old Kingdom to moral treatises on character and things pleasing to the gods, and ultimately to fatalism, can be traced in the Instructions and aphorisms that have survived the ravages of time.

Several texts from the late period graphically illustrate the nature of grammatical exercises assigned to students. These practice writings cover a wide range of grammar and syntax, but they also include lists of familiar things. They give the forms of verbs in first, second, or third person, masculine and feminine; uses of prepositions and infinitives; prefix and suffix conjugations; relative sentences; and so forth. Occasionally, they indicate Greek influence in the ordering principle, but often the arrangement of the items seems altogether random. Lists include names of gods, kings, places, birds, fish, bees, animals, types of trees, flowers, names of months, festivals, and occupations. Hieroglyphs in one papyrus depict men standing, women crouching, men falling, animals, and parts of the body. Onomastica of this kind throw fresh light on the classroom in the last centuries before the Common Era. They also provide anomalies such as this sequence: verbs in first person, second person, third person masculine singular; then third and second person feminine; then plural third person, first person, and second person.[26]

This brief account of education in Mesopotamia and Egypt illuminates the intellectual context of the world in which ancient Israelites took their place. To what degree Israel's in-

---

[26] Ursula Kaplony-Heckel, "Schüler und Schulwesen in der Ägyptischen Spätzeit," *Studien zur Altägyptischen Kultur* 1 (1974) 227–46, especially 230.

telligentsia participated in this lively culture is debatable. Interpreters who view Israelite wisdom literature as a product of the royal court will naturally emphasize the many affinities with a parallel phenomenon in Egypt and Mesopotamia. Those who think wisdom literature arose primarily among ordinary people in small villages will downplay the links with other cultures. The magical component that lies at the heart of wisdom in Mesopotamia is completely missing in biblical wisdom literature, and the theoretical, or philosophical, dimension of Israelite wisdom plays a minor role in Egyptian wisdom, where aphorisms and Instructions abound. Nevertheless, similarities between Israelite wisdom and that of its neighbors demand that interpreters take into consideration all three bodies of knowledge. The difficulty of mastering the literature written in so many different ancient languages is staggering, as is the necessity of controlling the secondary literature in all three branches of knowledge. The present analysis of biblical wisdom owes much to specialists in Egyptian and Mesopotamian literature, who will surely find many things with which to take issue. Perhaps the inadequacies in this interpretation will prompt them to reflect more fully on ancient education.

We began by observing that education grows out of a desire to structure one's existence for beneficial ends. In the process of ordering our lives we construct a symbolic world that exists only in our imagination. Nevertheless, we bestow on this imaginary world the task of ordering and explaining our existence. In the end, we become subject to this symbolic world. Hence the presence of intuitive familiarity occasions little surprise; another kind of discovery, effective surprise, impels one beyond ordinary experiences into wholly new ways of understanding the world.[27] Here mythos and logos come together, producing compelling belief. This symbiosis of human effort and instinctual memory suggests that knowledge participates in the sacred.

Teaching takes place in one of two modes, the expository and the hypothetical. The former emphasizes the teacher's authority and depends heavily on the power of example. It reminds students that the instructor has achieved a high level of knowledge and urges them to emulate the elder. The latter mode, the hypothetical, shifts the focus to students, who are challenged to engage in an exciting quest to discover answers to intriguing questions. Biblical wisdom employs both techniques; aphorisms and Instructions weigh in heavily on the expository side, while the highly reflective texts, Job and Ecclesiastes, encourage readers to discover new insights through a process of hypothetical reflection.

[27] Jerome S. Bruner, *On Knowing* (Cambridge: The Belknap Press of Harvard University Press, 1966) 18, 22.

Chapter One

≈

Literacy

*"A writing cannot distinguish between
suitable and unsuitable readers."*

SOCRATES

The shift from an oral culture to a literary one was not greeted with open arms. According to Plato (*Phaedrus* 274C–275B), the discovery of writing threatened a time-honored reliance on memory. The enthusiasm of the god Thoth, credited with the invention of writing and therefore honored as patron of scribes, was dampened by a warning from the king of the gods, Thamous, that writing would bring in its wake an unwanted lapse in memory. Actually, the new invention did not replace the reliable storage of information in the brain but complemented it. Much knowledge continued to be passed on from generation to generation without benefit of the written word.

Initial efforts to forge a language by means of visible signs suggest an awareness that something was needed to assist the memory. The revolutionary shift from an oral to a written culture was prompted by more than a sense of the artistic or a feeling for the power residing in signs and symbols.[1] The discovery of the alphabet made it possible to move beyond a complex language of signs to a relatively simple means of written communication. It also altered forever the medium for the written word; papyrus and leather parchment replaced clay, and ink made obsolete the stylus for pressing wedge-shaped marks into soft clay.

It had not taken long for royal administrators to discover uses for newly invented signs and the ensuing art of writing. First in Mesopotamia, and subsequently in Egypt by "stimulus diffusion," the new mode of communication served as a means of monumental display.[2] The actual meaning of the words was at first restricted to a few learned scribes, but the general populace may have considered the markings power-laden. Later inscriptions in burial chambers within Syria-Palestine probably reflect such a magical understanding of writing, inasmuch as ordinary grave robbers in tenth-century Byblos would hardly have possessed an ability to read the ominous message: "Beware! There is danger for you below." Magical incantations throughout the Near East

---

[1] Denise Schmandt-Besserat, "Record Keeping Before Writing," 2097–2106 in *Civilizations of the Ancient Near East*, vol. IV, believes that "the system of nonverbal communication based on tokens played a major role in the ascent of civilization" and "led to the invention of writing" (2105). According to her, this type of record keeping began about 8000–7500, attaining new forms about 4000–3500. Once the envelope (case) for holding several tokens was marked for easy identification, it ushered in a new phase, with signs on tokens becoming the message. Pictographic writing then followed, as did abstract counting. Herman Vanstiphout, "Memory and Literacy in Ancient Western Asia," 2181–2196 (especially 2184) in *Civilizations of the Ancient Near East*, vol. IV, thinks that something is missing in this theory. In his view, writing was invented at Uruk between 3200 and 2900. Vanstiphout has high praise for the school, "which was not only devoted to writing but whose whole existence and intention was meant to elaborate, foster, and perpetuate literacy" (2193). He also thinks that "literacy was more extensive than primary sources report" (2188).

[2] The expression "stimulus diffusion" comes from Baines, "Literacy and Ancient Egyptian Society," 575.

continued to rely on the notion of the special power inherent in letters and words, both spoken and written.

Paintings on the walls of tombs in Egypt during the Late Bronze Age depict scribes as they go about their daily task of recording estimates of crop yields at harvest time. Later they would write down the actual results as a reliable means of calculating the amount of taxes to levy on a farm. Their ancestors in Palestine scratched the names of pharaohs on jars and in seal impressions (bullae) during the Early Bronze Age. Palestinian evidence of cuneiform comes from the Middle Bronze Age, with considerably more from eighteen locations in the Late Bronze Age. By this time writing had acquired a power to stabilize society; through its use, rulers were able to keep track of payments received, expenses incurred in carrying out the daily affairs of government, and inventories of all sorts. Such written records strengthened a ruler's control over subjects, who existed to serve their patron. Monumental inscriptions reminded them of the heroic exploits undertaken by sovereigns on their behalf, and such propaganda portrayed kings as larger than life. Some inscriptions served a legislative function, identifying principal royal statutes relating to life in society and highlighting specific laws governing the community.[3]

---

[3] On early writing in Palestine, see Amihai Mazar, *Archaeology of the Land of the Bible* (ABRL; New York: Doubleday, 1995) 361–63, 514–20; Alan R. Millard, "An Assessment of the Evidence for Writing in Ancient Israel," *Biblical Archaeology Today: Proceedings of the International Congress of Biblical Archaeology, Jerusalem, April 1984* (Jerusalem: Israel Exploration Society, 1985) 301–11; "The Knowledge of Writing in Iron Age Palestine," *Tyndale Bulletin* 46 (1995) 1–10; "The Knowledge of Writing in Late Bronze Age Palestine," *42e Recontre Assyriologique Internationale, Leuven, July 3–7, 1995;* "The Uses of the Early Alphabets," *Phoinekeia Grammata: Lire et écrire en Mediterranée,* eds. Cl. Baurain, C. Bonnet, V. Krings (Collection d'Études Classiques; Liege: Namur, 1991) 101–14.

In addition to its magical and executive function, writing greatly expanded the geographical scope of activity, royal or otherwise. In a real sense, written messages momentarily united individuals separated by vast distances. Letters even communicated across generations, for they survived long after the ones who wrote them breathed their last breath. In short, "the literate can extend their communication in space and time, and their memory in compass and duration."[4] Writing thus cemented relationships; written documents also attested various official enactments—marriages and divorces, purchases of land, rights of inheritance, and so forth. Impressions of seals made from semiprecious stones pressed into soft clay, which then hardened and were attached to important documents and contracts, bear abundant witness to binding contracts in Syria-Palestine from biblical times.

Some written texts went beyond mere utilitarian value, eventually becoming classical literature. Here art for art's sake resulted in texts of exceptional rhetorical beauty and intellectual merit. Because of the limited clientele capable of understanding these works of literature, they assumed ancillary importance as texts assisting scribes in the process of acquiring an education. By copying classical literature, aspiring scribes improved both their minds and their writing skills. The time-honored copying of texts in Mesopotamia and Egypt—e.g., the *Gilgamesh Epic* and the creation narrative, *Enuma elish*, and the *Book of the Dead* and *Khety*, respectively—was followed in Palestine, where a copy of a

---

[4] Baines, "Literacy and Ancient Egyptian Society," 593. Only forty-eight letters in Hebrew have been discovered for the period from 700 B.C.E. to 135 C.E., most from military contexts. About one fourth of these come from postbiblical times, the Bar-Kochba revolt. On letters, see Dennis Pardee, *Handbook of Ancient Hebrew Letters: A Study Edition* (Chico: Scholars Press, 1982).

narrative about Balaam, the son of Beor, discovered at Tell Deir 'Alla, and possibly a royal statement from Arad, Ostracon 88, are believed to go beyond ordinary uses of texts and assume a classical "canon" that could be consulted.

Writing also had religious significance, whether communicating priestly prayers to the deity or reducing myths to the written word. Ritual thrived on its use, and priests transmitted sacred lore from generation to generation in writing. Together, word and symbol pointed beyond themselves to deeper mystery. Even nonsensical words signified the unknown and unknowable quality of transcendence, and icons implied that words alone could never suffice in describing sacred reality. In this way priests managed to come to terms with both media, icon and written text, for each one told a story in its own way. Furthermore, these two different modes of communication reached the learned and the unlearned, the few who could read and the many who lacked the capacity to do so. The richly decorated floor of the synagogue at Beth Alpha illustrates this point nicely. Both word and picture reinforce the message of the mosaic portraying the story of Abraham's near-sacrifice of his son Isaac. The combination of Jewish motifs and the zodiac at this site shows how competing cultures could coexist in the same way that the complementary modes of communication did.

Another form of writing falls under the category of idle doodling. This involuntary scrawl helped individuals while away restless hours of boredom in faraway places. Often taking the form of alphabetic writing, these meaningless sequences of consonants rival repetitious consonants of the alphabet, sometimes transposed to yield a different order, as at the border fortress Arad, where one finds both spellings,

Adar and Arad. The two different spellings may have resulted from confusion between *r* and *d* over time, or they
may reflect a metathesis in oral reproduction. The spelling
ʿrd seems correct. At other times the abecedaries may have
served as a rough draft for an envisioned text, perhaps even
as ornamentation. Still other texts of this nature belong to
the category of graffiti, presumably providing a sense of sat-
isfaction to the person who succeeded in forming the intended letters of the alphabet.

The earlier reference to impressions on clay seals suggests a singular way in which written words touched the
daily lives of many people engaging in official business.
Writing served to identify individuals and to mark off their
possessions. The characteristic letter for "belonging to,"
plus a personal name, on a clay seal indicated that this particular document belonged to so-and-so. In this way personal property of all kinds was set aside from that of other
persons, and, by extension, this indication of ownership
marked off ceremonial gifts as well.

To sum up, the written word lent itself to multiple uses—
executive, magical, universalizing, religious, entertainment,
and identifying.

Although writing seems to have flourished in Israel during the last century and a half of the monarchy, that is, from
just before the collapse of the capital city of the north, Samaria, in 722 until the fall of Jerusalem to Babylonian soldiers in 587, substantial written evidence from earlier times
has survived.[5] Its presence despite the biodegradable nature

---

[5] The texts appear in Graham I. Davies, *Ancient Hebrew Inscriptions* (Cambridge:
Cambridge University Press, 1991).

of most writing materials, and the principle in archaeology that most finds date from the final stages of occupation at a given site, implies that writing was by no means an isolated phenomenon.

Some biblical books take writing for granted, although not specifically identifying those responsible for inscribing words and sentences on lintels or amulets. The author of Deuteronomy expects those anticipating divorce proceedings either to be able to write or to be sufficiently affluent to secure a professional scribe for this purpose. Furthermore, the homiletician goes so far as to use symbolic language in connection with the verb for *writing*, urging readers—hearers in the literary fiction of the book—to write the divine instructions on tablets of the heart. Indeed, the Decalogue was thought to have been inscribed on tablets of stone by the finger of the deity (cf. Exod. 32:15–16 and 34:1, but contrast 34:27–28; also Deut. 5:22). The Deuteronomistic historian mentions a youth from Succoth who writes down the names of seventy-seven people, records an incident in which Queen Jezebel sends letters to powerful officials, whom she bribes to orchestrate Naboth's execution, and implicates David in arranging the death of his loyal soldier, Uriah, through a letter sent to Joab, his commander on the battlefield.

The prophet Jeremiah, active near the time of the composition of the Deuteronomistic history, sends letters to exiled Judaeans in Babylonia and draws up written contracts detailing the purchase of land. This same prophet employs an amanuensis to write down his oracles, and after King Jehoiakim burned the original scroll, generates a much-expanded version and dictates the words to the scribe, Ba-

ruch, who then puts everything into writing. The story goes
on to say that many other words like them were added, either through the prophet's dictation to his secretary or, less
likely, at Baruch's own initiative. Nevertheless, mention of
witnesses in Jer. 32:12 does not necessarily prove that they
were literate, for they may only have made a mark in this
connection, one equivalent to an *X*.

More than a century earlier the prophet Isaiah acknowledged that some people were illiterate, for when handed a
scroll they would respond, "I do not know how to read" (Isa.
29:12). Others, however, had acquired a knowledge of both
reading and writing. Such a one would assume the task of
recording the names of the chosen remnant (Isa. 10:19)
whom YHWH intended to spare. A huge chasm separated
the professional scribe from persons whose knowledge of
writing was only superficial. Menahem Haran likens the latter to individuals in the Bible who possessed some familiarity with various skills such as cutting wood, maneuvering
vessels at sea, working with metal, hunting, playing a musi-
cal instrument, and reciting laments on occasions of fu-
nerals.[6]

Classical prophets may well have delivered their oracles
orally, and these treasured utterances probably survived for
decades in the memory of close associates before finally being committed to writing. Nevertheless, both the prophets
and their audiences were undoubtedly aware of written
texts. Their testamentary value is attested in Isa. 8:16, Job
19:26, and Hab. 2:2. Whether witnessing to the authenticity

[6] "On the Diffusion of Literacy and Schools in Ancient Israel," *VTS* 40 (Congress
Volume, Jerusalem; Leiden: Brill, 1988) 81–94, especially 83–84.

of prophetic utterance in Isaiah, or to a faithful servant's undeserved affliction in Job, or to firm resolve in the face of contradictory reality in Habakkuk, these written texts stand as verifiable artifacts reinforcing the spoken word.

These three biblical texts refer to an equal number of media for writing—a scroll, either made from leather or papyrus, a stone, and a wooden tablet. Numerous seal impressions from Palestine indicate a widespread use of papyrus for valuable documents, although only one fragment of papyrus, discovered at the arid Wadi Murabba'at, has survived. For particularly prized writings such as canonical texts, parchment became the medium of choice, as illustrated by the well-known discoveries from the Judaean desert, the so-called Dead Sea Scrolls. One text from this cache, containing a catalog of hidden treasures, including vast amounts of gold and silver, but also precious garments and other items, was written on copper, an even more precious medium than parchment.

More modest writing vessels were the wooden tablets used by schoolboys of later times, as well as tablets with a smooth wax surface. These, too, could give way on occasion to slate and even ivory—for instance, the seventh-century Marsiliana writing board carved from ivory, which has the alphabet around the edge.[7] For occasional messages and early drafts, broken pieces of pottery or limestone flakes sufficed. Copious examples of these ostraca have survived, including 102 from Samaria, more than seventy from Arad, thirty from Jerusalem, and several from Lachish. Thanks to

---

[7] Alan Millard, "The Uses of the Early Alphabets," *Phoinikea Grammata. Lire et écrire en Mediterranée*. Collection d'Études Classiques, 6. Studie Phoenicia (Liege: Namus, 1991) 112.

the recent practice of dipping potsherds, as opposed to the previous practice of vigorous scrubbing, which often removed any writing, the number of inscribed ostraca has increased notably.

Scribes exercised their skill in other ways as well. Many of them wrote on the handles and rims of vessels containing wine or grain, for example, "Belonging to Yahzeyahu, wine of *khl*."[8] They inscribed ritual objects and gifts, such as five bronze arrowheads discovered near El Khadr, south of Bethlehem, with the words "arrow of '*Abd lb't*." On the obverse, one of these has the words "Ben Anat."[9] Scribes wrote on weights, indicating the particular value and thus stabilizing the economy to some degree. Talismans also received the exacting attention of scribes, as did objects of art, including an ivory pomegranate-shaped ceremonial scepter with the words "Belonging to the hou[se of YHWH] holy to priests." Even a priestly blessing occurs in tiny letters in a silver amulet from a tomb, Ketef Hinnom near Jerusalem. This blessing from Num. 6:24–26 was written fully and also in an abbreviated form on another amulet, the words carefully concealed from view but very much present in the mind of the wearer. Trained scribes also wrote names on seals, some of which were beautifully decorated, like the well-known seal of Shema', with its exquisite depiction of a lion. A number of seals belonging to governmental officials have either survived or are attested by copious bullae.

To what extent ordinary Israelites and Judaeans could write remains a mystery. Like most things in the ancient

---

[8] Mazar, *Archaeology of the Land of the Bible*, 516.
[9] *Ibid.*, 362.

world, literacy was affected by three factors: environmental, political, and social. An agricultural economy such as that prevailing in Judah and Israel provided few inducements to formal education, despite the rhetoric in Deut. 6:9 encouraging the people to write the commandments on doorposts and gates. In fact, the demands of daily chores—tending sheep and goats, preparing land for cultivation, attending to olive groves and vineyards—discouraged formal schooling. In addition, the modest economic rewards available to trained scribes and the limited prospects of advancement did little to offset this situation. Few families could afford the luxury of sending boys away to school, especially during the labor-intensive seasons of planting and harvesting crops. In all probability, most scribes belonged to guilds, and self-interest moved them to adopt a policy of manipulating scarcity, restricting scribal expertise insofar as possible. The simplicity of the Hebrew alphabet encouraged literacy, although no correlation between a simple script and mass literacy has been established. Japan, with its complex script but widespread literacy, stands as a warning against thinking that a simple alphabet necessarily leads to wholesale literacy, or that a complicated script necessarily implies widespread illiteracy.

The political well-being of various monarchs rested more on the shoulders of trained soldiers than on a coterie of intelligentsia, but the latter had their place under certain kings, most notably during Hezekiah's reign. At no time did an Israelite or Judaean monarch institute a program to educate the populace—except for Josiah's attempt to buttress his revolutionary practices by appealing to a newly discovered, or recently forged, ancient document. This instruction, however, was oral and aimed at moral renewal. Nor did social pressure exist for establishing schools and encouraging citizens to constitute a learned community. Biblical kings remain silent about this important feature of culture; they do not even claim to possess extraordinary intellectual prowess, although tradition attributes unique wisdom to Solomon. Perhaps the rhetoric in Deut. 6:9 stands as an exception and served as an incentive to literacy, but its demands could easily have been fulfilled by professional scribes.

EGYPTIAN LITERACY

John Baines has estimated that literacy in Egypt seldom exceeded 1 percent; in some ways, he thinks, Egypt resembles an oral culture rather than a literate one.[10] Under such circumstances, writing served administrative purposes as well as religious ends; it reinforced a centralization of resources that eventually contributed to the impoverishment of the illiterate. Writing also enhanced the prestige of administrators and priests, only gradually and superficially addressing popular needs and interests.

The complexity of the different scripts over the centuries—hieroglyphics, hieratic, and demotic—and the skillful management of scarcity by an administration with little demand for scribes, with a few exceptions, gave rise to a distinction between a core elite and a sub-elite. Scribes be-

---

[10] "Literacy and Ancient Egyptian Society," 572.

longed to the second of these. Literacy covered a wide spectrum, from an ability to read and write to mere reading of a few signs, and everywhere between these extremes. Many scribes of later times could not read hieroglyphics, and the opportunities open to them were often quite pedestrian. Pictorial reliefs, highly stylized, show them at work in various circumstances: sitting with legs crossed (mostly in statuary), working while seated in chairs, sitting on the ground and working at tables, kneeling on one knee, writing on well-lit porches and in a dark storeroom illuminated by an oil lamp.

Although some scribal texts give the impression that the military offered the most attractive alternative to the profession of scribe, a reference in Herodotus gives a different perspective on vocational opportunities. According to this fifth-century author, Egyptian society was divided into seven classes: priests, warriors, cowherds, swineherds, tradesmen, interpreters, and boatmen. The first of these, priests, teamed up with administrators, zealously guarding literacy and its magical power. With sacred writings came a sense of order, both in this world and in the next. Making preparations for the realm of the dead placed extraordinary demands on the time and energy of scribes, as Egyptians "searched for permanence beyond the initial threshold of death."[11]

Royal administrators promulgated an appreciation for the past, and literacy supported such history by means of annals and narrative, which lent themselves to celebrating the exploits of rulers, real or imagined. The prestige bestowed on

[11] *Ibid.*, 577.

the literate was real, but not sufficient to entice them to do the tedious job of writing texts. That task they delegated to scribes, the sub-elite. In iconography, members of the nobility preferred to be depicted while engaged in fishing and fowling, not toiling as scribes. During the Early Dynastic and Old Kingdom periods, however, kings acquired an education and expected their sons to do likewise. They even wrote instructions to their sons, offering them the benefits of long experience in forming character. These instructions covered a wide range of topics, such as proper etiquette, control of passions, appropriate behavior in office, effective speaking, psychology, and much more.

During the Old Kingdom, writing served an administration's wishes by recording important annals, legal statutes, significant biographical data, and religious teachings. Stone stelae gradually came to be used for this diverse matter, although at first limited to legal proclamations. In the Middle Kingdom, kings issued royal inscriptions comparable to earlier biographical texts. In addition, "literary" texts came into existence. These include Instructions, mythological tales, hymns, and texts covering specialized topics such as medicine, magic, mathematics, astronomy, and calendrical facts. Onomastica, or lists of categories, give evidence of an attempt at systematizing available knowledge on a given topic. Monumental texts come to resemble literary texts. The New Kingdom witnessed the rise of superficially popular genres, with the requisite simpler style, such as folklore motifs and love poems. According to Baines, the folklore elements in this literature must be taken with a grain of salt; the texts were addressed to the literate, a tiny percentage of the population.[12] Because of the absence of breaks between words, reading was quite difficult; rarely did anyone read for pleasure.

Egyptian scribes were certainly elitist and self-sustaining. From the earliest dynasties, writing enhanced a king's prestige, prompting pictorial representations of literary activity on the part of pharaohs. The exclusive nature of literacy contributed to esoteric knowledge and texts; the *Book of Amduat*, or "hidden space," depicts the underworld in pictures and text and concentrates on knowledge as such.

In principle, classical texts were preserved exactly as written. Actually, however, they fell victim to incompetent and/ or careless scribes. Religious and magical texts were also highly prized, great care being taken to assure accurate renderings of important ritual and language. Archaism in both art and literature grew out of respect for the values of the past. One type of literature, the harpists' songs, questioned the usual optimism about life after death. Used in association with funeral rituals, these songs juxtapose optimistic and pessimistic beliefs and question the value of assiduously preparing for the next life.

LITERACY IN GREECE AND ROME

The conclusions of William V. Harris about literacy in ancient Greece and Rome are not appreciably different from

[12] *Ibid.*, 586.

those regarding Egypt and Mesopotamia.[13] Even where the upper classes valued education, they looked down on teachers as socially inferior. Furthermore, the small monetary gains from acquiring an education did not sufficiently compensate for loss of labor on farms or among artisans. Greco-Roman society, like the Israelite, was largely rural, and even in classical Greece literacy rarely exceeded 10 percent. Evidence from papyri overwhelmingly suggests a high degree of inability to sign one's name, much less read and write. If one were to use the idea of cultural illiteracy as the norm, the picture would be bleaker still—and this understanding of illiteracy was certainly familiar, giving rise to the designations *agrammatos* and *illiteratur.*

Schools in Greco-Roman antiquity were not subsidized, except in a few Hellenistic cities. In the late third century B.C.E., Polythrous of Teos donated 34,000 drachmas, the income of which was to pay teachers an annual salary. At Miletus in 200–199, Eudemus gave a sum producing 480 drachmas a year for each of four teachers, plus a sum for athletic trainers. In 160 Attalus II of Pergamum gave 18,000 drachmas to Delphi as payment for teachers, and his brother, Eumenes II, contributed 280,000 bushels of grain, the largest gift by far, to subsidize teachers in Rhodes. The donor of the gift to Teos specified that it was to be used for "universal" education—for all free boys and some girls, but early marriages and social exclusion prevented girls from getting an education.

[13] *Ancient Literacy* (Cambridge and London: Harvard University Press, 1989). The following discussion relies on the results of Harris's research, to which one may compare Stanley F. Bonner, *Education in Ancient Rome: From the Elder Cato to the Younger Pliny* (Berkeley and Los Angeles: University of California Press, 1977).

Writing materials were expensive, beyond the reach of many people, and potsherds were a convenient substitute for use in ephemeral writing. In 408–407, 16 obols purchased two rolls of papyrus, and during the early fourth century, one roll cost as much as 21 obols. With subsistence wages at the time amounting to 3 obols a day, this placed papyrus out of the reach of ordinary citizens. Tablets of wood were widely used and, like papyrus, they could be re-used. Writers of Greek tragedies mention writing tablets as commonplace; these authors depict men as readers, but also an occasional woman. Although fifth-century Athenian vases portray women reading or carrying books, they usually represent Muses or Sappho, the renowned poet from the island of Lesbos, and hence reflect an ideal rather than reality. In some wealthy households, however, women could read and kept careful accounts of household items and expenses.

What functions did writing serve in Greco-Roman society? According to Aristotle, it contributed to the making of money, management of the household, instruction, and civic activities. Diodorus went so far as to insist that education based on the written word is the cause of the good life. Writing possessed an inherent dignity, which lent itself to propaganda. It had to compete with memory, as Plato suggests, and education consisted largely of memorization. Exactness was not expected, and specialists in memorization persisted, although these persons were also literate.

The ancients realized the enormous power of literacy—the resulting control over the lives of the illiterate. Religious authorities used written texts to exercise a measure of control over people, as did politicians, especially in matters of

taxation but also in military affairs. Positively, literacy contributed to an entrenchment of knowledge through a
canon—the *Iliad, Odyssey, Aeneid*—and made the culture
more rational, skeptical, and logical. Moralists such as Hipparchus used writing for propaganda, erecting herms along
the road with moral advice. In 510–508 Athenians adopted
the practice of ostracism, and by about 480, six thousand
written votes were needed to ostracize a citizen. Other cities
followed this practice—Argos, Syracuse, Megara, and Miletus. Nevertheless, many citizens could not write their
names, for in one instance of 191 negative votes, only four-
teen different signatures are discernible.

Although writing in archaic times occurred primarily in
commerce and among craftsmen to designate ownership,
it increased rapidly in the sixth century when Pherecydes wrote his cosmogony in prose. By the fifth century,
legal documents, treaties, inscribed weights and measures,
minted coins, and vases evidence widespread use of writing.
Written curses and even Delphic oracles began to appear in
the sixth century. The earliest known letter dates from this
century, about 520. Slightly later, in 496, a roof collapsed
in Chios, killing 120 boys who were studying letters. This
elementary education probably grew out of choral training
for religious festivals. Vases dating from the fifth century
depict children learning letters, not just studying music and
learning athletic skills. They gained social prestige from
such education but little monetary advantage.

In fifth-century Athens, administrative use of writing
took place in legal contexts; a court clerk wrote a record of
proceedings and, beginning with Pericles, pleadings were
based on a written text. Evidence could take the form of

written testimony, but it had to be confirmed by oral testimony. The names of debtors and convicted criminals were posted, as well as public announcements. Writing was also widespread among wealthy merchants and high-ranking soldiers, who sent and received sensitive messages. Lists of tribute had to be maintained, and junior clerks existed for this purpose as early as 405 in Athens. Governmental proclamations were normally delivered by heralds; for written messages, the illiterate had to rely on intermediaries to convey the sense of the text.

The historians Herodotus and Thucydides preferred oral testimony to written, although Thucydides was more open to documents than Herodotus. Tragedy and forensics contributed to the popularity of reading, and by the last quarter of the fifth century trading in written documents took place. In 405 Euripides refers to his own personal collection of literature, and three quarters of a century later Alexander took Callisthenes, a historian, on his military campaigns to provide propaganda.

Although religious texts and ritual were written, the masses seldom felt the effect of literacy. Priests at Epidaurus did appeal to written texts to authenticate Asclepius' cures. Funeral epitaphs served a number of purposes unrelated to the populace at large—to assuage grief, claim social standing, and perpetuate memory. "Most Greeks were small farmers or artisans with little or no surplus to spend, but with a powerful incentive to make their sons work from an early age."[14] Because parents had to pay for school, only the wealthy could afford to send their sons. Nevertheless,

[14] Harris, *Ancient Literacy*, 102.

Plato's *Laws* (Book VII) envisions universal education for boys and girls, and Aristotle recommends compulsory education, beginning at age five. Phaleas of Chalcedon was probably the first to argue for universal education, although Diodorus Siculus claims that honor for Clarondas of Catana.

During the Hellenistic period writing proliferated and every city had a school. By the third century work contracts and estimates were given in writing, although much evidence comes from Zenon's archives, which may not be broadly representative of the general populace. As accountant for Appollonius, a senior government official in Egypt, Zenon kept a record of every business transaction in which he was involved. An enormous amount of papyrus was required for this task. In 258–257, Apollonius received 434 rolls of papyrus in thirty-three days. Superintending the gathering of revenue required exact records. Technical manuals also flourished, covering such topics as medicine, rhetoric, military tactics, engineering, mining, dyeing, agriculture, and beekeeping. Examinations occurred in schools, and at Pergamum girls competed in calligraphy. Herodas' third miniamb, "The Schoolmaster" (280's or 270's), refers to a grown boy who had difficulty reading and writing. It takes for granted that to be Greek is to be educated, and that a woman could be literate.

A certain contradiction lies at the heart of the Greco-Roman culture. On the one hand, education was held in high esteem, both for its symbolic value and for its utility in commerce, government, and thinking. On the other hand, those who transmitted learning to the young, the schoolteachers, were held in contempt by the socially elite, who in a real sense depended on their expertise. This attitude prevented the subsidization of education by the government and discouraged private philanthropy. Occasionally something forced the decision-makers to reexamine the situation. Contact with barbarians, for example, may have encouraged Hellenistic leaders to place more emphasis on transmitting *paideia* to the next generation. Still, with a few exceptions, particularly the southeastern Aegean, most Greeks and Romans remained illiterate.

Chapter Two

⁓

The Contemplative Life

"Set sail and flee from every form of paideia."
EPICURUS

W hen the sages of ancient Egypt, Mesopotamia, and Israel contemplated reality, they assessed matters in two distinct ways, the one firmly grounded in experience, the other abstract and philosophical.[1] Central to both modes of understanding reality, the principle of analogy facilitated a moving from the better known to the less well known.[2] From the beginning, philosophical ponderings of life's enigmas took the form of extensive dialogue in which opposing viewpoints found expression and vied for acceptance. In contrast to this dialogic way of addressing the world around them,[3] others observed what was accessible to

---

[1] Gerhard von Rad, *Wisdom in Israel* (Nashville: Abingdon Press, 1972); James L. Crenshaw, *Old Testament Wisdom* (Atlanta: John Knox Press, 1981); and Buccellati, "Wisdom and Not: The Case of Mesopotamia," *JAOS* 101 (1981) 35–47.

[2] Some interpreters begin with an overarching concept, usually creation or theodicy, and move from this theme to discuss the way it affects everything else, but others discern several thematic interests of the sages and study the development of each line of thought.

[3] Sara Denning-Bolle, *Wisdom in Akkadian Literature: Expression, Instruction, Dialogue* (Ph.D. dissertation, University of California, Los Angeles, 1982), emphasizes the

the naked eye and crystallized insights about human beings or nature in brief aphorisms, riddles, and popular sayings. In time the gnomic apperception of reality receded as teachers expanded earlier insights in an effort to communicate with students. Modern scholars therefore distinguish between sayings and Instructions. Stimulated by the natural tendency to view the universe in terms of binary opposition, for example, light and darkness, good and evil, this approach encouraged an exploration of deeper reasons for the presence of troublesome aspects of reality along with the good. The two ways of viewing reality therefore reinforced one another.

THE LITERATURE

Instructions

In Egypt a technical term, *sbꜣyt*, designates Instructions, although the expression also refers to other forms of literature. Among the earliest Instructions are some that purport to offer advice from pharaohs to their young sons, the heirs apparent. Hence the subject matter was essentially directed toward preparing princes and their high officials for later responsibilities in government: e.g., appropriate etiquette, table manners, conduct in the presence of officials, eloquence, restraint, behavior with respect to women, control of passions, knowing when to speak and when to be silent.

---

importance of dialogue to ancient sages in Mesopotamia. She writes: "Wisdom is a matter of communicating, enlightening, and instructing; dialogue is its vehicle" (280).

Not all Instructions were restricted to royalty, for the majority of texts are attributed to courtiers wishing to prepare their sons to succeed them at the royal court. The late Demotic Instructions were probably written by ordinary citizens—though literate—as a sort of manual for self-improvement.

Over the two millennia from the earliest Instructions to these products of popularizing reflection, a decisive change is discernible. At first those who formulated these teachings confidently looked on the order of the universe and took the deity's control for granted. In their view persons deserving favor received it, and those whose conduct merited punishment did not prosper. With the coming of the Middle Kingdom optimism such as Ptahhotep's "Baseness may seize riches, yet crime never lands its wares" waned and an altogether different mood apparently set in, with serious consequences. Accompanying the anxiety generated by notable social changes was a piety in which individuals sought to secure divine favor by prayer and virtue. During the Demotic period the power of fate began to dominate the surviving Instructions, chiefly *Ankhsheshonqy* and *Papyrus Insinger.* Both Instructions stressed the necessity of pleasing the gods, never reconciling the contradiction between fate and the power of the gods but allowing the two notions to function in a complementary manner.[4]

Another decisive change occurred in these late Instructions, the adoption of a form that adhered to a single line for each saying.[5] Earlier teachings had begun with a conditional

---

[4] Lichtheim, *Late Egyptian Wisdom Literature in the International Context,* 133, n. 119.

[5] *Ibid.,* 4.

statement, followed by an observation and an explanation or justification for the comment. Because all Instructions seek to shape character and to stimulate action, they regularly employ imperatives, a feature biblical scholars have exaggerated in formal analysis.[6] *Papyrus Insinger* and *Ankhsheshonqy* link the imperatives together in chain fashion, with verbal links connecting anaphoric chains. Whereas older Egyptian Instructions influenced biblical Proverbs, the Demotic ones have left their impact on Qoheleth (Ecclesiastes) and Sirach (also known as Ecclesiasticus or Ben Sira), whose text is replete with paragraph-length Instructions.

The oldest Mesopotamian proverbs, the *Instruction of Šuruppak*, use the technical expression "my son" in the sense of student, a characteristic of Egyptian and biblical Instructions also.[7] The latter comprise the initial collection in Proverbs 7–9, as well as a section betraying the influence of the Egyptian *Instruction of Amenemope*, 22:17–24:22, and a brief unit attributed to King Lemuel's mother in 31:1–10. The Neo-Assyrian text *Counsels to a Prince* also belongs to this Instruction genre, as do *Counsels of Wisdom* and *Counsels of a Pessimist*.[8]

Sayings

No Egyptian collection of sayings has survived, but numerous traditional sayings and aphorisms are scattered throughout the Instructions and are embedded in other literary

---

[6] Above all, William McKane, *Proverbs* (Philadelphia: Westminster Press, 1970).

[7] Bendt Alster, *The Instruction of Šuruppak: A Sumerian Proverb Collection* (Copenhagen: Akademisk Forlag, 1974).

[8] For the texts in translation, see James B. Pritchard, *Ancient Near Eastern Texts Relating to the Old Testament* (Princeton: Princeton University Press, 1969).

forms, especially narrative. Collections of proverbs exist in Sumerian and Old Babylonian, just as they do in the Bible, chiefly in Proverbs but also in Qoheleth and Sirach. An Aramaic collection of riddles and proverbs, *The Sayings of Ahiqar*, resembles Mesopotamian texts and thus renders plausible its narrative framework about a Mesopotamian setting.[9]

Dialogue

The other way of assessing reality, philosophical reflection, deals with weighty matters, especially the problem of life's inequities. Only one text from Egypt, *The Admonitions of Ipuwer*, addresses the issue of theodicy as such, and this particular section may be a later addition.[10] Other works take up many issues typically found in theodicies—life's misery, chaotic social conditions—especially *The Harper's Songs*,[11] *Dispute of a Man with his Ba*, and to some extent *The Protests of the Eloquent Peasant* and the *Book of the Dead*. Two biblical exemplars of this genre, Job and Qoheleth, have greatly influenced Western thinkers. Both Sirach and the Wisdom of Solomon contain mini-discussions of the anxiety generated by evil in a universe supposedly created and ruled by a benevolent deity. A few Psalms also broach the issue, either to deny that any problem exists, as in Psalm 37, or to forge new insights, as in Psalms 49 and 73.

[9] James M. Lindenberger, *The Aramaic Proverbs of Ahiqar* (Baltimore and London: The Johns Hopkins University Press, 1983).

[10] Ronald J. Williams, "The Sages of Ancient Egypt in the Light of Recent Scholarship," *JAOS* 101 (1981) 1–19, especially 8.

[11] Michael V. Fox, *The Song of Songs and the Ancient Egyptian Love Songs* (Madison: The University of Wisconsin Press, 1985), demonstrates the relationship between Egyptian and biblical erotic poetry.

Several examples of theodicy derive from Mesopotamia. *The Sumerian Man and his God* is the oldest known expression of the problem addressed in the Book of Job, but the later *I Will Praise the Lord of Wisdom* and *The Babylonian Theodicy* develop the form in the direction that the biblical Job adopts. The author of *A Dialogue between a Master and his Slave* struggled with the problematic nature of reality that caused such consternation in Qoheleth.[12] These Mesopotamian texts set precedent for: blaming the gods; recommending repentance and correct ritual; arguing with a friend about God's justice; introducing and concluding poetry with a mythological framing narrative; and considering both sides of opposing intellectual positions.

COMPOSITION

Myths

What prompted the authors of these sapiential insights to adopt forms of expression intended to convey their meaning to a wider public? A didactic impulse seems to have accompanied dialogue and Instruction—perhaps even sayings—from their inception. This inherent didacticism does not exclude a conscious attempt at a later time to turn simple statements into *literary* products. The functional aspect of knowledge prevailed, its capacity to enrich life in quite tangible ways. According to a royal myth echoed in Prov. 25:2,

---

[12] W. G. Lambert, *Babylonian Wisdom Literature* (Oxford: Clarendon, 1960) and Benjamin R. Foster, *From Distant Days: Myths, Tales, and Poetry of Ancient Mesopotamia* (Bethesda, Maryland: CDL Press, 1995) 295–329.

deity and king enacted a reciprocal drama by hiding and seeking valuable facts about the universe and its inhabitants. Presumably, the creator concealed such data in observable reality and thereby presented a challenge for humankind, especially its representative leader, to search for insights that would facilitate steering life's course into safe harbor. The operative word, "What is good for men and women?" survived the very questioning of the intellectual quest's validity. Qoheleth retained the myth of the deity's concealing essential data (3:11) but pronounced a negative judgment on human ability to profit from this dubious gift. Similarly, the author of Job 28 restricted something called wisdom to the deity, announcing that no one else came any closer to it than secondary reporting. Sirach goes a step further, attributing secrecy to wisdom itself.

Underlying this myth was a significant theological issue—the freedom of God. That prerogative of a deity to act without restraint from external sources seems threatened by the sapiential notion of an order governing the universe. In Egypt the principle of *Ma'at* represented this divine order that assured governmental, societal, and individual well-being. A corresponding principle in Mesopotamia seems to be implied by the Tablets of Destiny, *ME*. The Israelite concepts of justice, *mišpāṭ*, and right dealing, *ṣedāqâ*, functioned in the way *Ma'at* and *ME* did elsewhere.

At first glance this objective order appears to compromise the deity's freedom, but even this principle remained subject to God's free will. At the same time, sages spoke openly of deeds that carried within them the capacity to set into motion events commensurate with the originating act, whether for punishment or for reward. Occasional canonical sayings within the Book of Proverbs accentuate the fundamental limits imposed on the human intellect; these reminders that "humans propose but God disposes" resemble sayings in Egyptian Instructions. The latest surviving Egyptian Instruction, *Papyrus Insinger*, has developed this notion of fate into a refrain while also acknowledging the deity's active involvement in shaping human destiny. Resolving apparently contradictory statements was not essential in the ancient world; rigorous thinkers have always managed to flourish without pressing for closure on disputed matters.

Forms

This open-ended worldview of sages achieved expression in specific forms, chiefly sayings and Instructions, but also in related ones.[13] Interpreters generally assume that the elemental form, the saying, existed initially as a product of popular insights. Brief maxims and aphorisms simply registered the way things were without pronouncing judgment or advocating corrective action. Several traditional sayings have survived in the narrative and prophetic literature of the Bible; others, in expanded form, may be embedded in the wisdom corpus. Occupying a transitional stage between popular saying and didactic poem, riddles captured the surprise of discovery and directed it toward the teaching task. Only Mesopotamian wisdom has preserved riddles intact, but once again Israelite narrative, more particularly, the story of Samson in Judges 14, fills the gap left tantalizingly open by explicit references to riddles as a sapiential concern

[13] James L. Crenshaw, "Wisdom," 225–64 in *Old Testament Form Criticism*, ed. John H. Hayes (TUMS 1; San Antonio: Trinity University Press, 1974).

(Prov. 1:6; Sir 39:1–3). Several proverbs structured by ascending numbers betray affinities with riddles, and in one instance the specific allusion to numbers has vanished but the normal interrogative form of riddles takes its place (Sir. 1:2–3).

The popular saying, often only a half-line, commanded assent by its content alone. Instructions relied on motivation clauses and warnings to persuade others that their teachings were valid. This extended discourse developed into didactic poems, which treated single themes at greater length than occurred in sayings and Instructions. At this point erotic overtones color the expression of paternal will, either in the form of positive seduction to the intellectual enterprise or in the guise of negative warnings about strange women who lured young men to the grave. Other didactic poems tackle the vexing problem of aging and its final victory, they acknowledge the tyranny of time over all flesh, or they celebrate the worth of a good woman. An impressive group of poems explores the means through which the deity communicates with mortals, at first envisioning nothing more than poetic metaphor but afterward contemplating an actual expression of the divine will in legal form, and eventually opting for a virtual hypostasis in which the deity becomes manifest on earth. Echoes of a polytheistic environment persist in this mytho-logos, with features deriving from Egyptian *Ma'at* traditions and Isis aretalogies. Didactic poems delve into the wonder and majesty surrounding the creative process, both the divine act by which everything came into existence and the human intellectual adventure that endeavors to make sense of reality as it presents itself to inquiring minds.

Pedagogic interests generated yet another form of communication, the exemplary tale. The autobiographical character of these stories bestows on them credibility and authority. A concerned teacher reports on the fatal attraction of two people who come together for illicit sexual pleasure, an older person recalls near-disastrous personal decisions during his youth, an astute observer calls attention to the undesirable results of laziness, a fictional monarch sums up his life's work and assesses its worth, a sober social analyst registers dismay over society's lack of appreciation for the contribution of scholars, and so on.

Such communicative devices gave birth to related ones, for example, exemplary tale to parable, parable to allegory, and dialogue to dispute. One parable uses the ant's furious pace in preparing for winter's scarcity as incentive to action. Such appeal to lessons from nonhuman creatures played a significant role in ancient wisdom. Mesopotamian disputes between animals or trees over the merits of different species reflect a similar epistemological assumption that nature itself functions as a bearer of knowledge. That polytheistic environment also encouraged informed evaluation of rival deities through disputes. In Israel the dispute form developed into internal debate, a conversation with the self in which Qoheleth considers what he has seen and draws rational conclusions from the available evidence. The Egyptian *Dispute of a Man with his Ba* differs dramatically in its view of an entity, the *ba*, that survives death. The arrangement of aphorisms into a statement, then a contradiction, an objection, or a confirmation demonstrates the sages' fondness for dialogue.

Not all stylistic devices employed by the sages are unique

to their literature. The Book of Job makes copious use of the lament form, common to the Psalms and to comparable texts from Mesopotamia. Later wisdom, especially Sirach, introduced prayer and hymn into the sapiential vocabulary. Prior to this embracing of religious language, the only prayer occurs in the late excerpt attributed to Agur (Prov. 30:7–9) and the nearest semblance to a hymn (Job 9:5–10; 5:9–16) heightens the tension between Job and his friends by pointing to the mystery of the universe and its maker. The hymnic praise of the creator comes into its own in Sirach; in addition, Ben Sira adapts a Hellenistic form, the encomium, to heap accolades on heroes of the past.

Social Settings

Do these rhetorical devices indicate the social setting for their use? Unfortunately, one cannot move from literary genre to precise locations in society.[14] This issue must be addressed from country to country, and even within a given environment distinctions readily surface. Egyptian Instructions presuppose a royal context, but this intimate connection with the court is not absolute. Scribal schools existed primarily as a function of area temples, instructing religious

[14] Michael V. Fox, "The Social Location of the Book of Proverbs," 227–39 in *Texts, Temples, and Traditions: A Tribute to Menahem Haran*, eds. Michael V. Fox et al. (Winona Lake: Eisenbrauns, 1996); Franz Crüsemann, "Die unveränderbare Welt. Überlegungen zur 'Krisis der Weisheit' beim Prediger (Kohelet)," 80–104 in *Der Gott der kleinen Leute*, eds. Willi Schotroff and Wolfgang Stegemann (Munich, 1979; ET, *The God of the Lowly*, Maryknoll: Orbis, 1984); R. N. Whybray, "The Social World of the Wisdom Writers," 227–50 in *The World of Ancient Israel*, ed. Ronald E. Clements (Cambridge: Cambridge University Press, 1989); Joseph Blenkinsopp, *Wisdom and Law in the Old Testament: The Ordering of Life in Israel and Early Judaism* (Oxford: Oxford University Press, 1995); and Claus Westermann, *Roots of Wisdom: The Oldest Proverbs of Israel and Other Peoples* (Louisville: Westminster John Knox Press, 1995).

personnel in the necessary ritual and in theological texts. The language and themes of individual Instructions do not provide easy access to the social location of the authors. Villagers can readily discuss royalty and their doings, just as courtiers can talk about agrarian tasks. The fact that only about one-tenth of *Ankhsheshonqy's* sayings deal with agricultural topics hardly settles the question of origins. The Sumerian school, *edubba*, may have served as a locus for learned discourse, as well as for education at all levels of instruction. Here, as also in Egypt, noun lists, or onomastica, assisted in the study of language and grammar, perhaps also in providing data for a broader education itself.

Ancient Israelite literature derives from several different social contexts. The authors of Proverbs, Job, Ecclesiastes, and Sirach occupied distinct social worlds, and a single book like Proverbs reflects several settings. To be sure, most of the sayings revolve around life in small villages and restrict themselves to the nuclear family. The latter point detracts from the hypothesis of clan wisdom, for members of an extended family are never mentioned. The Instructions are directed to yet another group, young urban men, possibly potential officials at the royal court. Given the court's minor role in these sayings and Instructions, perhaps one should assume that both forms eventually played a significant role in the scribal school, for which the earliest firm evidence is the second century B.C.E. remark by Ben Sira. Inscriptional evidence has generated a hypothesis of widespread schools in Palestine from early monarchic times, but these data, particularly abecedaries, exercise tablets, crude drawings, and foreign language texts, can be readily explained without resort to the claim of a vast educational network. As we have seen, literacy in the ancient world rarely exceeded 10 percent, and in most instances it ran considerably lower. The modern advance in literacy is a direct result of several factors: the invention of the printing press; the Industrial Revolution's need for trained workers; state sponsorship of education, assisted by exceptional philanthropists; Protestantism's emphasis on knowing the Bible; the availability of eyeglasses; population density sufficient to support public education; and affordable writing materials. Ancient literacy was ordinarily restricted to males with administrative legal functions; exceptions occurred only with respect to the daughters of a few rulers or high officials.

At least three social groups factor into the discussion of the Book of Job, according to a recent plausible theory.[15] Two wealthy groups, one of which objects to taking advantage of the poor, contend for supremacy. The cruel upper class against which Job rails has no compassion for the underprivileged, who in the wealthy's view exist only to be used. Qoheleth belonged to an acquisitive society, one in which financial success counted heavily. He has been accused, with dubious justification, of membership in a cruel, calculating upper crust that held the poor in contempt.[16] Such a harsh reading of the book ignores the pathos of Qoheleth's observation about defenseless victims of oppres-

---

[15] Rainer Albertz, "Der sozialgeschichtliche hintergrund des Hiobbuches und der 'Babylonischen Theodizee,'" 349–72 in *Die Botschaft und die Boten* (Neukirchyen: Neukirchener-Vluyn, 1981).

[16] Crüsemann, "Die unveränderbare Welt. Überlegungen zur 'Krisis der Weisheit' beim Prediger (Kohelet)"; for another view, see James L. Crenshaw, *Ecclesiastes* (Philadelphia: Westminster Press, 1987).

sion. Strictly speaking, one can only conclude that Qohel-eth's *audience* possessed the means to enjoy life that he recommends as a way of dealing with absurdity everywhere.

Although Egyptian and Mesopotamian wisdom had a positive relationship with the royal court, Israelite attitudes toward kingship and a discernible enthusiasm for simpler societal structures produced conflicting texts. Despite a royal myth that includes attributing collections of sayings and even two entire books, Ecclesiastes and the Wisdom of Solomon, to a king, the nature of the proverbial sayings and the celebration of Edomite sagacity imply that in some cir-cles marginal existence apart from society's corrupting in-fluence was viewed as more pristine. Presumably, in that purer state knowledge came much more naturally.

THEMES

Creation

The fundamental themes of wisdom literature are religion and knowledge.[17] Beginning with an assumption that truth applies universally and thus was not confined to private ex-perience or limited to any geographical area, sages concen-trated on the initiating event that made life possible in its manifold localities and variations. In Israelite wisdom the

---

[17] James L. Crenshaw, "The Concept of God in Old Testament Wisdom," 1–18 in *In Search of Wisdom: Essays in Memory of John G. Gammie*, eds. Leo G. Perdue, Bernard Brandon Scott, and William Johnston Wiseman (Louisville: Westminster John Knox, 1993) and *Urgent Advice and Probing Questions*.

creative act was placed under the umbrella of divine justice, for it was believed that appropriate reward or punishment could be dispensed only by one who controlled the universe. Even social distinctions on the basis of access to property failed to efface the unique feature uniting all humanity in a single community—their mortality—or to compromise the fact that rich and poor had the same maker. Radical dissenters like Qoheleth did not challenge the common conception that the created world was a thing of beauty, despite occasional examples of twistedness. According to the wisdom myth, the original act of creation culminated in rejoicing on the part of the morning stars and, in one bold text, the creator's youthful female companion, Wisdom, unless one accepts the alternative reading and views her as a master craftsman.

One type of creation myth included a battle between the power representing order and an opposing force characterized by instability. This "struggle against chaos" has left its imprint on numerous hymnic texts within the Bible, especially those incorporated in Deutero-Isaiah and the Psalms.[18] This version of creation in which the Israelite deity prevails over chaos has close parallels in ancient Babylon, best known from the conflict between Marduk and Tiamat recorded in *Enuma elish*. The belief that a violent event fashioned the arena for life's drama evoked similar myths throughout the ancient world, competing with the explanation of origins in natural or sexual imagery. Some interpret-

[18] Jon D. Levenson, *Creation and the Persistence of Evil: The Jewish Drama of Divine Omnipotence* (San Francisco: Harper and Row, Publishers, 1988).

ers think the struggle between Baal and Yamm in Ugaritic myth actually disguises the creative act under the story about constructing a palace for Baal.

Israelite sages transformed the chaos myth into a story about domesticating the forces of evil or, more accurately, restricting their scope. Thus the deity who spoke to Job in the whirlwind boasts about setting limits for the chaos monster, circumscribing its movement and wrapping it in swaddling bands. In this version of the myth the real problem of chaos shifts to the human arena, and the faintest hint of divine weakness against this evil probably achieves expression. In its social dimension evil poses a constant problem requiring perpetual vigilance on the part of the deity and virtuous mortals.[19]

Fear of God

The sages' emphasis on creation acknowledged major indebtedness on the part of human beings toward the deity, for life itself derived from the creator. Occasionally this knowledge led to the rejection of any claim with respect to the deity based on virtuous conduct, for no gift to or from God could ever rival the one already freely bestowed on mortals. Given this situation, it is a little surprising that a concept of reward and retribution became common belief, virtually hardening into dogma. At the same time, the sages also recognized their complete dependence on the creator's goodwill, hence the necessity for proper fear. This notion

---

[19] James L. Crenshaw, "When Form and Content Clash: The Theology of Job 38:1–40:5," 70–84 in *Creation in the Biblical Tradition*, eds. Richard J. Clifford and John J. Collins (CBQMS 24; Washington D.C.: Catholic Biblical Association, 1992).

of fear before the deity included the sense of dread in the presence of a potential threat as well as genuine submission in obedient love. In its fullest sense the expression "fear of God" is the closest the sages ever came to the modern idea connoted by the word *religion.*

Although the evidence lacks clarity, some interpreters think the sentiment expressing fear of God was originally missing from the sayings. In modern categories, they would have been thoroughly secular. This understanding of the sayings underscores the fact that several aphorisms whose form bears the marks of great antiquity are remarkably silent about any deity, relying solely on human action without regard to transcendent motivation. Such silence does not necessarily mean that the authors of these texts were irreligious. Egyptian wisdom literature also betrays a growing overt pietism as a direct consequence of the collapse of traditional values during the era immediately preceding the composition of the *Instruction of Anii* (Eighteenth Dynasty). In this work and in subsequent ones, personal piety replaced the strong sense of self-reliance characterizing earlier wisdom. One seems drawn to the conclusion that the world was viewed as less penetrable than had been the case during the early days of Egyptian and Israelite wisdom.

The failure of traditional belief may have affected only a small segment of the population, whereas secular sayings may have derived from well-placed individuals at the palace. Perhaps the authors of these precepts saw no need to articulate self-evident views that temple functionaries explicitly mentioned in their literature. A conviction that a person could cope with every eventuality may easily have existed alongside the belief that divine assistance was essential to successful endeavor. Hence modern attempts to discern an increase in piety reflecting a crisis of confidence may be correct for only a select group of ancient thinkers.

Although the formula "Let the initiate instruct the initiate; the uninitiated may not see" does not always imply esoteric knowledge, certain texts in Egypt and in Mesopotamia, intentionally secret, suggest an elitist—perhaps even a mystical—tradition as early as the second millennium, one that goes far beyond the elitism accompanying literacy and possession of information concerning magical ritual. Egyptian initiation texts, e.g. the *Book of Amduat*, the *Book of Gates*, the *Book of the Heavenly Cow*, and the *Book of the Dead* (ch. 148), restrict gnosis to a select group or claim extraordinary knowledge of ritual for a chosen person such as the vizier User. Mesopotamian mystical and mythological explanatory works employ the numerical device *gematria*; comment on mystical numbers and names of deities; identify gods with various parts of the world through analogy and/or specification; offer mystical descriptions of gods; explain state rituals in terms of the myths by which people lived; and interpret the god's (Marduk's) ordeal existentially. Some of these texts state that the contents are "a secret of the scholar," adding that "the uninitiated shall not see." Occasionally, a scribe expects readers to know another text by heart; for instance, one scholar cites only the first line of *Enuma elish*. An aim of a few texts was identification with a deity, sharing mythic conflicts and victories.

Within seventh-century Israel a quasi-mystical surge in the thinking of two prophets, Jeremiah and Ezekiel, may have taken place. Claiming to have been given access to the divine council, Jeremiah insists that his opponents were not similarly gifted. He even uses language that accords with a mystical understanding of the Word, which he characterizes as a fire and a hammer (23:29). His contemporary Ezekiel describes the divine departure from the Temple of Jerusalem in mystical categories, leading to later restrictions on just who could read these visions. Prophetic books such as Joel cite earlier prophecies and interpret them in new ways; thus an exegetical tradition emerges to prominence in post-exilic and Hellenistic Judaism.[20] Apocalyptists soon boasted of esoteric knowledge, comparable with Jeremiah's claim to special disclosure. An elitist tradition flourishes at Qumran and in Pseudepigraphic literature, partly because some contemporaries believed that revealed writings necessarily derived from ancient worthies.

Personified Wisdom

The tension between self-reliance and dependence on the deity in special circumstances, or indeed in all circumstances, was eventually eased through a remarkable myth.[21] Israel's poets frequently spoke of abstract divine qualities in a personified manner, for example, picturing righteousness and truth as kissing each other. The wisdom of God naturally lent itself to such personification, as did divine power and speech, which were personified by the Aramaic terms

[20] Siegfried Bergler, *Joel als Schriftinterpret* (BEATAJ, 16; Frankfurt, am Main/Bern/New York: Verlag Peter Lang, 1988) and James L. Crenshaw, *Joel* (AB; New York: Doubleday, 1995).

[21] Roland E. Murphy, *The Tree of Life* (ABRL; New York: Doubleday, 1990), "The Personification of Wisdom," 222–33 in *Wisdom in Ancient Israel;* Judith M. Hadley, "Wisdom and the Goddess," 234–43 in *Wisdom in Ancient Israel;* and Bernhard W. Lang, *Wisdom and the Book of Proverbs: An Israelite Goddess Redefined* (New York: The Pilgrim Press, 1986).

Geburah and *Memra*. Wisdom, *ḥokmâ*, represented the divine logic by which the universe took shape, the structuring of things into a coherent order.

The erotic dimension inherent to all knowledge found suitable expression in this personification of the thought processes, the inexplicable seduction of the human mind by the unknown. Curiously, Israel's stout resistance in official circles to fertility religion did not prevent enthusiastic development of an erotic relationship between students and Wisdom. The sages spoke freely about Wisdom as a seductress who lures young men to her banquet, but they also conceded that she had a rival in this game of love, one who capitalized on her exceptional physical attributes, inflaming youthful passions by smooth limbs and speech. *Ḥokmâ* thus was forced to adopt extreme measures, hence the emphasis on her turning to human beings in love, a notion that does not appear in Egyptian description of a comparable figure, *Maʿat*, the goddess of "right order." In Israelite wisdom, seekers of knowledge are invited to pitch their tent near Wisdom's and to pursue her relentlessly, ignoring her initial rebuff in assurance that perseverance will reap rich reward. A partial defusing of this myth occurs in the Hellenistic Wisdom of Solomon, where the intellectual quest has achieved its goal and gained Wisdom, now the familiar *sophia* from Greek philosophy, as wife. Here love's ardor burns under the protective canopy of piety.

Quite a different redirection of erotic ardor takes place in Sirach, where daughters in particular do not receive adequate appreciation—despite Ben Sira's enthusiasm for some women and an appendix to the book that is arguably rich in eroticisms. The development by certain psalmists of something called Torah piety led Ben Sira to a bold move, the identification of the Torah with God's wisdom. In this way a divine attribute has taken up residence in Jerusalem, assuming visible form in the Mosaic covenant, the Law. Furthermore, this wisdom evokes comparison with knowledge in the story of the fall, for the paradisaic myth of the rivers recurs here in Ben Sira's musings about the composition of his book.

Why this striving to mediate Transcendence in a tangible manner? The sages' concept of God is remarkably silent with regard to the saving deeds extolled within official Yahwism. This theological position is a corollary of an ethical view emphasizing self-worth, a coping with life on one's own. As confidence in one's ability dwindled, particularly after the collapse of the concept of the extended family and later the state, sages began to recognize their own reliance on divine compassion. Wisdom mediated God's concern for mortals. The transcendent creator draws near and makes known the secrets to success and happiness. Most revealing of all, for those who think of the divine law as oppressive, the person who equates wisdom and the Torah also introduces the attribute of divine mercy into the discourse of the sages to a degree unprecedented in his time.

Formation of Character

How did wisdom express itself in the lives of sages? Both in Egypt and in Israel, four character traits distinguish wise from foolish, good from evil: silence, eloquence, timeliness, and modesty. The first requires control over passions; the silent person does not permit anger, lust, greed, or envy to dominate thought or action. The opposite, the heated individual, gives passion a free rein. The second quality enables sages to persuade others and to communicate effectively, while the third implies an awareness about the appropriate moment for speaking, valuing nonspeaking as a powerful form of communication. The fourth, modesty, indicates humility arising from knowledge that life's mysteries will never fully divulge themselves to those who search for truth.

The premise underlying the sages' elevation of these characteristics is clearly opportunistic. Some interpreters prefer the term eudaemonistic. The fundamental question, What is good for men and women? reveals their anthropocentric orientation. Nevertheless, the sages believed that their virtuous conduct did more than guarantee good rewards in the form of wealth, health, progeny, and honor. They also thought their actions sustained the order of the world, preventing a return to chaos. Hence eudaemonism was rooted in ethical philosophy, transforming an apparent selfish act into a moral and religious deed. In their view, the world was always at risk. This fear explains their incessant struggle against those who posed the most formidable threat, fools, and the fervent pleading with vulnerable students, called sons, that they adopt their teacher's worldview.

Sporadic victories by representatives of evil called into question the comfortable eudaemonism and forced sages to reckon with suffering and mortality. The lyrical "I" soon led to a heightened ego, an almost inevitable consequence of the hurting self, and eventuated in uncommon pride of authorship, at least for Ben Sira. With Qoheleth, egoism affects the form of expression, the teacher daring to assess everything as absurd on the basis of his experience. The union of epistemology and theology persists in Qoheleth, who drew the painful conclusion that human beings cannot discern whether or not the deity turns to them in love or hate, all the while speaking effusively about divine gifts. The problem lay in the changed status from one who earned life's rewards to a person depending on divine handouts over which the recipient had no control. More specifically, the apparent arbitrary conduct of the deity generated increased anxiety.

FUNCTION

Education

The literature produced by ancient Near Eastern sages served several purposes, all of which belong to the general category of education. Egyptian and Sumerian school texts assisted in the task of instructing students for the many demands of professional life, potentially at the court, but also as scribes responsible for all sorts of economic transactions. Training in requisite languages, contract forms, epistolary style, and regulations pertaining to international commerce probably occurred in the schools, and such instruction required paradigms and exemplars of diverse kinds. Sample examination questions have been identified among surviving Egyptian scribal texts, particularly in *Papyrus Anastasi I*, indicating that students learned considerable general knowledge of local geography, perhaps while practicing grammar and calligraphy. The complex hieroglyphs and cuneiform signs necessitated close attention to detail beyond

the aesthetics of nicely shaped letters. The abecedaries re-
covered from Palestine probably indicate scribal practice in
forming the vastly simpler Hebrew alphabet, but the silence
in Hebrew literature concerning schools has elicited opposite explanations: no schools existed; schools were so prevalent that no one ever thought about mentioning them.

Debate

Possibly the most useful texts in implementing pedagogical
strategies for advanced students, the philosophical debates
covered a wide range of responses to difficult intellectual
problems. Such literature offered alternative solutions to
the vexing issues encountering the populace every day, although the stellar example of this genre in Israel, the Book
of Job, portrays its disputants as pastoralists rather than as
scribes or sages. This unusual feature highlights the simple
fact that ancient learning, however academic, did not occur
within the confines of an ivory tower but took place at the
center of daily activity and addressed pressing questions that
directly affected human lives. The same point underlies the
description of Wisdom in Proverbs as a rhetor practicing
her trade in busy streets where she had to compete with ven-
dors of all types. In this respect the similarity with Hellenistic peripatetic philosophers comes to mind.

Entertainment

Debate did not always focus on serious existential issues, for
the sages found time to enjoy the art of storytelling and the

clever defense of an intellectual position. An example of the former is the remarkable contest of Darius' guards recorded in 1 Esd. 3:1–4:41, which examines the relative merits of wine, king, woman, and truth under the rubric, "What is greatest?"[22] An intriguing remark by the servant in the *Dialogue between a Master and his Slave* suggests that intellectual exchange occurred at banquets, hence that symposia played a significant role in early education. That incidental remark has parallels in Egyptian wisdom literature also, and the pseudepigraphic Epistle of Aristeas develops the notion of scintillating conversation during meals in great detail. Mesopotamian fables served a dual purpose of entertainment and practice in defending a particular viewpoint. These fables sometimes required students to make discerning judgments about the relative merits of various aspects of society—e.g., tools, animals, vocations, deities. The combined sayings and Instructions reflect societal values about numerous topics, but they do not constitute a complete moral code, for some important dimensions of life are strangely missing.

Taxonomies

A few texts from Egypt and many more from Mesopotamia comprise zoological and botanical taxonomies, an exhaustive list of various species. A curious legend in 1 Kings 4:29–34 (Hebrew, 5:9–14) attributes this sort of learning to

[22] James L. Crenshaw, "The Contest of Darius' Guards in 1 Esdras 3:1–5:3," 74–88, 119–20 in *Images of Man and God: The Old Testament Short Story in Literary Focus*, ed. Burke O. Long (Sheffield: Almond Press, 1981).

Solomon, who is said to have compiled proverbs about trees, beasts, birds, reptiles, and fish. Those interpreters who consider this text historically credible understand Solomon's contribution to the genre to be the actual formulation of poetic sayings incorporating such taxonomies. Encyclopedic lists in Egypt and Mesopotamia probably served a dual function, facilitating the practice of language and writing.

Ritual

Mesopotamian scribal texts served an important role in ritual, especially magic. Incantations dealing with all kinds of circumstances enabled society to reckon with multiple threats to existence. Liturgical paradigms such as *I Will Praise the Lord of Wisdom* enjoined proper religious response to calamity. Egyptian ritual incantations also claimed the attention of learned scribes, and the biblical Job's protestations of innocence in chapter 31 resemble oaths of innocence in Egypt and Mesopotamia. Otherwise, biblical wisdom practiced restraint with respect to religious ritual prior to Ben Sira, whose priestly leanings led to unchecked exuberance at witnessing the high priest in procession on a holy day. This late biblical sage also compiled an expansive eulogy honoring great men of the past; in doing so he incorporated Yahwistic tradition into wisdom thought.

Polemic

Some sapiential texts functioned polemically to defend the scribal profession, perhaps necessitated by harsh measures employed in the classroom, for which several scribal texts in Egypt and at least one school text from Sumer provide vivid documentation. Ben Sira's defense of the scribe's vocation has some affinity with the much earlier Egyptian *Instruction of Khety*, although the phenomenon of polygenesis may be at work here rather than direct literary dependence. Naturally, opposing views among the sages resulted in literature rich with polemic. Sometimes polemical attacks on outsiders intrude into sapiential texts, as when Ben Sira's anger explodes against traditional enemies of Israel and the Wisdom of Solomon launches a verbal assault against Egyptian idolaters.

Counsel

Just as Egyptians had officials at the royal court who needed instruction, Mesopotamians also employed scribes for whom appropriate guidance was necessary, as the story of Ahiqar implies. Whether or not an actual royal counselor advised biblical kings remains unclear, although the story about David mentions two counselors, Ahithophel and Hushai (2 Sam. 16:15–17:23). The obscure title "men of Hezekiah" alluded to in Prov. 25:1 indirectly links these sayings with royalty.

CONCLUSION

A significant literature from ancient Egypt, Mesopotamia, and Israel possesses sufficient thematic and formal unity to suggest a "common context of origin" and purpose, allowing for distinctions in the several areas. Those texts comprise the ancient effort to acquire knowledge and to embody wisdom in personal character. To achieve that worthy goal, the sages collected traditional insights of the populace and added their own learned conclusions about reality. In doing so, they bequeathed an important legacy to posterity.

Excursus

Foreign Woman

> Beware of a woman who is a stranger,
> One not known in her town;
> Don't stare at her when she goes by,
> Do not know her carnally.
> A deep water whose course is unknown,
> Such is a woman away from her husband.
> "I am pretty," she tells you daily,
> When she has no witnesses;
> She is ready to ensnare you,
> A great deadly crime when it is heard.

> *Instruction of Anii*

> You will be saved from the loose [strange] woman,
> from the adventuress with her smooth words,
> who forsakes the companion of her youth

and forgets the covenant of her God;
for her house sinks down to death,
and her paths to the shades;
none who go to her come back
nor do they regain the paths of life.

Prov. 2:16 (cf. 5:20; 6:24; 7:5)

⁀

Good Deeds

Do a good deed and throw it in the water;
when it dries you will find it.

Ankhsheshonqy 19:10

Cast your bread upon the waters,
for you will find it after many days.

Eccles. 11:1

⁀

The Shame of Begging

Better is the short time of him who is old
than the long life of him who begs (or has begged).

P. Insinger 17:19

My son, do not lead the life of a beggar;
it is better to die than to beg.

Sir. 40:28

Human Plans and Divine Action

God is ever in his perfection,
Man is ever in his failure.
The words men say are one thing,
The deeds of the god are another.

Amenemope 19:14–17

The plans of the god are one thing, the
thoughts of [men] are another.

Ankhsheshonqy 26:24

The plans of the mind belong to man,
but the answer of the tongue is from the Lord.

Prov. 16:1

Many are the plans of the mind of a man,
but it is the purpose of the Lord that will
be established.

Prov. 19:21

On Disciplining One's Son

> Withhold not thy son from the rod, else thou
> wilt not be able to save [him from
> wickedness]. If I smite thee, my son, thou
> wilt not die, but if I leave thee to thine
> own heart [thou wilt not live].
>
> > *Ahiqar, Saying 4*

> He who loves his son will whip him often,
> in order that he may rejoice at the way he
> turns out.
>
> > *Sir. 30:1*

> He who spares the rod hates his son,
> but he who loves him is diligent to
> discipline him.
>
> > *Prov. 13:24*

> You beat my back; your teachings entered my ear.
>
> > *P. Lansing*

Old Age

O king, my Lord!
Age is here, old age arrived,
Feebleness came, weakness grows,
Childlike one sleeps all day.
Eyes are dim, ears deaf,
Strength is waning through weariness,
The mouth, silenced, speaks not,
The heart, void, recalls not the past,
The bones ache throughout.
Good has become evil, all taste is gone,
What age does to people is evil in everything,
The nose, clogged, breathes not,
Painful are standing and sitting.

Ptahhotep

Remember also your creator in the days of
your youth, before the evil days come, and
the years draw nigh, when you will say, "I
have no pleasure in them"; before the sun and
the light and the moon and the stars are
darkened and the clouds return after the
rain; in the day when the keepers of the
house tremble, and the strong men are bent,
and the grinders cease because they are
few . . . the almond tree blossoms, the
grasshopper drags itself along and desire fails. . . .

Eccles. 12:1–7

[I was] a youth, [but now] my luck, my
strength, my personal god and my youthful
vigour have left my loins like an exhausted
ass. My black mountain has produced white
gypsum . . . my mongoose which used to eat strong
smelling things does not stretch its neck
towards beer and butter. My teeth which used
to chew strong things can no more chew strong
things. . . .

SUMERIAN *The Old Man and the Young Girl*

Chapter Three

⤳

Schools in
Ancient Israel

*"Don't kill someone whose virtues you know,
with whom you once chanted the writings."*

Merikare

In Egypt and Mesopotamia, where complex writing systems existed, scribal training occurred in official schools, sometimes associated with temples. According to J. D. Ray, "all the literate societies of the area needed to train an administrative class, and all probably approached the problem in much the same way: complex writing-systems required long training, with emphasis on rote-learning and reverence for the past, and the combination of tradition, didacticism, and repeatable sentiment encouraged the use of proverbs and rules for successful or ethical behaviour."[1] Such emphasis resulted in instructional literature, called *sb³yt* in Egypt, and loosely identified with the genre wisdom literature.[2] Similar training probably took place at Ugarit, where be-

---

[1] "Egyptian Wisdom Literature," 17–18 in *Wisdom in Ancient Israel*.

[2] The expression *sb³yt* occurs in widely different types of literature, not just in wisdom Instructions; similarly, the word "scribe" designated learned persons in various professions. *Some* wisdom texts can be called *sb³yt*, but many *sb³yt* are not wisdom Instructions, just as *some* scribes, but not all, occupied themselves with wisdom literature.

sides a cuneiform script for writing Akkadian there existed a simpler alphabetic script consisting of twenty-eight letters, three of which were *'alef* signs indicating a different vowel and useful in indicating Hurrian sounds. Royal administrative texts were deposited at Ugarit for consultation and safe-keeping.[3]

Evidence for schools in these areas is incontrovertible. The same cannot be said of ancient Israel, and much controversy centers on the very existence or nonexistence of schools before the second century B.C.E., when Ben Sira alludes to his own house of instruction. Learning took place; of that there is no doubt. The dispute rages over the nature and place of this instruction. For some interpreters, the locus of education was the home, with parents assuming full responsibility for teaching their children.[4] Most if not all such training was oral, the older generation passing along to the youth a wealth of insights it had gained through wide experience. The proverbial sayings in the Book of Proverbs encapsulate such instruction, which combined practical and moral learning. In addition, special guilds provided training in various occupations. These training centers were under the supervision of heads of families, and students were ordinarily drawn from members of their own households. In this way artisans and craftsmen received requisite training, and

---

[3] Loren R. Mack-Fisher, "The Scribe (and Sage) in the Royal Court at Ugarit," 109–15 in *The Sage in Israel and the Ancient Near East* and Anson F. Rainey, "The Scribe at Ugarit: His Position and Influence," *Proceedings of the Israel Academy of Sciences and Humanities* 3 (1969) 126–46.

[4] Golka, *The Leopard's Spots*, 10–11 ("Education presupposes a so-called master-apprentice system" . . . "The education of the Israelite boy, after he has been weaned, is his father's responsibility.")

society benefited from the skills of potters, weavers, leather workers, smiths, and the like.

None of this training required expertise in reading and writing. In addition to memory, a rudimentary system of record keeping existed prior to written texts, and society functioned reasonably well without resorting to writing, particularly when most people lived in small villages. Rural existence encouraged self-reliance, with each family mastering as many skills as necessary to eke out a living. Such circumstances also encouraged cooperation with neighbors, who possessed additional skills and who increased the number of laborers for tasks requiring communal collaboration.

Other critics insist that Israel possessed a complex system of formal education beginning either during Solomonic times or during Hezekiah's reign in the eighth century.[5] These scholars have in mind actual buildings set aside for instruction by paid teachers, who trained students to read and write by copying literary texts that eventually comprised a canon. Some of these classic texts make up the wisdom literature in the Bible, but the scope of scribal literature is not limited to religious texts. Such places of learning served the wishes of the royal administration, providing trained scribes for services as varied as political propaganda, record keeping, epistolary correspondence, and artistic representation. Only gifted scribes served as courtiers; the vast majority engaged in more modest tasks—assisting mer-

[5] Von Rad's hypothesis that a Solomonic enlightenment gave rise to wisdom literature, particularly the Joseph Narrative (!), has lost its attractiveness, although Walter Brueggemann still thinks the general concept has merit ("The Social Significance of Solomon as a Patron of Wisdom," 117–32 in *The Sage in Israel and the Ancient Near East.*

chants and drafting official documents such as wills, contracts for marriages or divorces, purchases of land, and so
forth.

If scribal training in Israel prepared students to read and
write foreign languages, particularly the complex writing
systems of cuneiform and hieroglyphics, the education required considerably more years of study than for the mere
mastery of a single language, written Hebrew. With the
widespread use of Aramaic for diplomatic correspondence,[6]
a different picture develops, one that required far less training to master the script than either cuneiform or hieroglyphics. It makes a great deal of difference, therefore,
whether an interpreter thinks Israel's schools evolved in the
tenth century, when knowledge of Akkadian and Egyptian
was essential for international relations, or in the eighth
century, when familiarity with Aramaic would normally
have sufficed. The inscriptions from the outpost at Kadesh-
Barnea, which employ a complete list of hieratic signs, suggest, however, that scribal training as late as the seventh and
sixth centuries required extensive knowledge beyond Hebrew and Aramaic, at least for some individuals.[7]

The picture becomes even more complicated when one
takes into account certain philosophical texts in the Bible.
While the Books of Job and Ecclesiastes may have originated in an oral culture, it is far more likely that their
authors wrote their thoughts from the outset. The first
epilogue to Ecclesiastes recalls Qoheleth's *writing* down
reliable sayings, and the Book of Job appears to be based on

---

[6] The adoption of Aramaic for diplomatic purposes also required a change in the
materials employed, stylus and clay tablet being replaced by brush, ink, and papyrus.

[7] Davies, "Were there schools in ancient Israel?" 210–11.

an oral folktale that an author uses as a point of departure for launching a literary debate about innocent suffering and an appropriate response to such misfortune.[8] Did Israel's schools provide a place for students and teachers to reflect on life's anomalies and to ponder the meaning of existence? An affirmative answer to this question forces one to imagine more advanced education than was required to master the art of reading and writing. Indeed, some interpreters conjecture that the land of Israel accommodated elementary education in small villages, secondary education in larger towns, and advanced training in the capital cities and in a few other urban centers.[9]

Assessing all available evidence is no easy task. The city of David, for example, has as yet yielded little inscriptional evidence to support a theory of administrative schools in Jerusalem. That paucity of evidence may indicate nothing more than failure thus far to dig in the right place, but it is much more likely that continued looting and burning of the city have destroyed all literary evidence that modern scholars seek. Unlike the other ancient Near Eastern sites that have produced evidence of impressive libraries and abundant texts,[10] Jerusalem presents special problems resulting from its continued occupation to the present. Moreover, the climate is not conducive to preserving texts written on leather or papyrus, the normal medium for important documents in Israel. Such material evidence has long since van-

---

[8] Recent views about the Book of Job are discussed in my entry, "Job, Book of," *The Anchor Bible Dictionary*, vol. III, ed. David Noel Freedman (New York: Doubleday, 1992).

[9] Lemaire, *Les Écoles et la formation de la Bible dans l'ancien Israël*.

[10] Jeremy A. Black and W. J. Tait, "Archives and Libraries in the Ancient Near East," 2197–2209 in *Civilizations of the Ancient Near East*, vol. IV.

ished, if it ever existed, and modern interpreters must rely on bits and pieces discovered throughout the land, mostly writings of an occasional nature on ostraca.

BIBLICAL EVIDENCE FOR SCHOOLS

The biblical authors never mention schools, and this silence can be read in two different ways: (1) the existence of schools was so well known that no one stated the obvious, or (2) there were no schools in ancient Israel. Arguments from silence often lack cogency, for the biblical authors were equally silent about other significant aspects of daily life that undoubtedly existed at the time. Nevertheless, failing to mention an institution such as a school, particularly in the Book of Proverbs, where one reasonably expects some reference to a place of learning, is not the same as remaining silent about training centers for various occupations like weaving, leather works, and so forth.[11]

    The only texts that may allude to formal schools can also be understood without positing such an institution, although the more natural way of reading them seems to indicate an actual place where students learned to read and write. The strange reference to childish babble in Isa. 28:9–13 apparently ridicules the pedagogical technique by which students practiced the alphabet by citing strings of consonants with various vowel sounds. The resulting nonsense resembles the meaningless prattle of drunks, made

---

[11] Contra Heaton, *The School Tradition of the Old Testament*, 1–2.

more ridiculous by the innocence of children barely weaned from their mothers' milk. The idea of three-year-olds assembled for the purpose of learning to read and write poses problems for interpreters, prompting efforts to understand the words as a corrupt version of Akkadian. However one reads the text, it seems to presuppose familiarity with a context of learning characterized by the recitation of recurring sounds. A school best fits such a description, even if the activity of the children comes in for mockery.

> Whom will he teach knowledge,
>> and to whom will he explain the message?
> Those who are weaned from milk,
>> those taken from the breast?
> For it is precept upon precept,
>> precept upon precept,
> line upon line, line upon line,
> here a little, there a little.
> Truly, with stammering lip
>> and with alien tongue
>> he will speak to this people,
>> to whom he has said,
>> "This is rest;
>> give rest to the weary;
>> and this is repose";
> Yet they would not hear.
> Therefore the word of the Lord
>> will be to them,
>> "Precept upon precept, precept upon precept,
>> line upon line, line upon line,
>> here a little, there a little,"

in order that they may go, and fall backward,
and be broken, and snared, and taken.

(*Isa. 28:9–13*)

This text describes the people's ridicule of the prophet, whom they accuse of instructing them in the same way teachers train children the basics of reading and writing. Isaiah scolds them for such insensitivity, threatening them with divine "nonsense" that will leave them vulnerable to the Assyrian menace.[12]

In Isa. 50:4–11, the third of the poems often identified by modern interpreters as servant songs, the mysterious servant claims to possess an instructed tongue.

The Lord God has given me
  the tongue of a teacher,
that I may know how to sustain
  the weary with a word.
Morning by morning he wakens—
  wakens my ear
to listen to those who are taught.

(*Isa. 50:4*)

The Hebrew *limmûdîm* (and with a preposition implying likeness, *kallimmûdîm*) suggests familiarity with something resulting from intentional training. The language does not apply exclusively to formal education, for it elsewhere de-

---

[12] A. van Selms, "Isaiah 28:9–13: An Attempt to Give a New Interpretation," *ZAW* 85 (1973) 332–39 translates this difficult text in light of Akkadian. He writes: "Go out! Let him go out! Go out! Let him go out! Wait! Let him wait! Wait! Let him wait! Servant, listen! Servant, listen!"

scribes the trained response of domestic animals. The passive adjective connotes the end product of such teaching; the servant has the ready tongue of one who has been taught. Moreover, he boasts that the instruction comes from the Lord, to whom the servant listens attentively after daily being roused from sleep.[13]

This language conforms to usage in the ancient Near East, where learning enters the ear rather than resulting from visual activity.[14] Because instructors made heavy use of oral recitation and depended on students to memorize what they heard, the servant's remark may indicate formal schooling as the analogy for divine instruction. The observation may just as plausibly reflect oral teaching within the home. As parents awaken their children and begin their day with sound advice that eventually takes hold and forms character, the divine Parent gently instructs the servant, who contrasts sharply with rebellious Israelites. In short, this text neither confirms nor refutes the theory of formal schools among exiled Jews in Babylon.

The bold assertion that the Lord tutors a selected individual is widened to include simple farmers in Isa. 28:23–29. Here the prophet observes that the Lord instructs farmers about their everyday tasks, teaching them to do all things at the right time and in the proper proportion. This revealing account of techniques in planting and harvesting functions to accentuate the controlled manner in which divine

---

[13] Golka correctly recognizes that the language of prophetic discipleship in this text designates the servant as one who has obeyed the divine commission (*The Leopard's Spots*, 7–8).

[14] Shupak, *Where can Wisdom be found?* passim. Qoheleth departs from this widespread usage, for he places the emphasis on what he has seen.

judgment takes place. The astonishing remark occurs in verse 26.

> For they are well instructed;
>> their God teaches them.

Often considered a prophetic text strongly influenced by the language of the sages, this lesson in effective agricultural practice concludes with the declaration that the Lord of Hosts excels in counsel and perspicacity. Although this text shares a common subject matter with the so-called Gezer calendar, it differs noticeably in religious tone and self-conscious pedagogy. There one reads:

> His two months are (olive harvest),
>> His two months are planting (grain),
>>> His two months are late planting;
> His month is hoeing up the flax,
>> His month is harvest of barley,
>>> His month is harvest and *feasting*;
> His two months are vine tending,
>> His month is summer fruit.
>>> *(ANET, 320)*[15]

Another biblical text that may reflect formal schooling is Prov. 22:17–21, but the relationship between it and the

---

[15] Other instances in which biblical prophets viewed everyday occurrences in nature from the perspective of careful manipulation by the deity include, among others, Amos' discussion of events based on the principle of cause and effect in 3:3–8 and the "liturgy of wasted opportunity" in 4:6–11, in which the prophet lists punitive actions that did not lead to repentance on Israel's part.

Egyptian *Instruction of Amenemope* reduces its value as evidence for Israelite practice.

> The words of the wise:[16]
> Incline your ear and hear my words,
>   and apply your mind to my teaching;
> for it will be pleasant if you keep them within you,
>   if all of them are ready on your lips.
> So that your trust may be in the Lord,
>   I have made them known to you today—yes, to you.
> Have I not written for you thirty sayings[17]
>   of admonition and knowledge,
> to show you what is right and true,
>   so that you may give a true answer
>   to those who sent you.
>   *(Prov. 22:17–21)*

The Egyptian setting for the thirty sayings of Amenemope, the formal education of royal courtiers, is reflected in the reference to accuracy in transmitting official sentiment. The crucial issue for understanding the function of the sayings in the Book of Proverbs has to do with the extent of carryover from one culture to another.[18] The modest overlap between the Egyptian Instruction and its Hebrew coun-

---

[16] Textual critics usually assume that the superscription "The words of the wise" has accidentally been incorporated into the actual text of this introduction to the collection resembling the *Instruction of Amenemope*.

[17] The meaningless form, *šlšwm (šālišîm,* Qere) has been explained with reference to the division of the *Instruction of Amenemope* into thirty chapters, representing the thirty judges who were believed to determine the fate of individuals.

[18] Glendon E. Bryce, *A Legacy of Wisdom* (Lewisburg, PA: Bucknell University Press, 1979), explores the manner in which foreign material is integrated into a different culture. Washington, *Wealth and Poverty in the Instruction of Amenemope and the Hebrew Proverbs,* concentrates on sociological factors.

terpart makes it hazardous to conclude that the two operate in similar contexts, despite the promise that accomplished individuals will serve kings (22:29). Education for courtiers does not play a major role in biblical wisdom,[19] and even in the collection introduced by Prov. 22:17–21, parental instruction claims the reader's attention. That humble setting stands out in Prov. 23:22.

> Listen to your father who begot you,
>> and do not despise your mother when she is old.[20]

The next verse encourages young people to purchase truth, which it then defines more broadly with three favorite expressions for knowledge—wisdom, instruction, and understanding.

The common elements between *Amenemope* and the biblical text may have arrived through popular teaching rather than as translations for use by scribes, but the advice about curbing one's appetite in the presence of a ruler hardly accords with such an explanation. The entire collection in Prov. 22:17–24:22 may have served as formal instruction for potential courtiers, but the matter cannot be settled on the basis of such an ambiguous text as this one.

The allusion in this text to buying truth recalls other

---

[19] W. Lee Humphreys, "The Motif of the Wise Courtier in the Book of Proverbs," 177–90 in *Israelite Wisdom*.

[20] On the basis of an article by Menahem Haran, "The Graded Numerical Sequence and the Phenomenon of 'Automatism' in Biblical Poetry," *Congress Volume VTS* 22 (Leiden: E. J. Brill, 1972) 238–67, Michael Fox thinks that the references to "mother" in such proverbial sayings are otiose ("The Social Location of the Book of Proverbs," 231). This balancing of the word for father with one for mother is neither absolutely required nor automatic, for the poet could easily have used another phrase of exact parallelism (your mother/the one who bore you).

places in the Book of Proverbs where people are urged to obtain wisdom by investing a sum of money (4:5, 7; 17:16). Some critics understand these references in the context of formal education, for which tuition was charged.[21] The first of these texts has four uses of the Hebrew imperative for buying something, twice in 4:5 and twice in 4:7. A fifth use of the root *qānâ* occurs in the latter verse, but in an infinitive construct. Only two objects appear in these verses, wisdom and understanding. The other text ponders an anomaly, a fool paying money for wisdom, although lacking the intellectual acumen or will to take advantage of such expenditure. The text clearly implies that payment for knowledge makes sense only for capable students.

Such language may be symbolic, there being no real analogy for payment of tuition in actual day-to-day living. This understanding of the vocabulary for buying something valuable is reinforced by prophetic rhetoric, for example Isa. 55:1–2, although the two verbs are different (forms of *šābar* and *šākal*).

> Ho, everyone who thirsts,
>   come to the waters;
> and you that have no money,
>   come, buy and eat!
> Come, buy wine and milk
>   without money and without price.
> Why do you spend your money
>   for that which is not bread,

---

[21] Davies, "Were there schools in ancient Israel?" 199–200 (citing my article "Education in Ancient Israel," 602 with reference to Prov. 4:7 and adding Prov. 17:16 and 23:23).

and your labor for that which
  does not satisfy?

Ben Sira's language in 51:23–25, 28 probably echoes this familiar text, particularly the allusion to thirst in the context of acquiring wisdom without paying money for it. In his mind, too, the rich reward far outweighed any cost; that is true whether one reads the more modest version in Hebrew or the lavish promise in Greek of gold in return for silver.[22]

Hear but a little of my instruction,
  and through me you will acquire silver and gold.
  (Hebrew)
Get instruction with a large sum of silver,
  and you will gain by it much gold. (Greek)

The sages certainly used similar metaphors when referring to scribal activity, for example, the admonition to write the laws of the Lord, or abstract qualities such as loyalty and faithfulness, on the tablet of the heart (Prov. 3:3; 7:3).

Further complicating this picture drawn from biblical literature is the probable existence of prophetic associates who gathered around Elijah, Elisha, and Isaiah, perhaps others as well. Although these loyal followers of influential prophetic figures comprised schools in a loose sense of the word, they do not qualify for the type of institution discussed earlier. Instead of teaching young boys the essentials of reading and writing, these schools preserved the oracles of their mentors

---

[22] Whereas the Hebrew text promises silver and gold as reward for a little instruction, the Greek text implies that one lays out a sum of silver in payment for an education but receives much gold in return.

until the revered tradition was eventually compiled into written texts.[23] Furthermore, the prophet Jeremiah had access to the services of a scribe named Baruch. One may reasonably ask where Baruch and others like him, Shaphan, for instance, acquired their ability to compose a literary document.

At this point, all sorts of incidental information from biblical literature become relevant to the discussion, for these texts presuppose the existence of some literate people in Israelite society from as early as the tenth century, if one can trust the narrative about David sending a letter to Joab at the hands of a condemned soldier, Uriah the Hittite. At the very least, the many references to literary activity within the Deuteronomistic history indicate that this sixth-century author assumed that writing belonged to the daily lives of quite a few citizens in Israel and Judah. Similarly, the later author of Dan. 1:3–20 took for granted a type of education within Hellenistic society that could be used by the Lord for noble ends. The same background may be postulated for Ps. 119:99, where the author brags about having more understanding than all his teachers, explaining that he meditates on the Lord's decrees.

[23] Susan Niditch, *Oral World and Written Word: Ancient Israelite Literature* (Louisville: Westminster John Knox, 1996) examines the evidence for the transition from an oral to a written culture in ancient Israel. In doing so, she demonstrates the staying power of orality long after writing has been introduced. For the interplay of orality and literacy, see Simon B. Parker, *Stories in Scripture and Inscriptions* (New York and London: Oxford University Press, 1997) 8–10.

EVIDENCE FROM
PALESTINIAN INSCRIPTIONS

In an effort to break out of the impasse resulting from inconclusive biblical material, André Lemaire shifted the emphasis to Palestinian inscriptions.[24] On this basis, he concluded that schools existed throughout Palestine from premonarchic times. In the process, Lemaire examined eleven different types of material: (1) abecedaries discovered at Lachish, Kadesh-Barnea, Kuntillet-ʿAjrud, and perhaps Arorer; (2) isolated letters of the alphabet or groups of letters, perhaps at Arad; (3) letters of the alphabet grouped by similarities in appearance, perhaps at Lachish; (4) words written several times at Arad, Kadesh-Barnea, and perhaps Kuntillet-ʿAjrud; (5) personal names, perhaps at Arad and Arorer; (6) formulary beginnings of letters; (7) lists of months at Gezer; (8) symbols at Kadesh-Barnea; (9) sequence of signs for numbers and units of measurement at Kadesh-Barnea; (10) drawings at Kuntillet-ʿAjrud and probably Lachish; and (11) exercises in reading a foreign language, Phoenician, at Kuntillet-ʿAjrud.

The nature of the evidence evoked considerable speculation, both with respect to actual content—the readings are

---

[24] *Les Écoles et la formation de la Bible dans l'ancien Israël.* Lemaire thinks major Canaanite cities such as Aphek, Gezer, Megiddo, Shechem, Lachish, and Jerusalem had schools, as did later Israelite centers (Shiloh, Shechem, Gilgal, Bethel, Hebron, and Beersheba). Furthermore, he conjectures that local schools such as Arad, Kadesh-Barnea, and Kuntillet-ʿAjrud concentrated on elementary education, whereas regional schools like that at Lachish were more advanced. Alongside these schools were, in Lemaire's view, priestly and prophetic schools. Teaching thus occurred at the gates, in temples, and at the royal palace. According to Lemaire, the Bible was composed in the process of providing literature for students to use in the classroom.

often ambiguous—and intention. Lemaire conjectures that numerous features of these inscriptions arose from students' efforts to master the Hebrew script and alphabet, to memorize correct epistolary form and essential information about the agricultural year, to acquire refined techniques in drawing, and to familiarize themselves with the spelling of proper names. He attributes poor drawing and large characters to learners, as well as mistakes such as transposed letters, and he understands the juxtaposition of characters of the alphabet that resemble one another as proof that students have begun to express their powers of discrimination.

Some of this evidence has considerable merit: the existence of a clear Phoenician script, indicative of a trained scribe; abecedaries; paleographic consistency, which seems to imply authoritative instruction in the art of writing; and the juxtaposition of kindred letters of the alphabet. Emile Puech's comprehensive evaluation of Lemaire's hypothesis narrows the evidence down to four things: (1) the abecedaries written on ostraca, to which he adds Ostracon 90 from Arad; (2) the isolated letters; (3) the repeated numbers, and (4) the lists of numbers in order.[25] Puech buttresses the argument by noting the consistency of spelling and the sequence of letters of the alphabet, along with the use of a stylus and ink.

Much of Lemaire's evidence may be explained differently. The size of the script may indicate poor eyesight, and the disparity in the quality of drawings may mean nothing more than that some people draw better than others. Various ex-

---

[25] "Les Écoles dans l'Israel préexilique: données épigraphiques," *Congress Volume: Jerusalem 1986* (VTS 40, 1988) 189–203.

planations for letters arranged in alphabetic sequence can be posited: they may comprise part of a personal name or place; they may represent attempts to decorate an object; they may constitute a few practice strokes by artisans preparing to decorate a vase; they may be graffiti; they may have some mysterious magical purpose, yet unexplained.

Some of the supporting evidence can be dismissed with confidence.[26] An abecedary discovered at Nahal Michmash, a single dwelling accessible solely by means of a rope ladder, hardly indicates a school at such a remote location. Similarly, the three abecedaries at Khirbet el-Qom, the letters ʿ, ʾb, and possibly nl, appear in the middle of a dark, underground tomb that must be entered through a narrow passageway and down a short shaft. Like the three abecedaries on a large pithos that was discovered in a bench room atop a steep hill in the desert at Kuntillet-ʿAjrud, these pose the questions, Where would students have come from and why would they have gathered at this place? The tiny room at Kuntillet-ʿAjrud, situated where people entering the building had to pass, would not have been conducive to learning. The second abecedary, ʿto t, varies the order of ʿp, unthinkable if it represents a student's attempt to copy the other two, which have the usual sequence ʿp. Similarly, a reversal of these two letters occurs in Lam. 1 and 2, which are alphabetic acrostics with the normal order of all letters except these two. The uppermost of the three abecedaries has ṭ to t

---

[26] Weeks, *Early Israelite Wisdom*, 132–56 submits the epigraphic evidence to a thoroughgoing examination, concluding that "the biblical and epigraphic evidence adduced for schools in Israel seems very weak indeed, and can certainly not support any hypothesis of a large, integrated school system" (153). His discussion has informed my analysis of the epigraphic evidence. Haran, "On the Diffusion of Literacy and Schools

and the lower *k to t*, both in cursive style, as opposed to the smaller script and squarer style of the second. Between the second and third abecedaries, the letters *sʿrm* appear twice, and two brief sentences begin with *ʾmr* and conclude with blessings. The claim that the repeated *sʿrm* indicates students' practice and that *ʾmr* shows them learning the epistolary formula overlooks the fact that the form can be the third masculine singular verb rather than the customary imperative. Besides, can one even speak of a formula on the basis of two occurrences in first millennium Northwest Semitic?

In one instance, the abecedary comes from a time that rules out an Israelite, or for that matter, Canaanite school. The ostracon from ʿIsbet Ṣarṭah consists of five lines, one of which may be an abecedary written from left to right, with the other four lines in proto-Canaanite script but undecipherable. The nearest location to this site, Aphek, three miles distant and a Canaanite city, was apparently destroyed in the thirteenth century, but the Israelite occupation began in the eleventh century, excluding the possibility of an Israelite studying at a Canaanite school. The three inscriptions from Lachish include an abecedary comprising the first five letters of the alphabet, with a symbol of a roaring lion at some remove. The location of the inscription on the rise of a limestone step would have required a writer to sit in an awkward position on a lower step while stretching out an arm in order to scratch letters diagonally across the corner

---

in Ancient Israel," dismisses most of Lemaire's evidence, as do I ("Education in Ancient Israel").

of the rise. A second inscription, partially erased, has three of eleven letters out of place and insufficient space for the missing letters. A third inscription includes a sign resembling an arrow, plus the clear letters *'bgd* (or *r*) on a fired jar. In view of the name *l'bgd* (Abigad) on a seal elsewhere, one may plausibly read a name here as well.

The copious evidence on a bowl from Arad consists of clumsy mirror writing, but the eight appearances of the word Arad lack consistency. Six times the letters are written from right to left, but with mirror writing, and twice from right to left in standard form. A student who knew how to form the letters correctly would likely have known the proper sequence. The confident writing of names in Ostracon 87 and 88, the appearance of names in Ostracon 50–57, perhaps for delegating priestly responsibilities, and the use in Ostracon 33 of *ḥṭm* (wheat) several times followed by numbers and hieratic signs for quantity, suggesting an inventory—these indications of a setting other than school encourage one to look for other explanations for the inscription on the bowl. An attempt to decorate the bowl commends itself as the best interpretation of the data, similar to a bowl from Deir 'Alla.

The two ostraca from Arorer probably contain personal names, despite the sequence *qr* on one of them. The only site that has a strong claim to represent writing exercises, Kadesh-Barnea, has yielded five ostraca. One fragment from the seventh century has the letters *zḥṭ* in excellent script; another features the words *ml'* and *wt'sr*, each repeated once; three others have lists of hieratic numerals, repeated in one as if the product of written exercises.

Graham I. Davies has recently assessed the evidence for

schools in ancient Israel and found it convincing, particularly the epigraphic data.[27] On the basis of his wide knowledge in this area, he appeals to little-known inscriptions
from Kadesh-Barnea that are written in columns and use
hieratic Egyptian signs for numbers. He points out that one
(no. 4) has the same number (2382) nine times; another (no.
3) has two columns of mixed numbers and units of measurement, and a third column contains the numbers 100 to 800
followed by the unit *qrh;* a third (no. 9) has the numbers
from 100 to 500 preceded by the shekel sign; most signifi-
cantly, one (no. 6) has nine columns, six on the recto and
three on the verso, with sequences of the numbers from 1
to 10,000. Sometimes these are found in conjunction with
signs for *ephah* (or *kor*) or shekel. Davies concludes that this
"can scarcely be anything but a practice exercise of a trainee
scribe, like the others from Kadesh-barnea."[28] He is puzzled
by such indications of scribal training in a remote fortress,
but the evidence leads him to suppose that similar instruction must have taken place in major centers of administration.

What about the well-known Gezer calendar, a tenth-
century oddly shaped limestone tablet? This palimpsest
(erasure) has been compared with three other tablets; an
eighth-century Phoenician tablet, an Aramaic one from Tell
Halaf, and a limestone tablet from Byblos with five lines of
clumsy script, some names, and erasures. Only the latter re-

---

[27] "Were there schools in ancient Israel?" He believes that prior to the eighth century, formal education may have been limited to capital cities and administrative centers dependent on them. Davies also thinks village elders may have presided over a
few local schools. In any event, he suggests, the more technical skills were probably
passed on through schools (210–11).

[28] "Were there schools in ancient Israel?" 210.

sembles the Gezer tablet, and two exemplars do not make a type. Stuart Weeks compares the Gezer tablet with incantation tablets from Arslan Tash, of debatable authenticity.[29] He asks an important practical question: Were such tablets preferable as writing instruments to wood or clay? The obvious answer to the question leads him to speculate that the Gezer tablet had a magical or votive function.

What about the argument for schools based on uniformity of script? Two observations seem to apply here. First, changes do occur in the script, with different styles overlapping in time, and second, the Hebrew alphabet offers little option in spelling, at least until the use of vowel letters. Orthographic variation in official correspondence from Arad and Lachish persists into the sixth century, and regional variation in representing vowels also occurred. Nevertheless, a remarkable uniformity of spelling and script must surely suggest standardized instruction; whether a scribal guild adequately explains this phenomenon remains to be seen.

If one concedes that sufficient inscriptional evidence exists to posit actual schools at the several locations, a problem surfaces immediately: Why do these student exercises lack any corrections by the hands of teachers? Similar texts from Egypt and Mesopotamia show clear corrections, thus indicating circumstances of actual pedagogy. If the Palestinian inscriptions had similar corrections, the evidence for schools would be much more compelling.

Did the demands of royal correspondence and archival preservation of important documents necessitate wide-

[29] *Early Israelite Wisdom*, 140–41.

spread schooling in monarchic times? The verdict is still out on this question, but a small coterie of trained scribes belonging to a single guild could easily have managed the essential correspondence and preservation of records in Israel and Judah. From the eighth century onward a single language, Aramaic, would have sufficed for foreign diplomacy. As for training to read and write Hebrew, its simplicity would have enabled students to acquire the necessary skills in a short time. Mastering complex linguistic systems required years of study. Although some interpreters have assumed that advanced scholars in Israel used literature as instructional aids, no evidence exists to support this claim. In all probability, scribal training for royal administrations in Israel had a purely pragmatic character. Potential scribes learned to write royal correspondence, keep records of inventory, and promote the reigning monarch through effective propaganda.

The sole reference to royal scribes in the Book of Proverbs, 25:1, uses the verb *he'tîqû*, which normally has the meaning "move," "remove," "overturn" (Gen. 12:8, 26:22; Job 9:5, 32:15). The LXX renders the verb with *exegrapsanto* ("copy") and the Vulgate uses *transtulerunt* ("transfer"). A tendency to elevate King Hezekiah to legendary stature within the Bible—attributing a Psalm to him in Isa. 38:9; identifying him as the subject of miracles in 2 Kgs. 18–20 and Isa. 36–38—suggests that this inscription belongs to the same trend. As is well known, a similar phenomenon surrounds David in the Psalter and Solomon in the wisdom corpus. The expression "men of Hezekiah" may indicate a special relationship to the king (cf. 1 Kgs. 10:8). If the verb *he'tîqû* in Prov. 25:1 retains its usual connotation, the superscription may suggest that the royal subjects either removed the ensuing collection of sayings, 25:2–29:27, from their earlier location alongside the Solomonic collection in 10:1–22:16 or reduced a more extensive collection to the smaller one in 25:2–29:17. Neither sense of the verb is very compelling in this context, as later translators and rabbinic interpreters attest.

ANALOGY WITH EGYPT
AND MESOPOTAMIA

None would question the existence of royal scribes in Egypt and Mesopotamia, as well as at Ugarit, but drawing analogies from these empires, more advanced than Israel and Judah, seems inappropriate. Comparative studies invariably confront a fundamental question: Are the two cultures being compared sufficiently alike to justify a transference of ideas and practices from one to the other? The answer to that question in this instance is probably no. The simple fact that both Egyptian and Mesopotamian texts provide ample witness to the existence of schools requires one to ponder the absence of similar attestations in Israel. One hesitates to make much of arguments from silence, but in this case the missing allusions to schools stand out as exceptional and therefore demand an explanation.[30] Why do the lists of royal

---

[30] Fox, "The Social Location of the Book of Proverbs," asks the following penetrating question: "If the ostensive setting really is just a cloak for a teacher-pupil school setting, why are the school teachers, for a period of some 2600 years, so determined to hide the instructor's role in Wisdom authorship?" (232). He goes on to argue that

officials in the biblical record omit any reference to an official in charge of instruction, and why do the sages of Israel
never mention schools prior to Ben Sira?

Similar features within Israelite wisdom literature and
that of Egypt and Mesopotamia make it difficult to deny
the appropriateness of argument by analogy. Nili Shupak's
analysis of affinities between Israelite and Egyptian wisdom
underlines this point, for the resemblances go beyond ideas
to verbal expressions. She identifies eight expressions in
Hebrew that have an exact equivalent in Egyptian, four of
which she terms "translations" and four "adaptations."[31]
Scholars have long recognized extensive Egyptian influence
on biblical wisdom, probably as a result of the identification
of the interconnection between Prov. 22:17–24:22 and the
Instruction of Amenemope. Besides the use of "my son" as addressee, these Egyptian influences include, among others,
the idea of order—reflecting Egyptian *Ma'at*—wisdom as a
child playing in the divine presence at the time of creation,
if not before; righteousness as the foundation of the throne;
the idea that wisdom holds righteousness in one hand and
life in the other; the notion of weighing the heart in accurate
scales; the use of steering as a description of sagacity; the
concept of a messenger of death; the garland of honor encir-
cling the neck; the description of fools as "heated"; the
praise of the scribes' vocation as superior to all other profes-

---

the Book of Proverbs preserves evidence that some of the sayings were written for
clerks who served major businesses and governmental officials at the court (232–39).

[31] *Where can Wisdom be found?* Four of these "wisdom terms" are literal translations
("heated man," "cool tempered," "weighs the heart," and "a well-constructed saying").
Others are adaptations from Egyptian ("chambers of the belly," "slow to anger,"
"short-tempered," [both *qeṣar 'appayim* and *qeṣar rûaḥ*]).

sions; and the expression "heaping coals of fire on an ene-my's head," presumably a ritual of expiation. In addition, the words for stylus and ink in Hebrew were borrowed from Egypt.

The affinities between biblical wisdom and Mesopota-mian literature extend beyond verbal expression to themes, particularly the vexing issue of theodicy in the face of death. Furthermore, in the proverbial literature of ancient Sumer, the person addressed is called "my son" and the spokesman is "father." Such resemblances between wisdom and com-parable literature from Mesopotamia cannot mask the fact that Babylonian wisdom placed extraordinary confidence in magic. Here, learned priests endeavored to manipulate the gods for human good; omen literature thus lies at the center of this endeavor. Interpreters who emphasize the connec-tions between the two areas must concede that the bor-rowing has been selective, and this admission weakens the argument from analogy.

This line of reasoning has also drawn attention to the ne-cessity for courtiers in Mesopotamia and Egypt, and by im-plication, in Israel. The administrative structure during the reigns of Solomon and to some extent David has strength-ened this argument, except for the crucial absence of a government official in charge of education. David W. Jamieson-Drake's examination of administrative control in Judah raises serious questions about the existence of schools before the eighth century.[32] Even if his archaeological data are flawed,[33] the evidence he studies—the number and size

[32] *Scribes and Schools in Monarchic Judah: A Socio-Archaeological Approach.*
[33] Davies, "Were there schools in ancient Israel?" 207–09.

of settlements, the extent of public works such as fortifica-
tions and public buildings, and the amount of luxury items
that presuppose specialists other than producers of food—
raises serious doubt about the complexity of administrations
during the tenth and ninth centuries. The real differences
between complex societies like Egypt and Mesopotamia,
on the one hand, and Israel, on the other, remain, and
Jamieson-Drake has underscored that fact. Nevertheless,
the degree of difference is relative, and Israelite society may
well have required the services of enough trained bureaucrats to posit official schools, as Graham I. Davies thinks.[34]
Whether or not a single scribal family with relatively
few active members could have trained sufficient personnel
to accommodate governmental demands is a matter of
judgment.

The argument from analogy pertains to another aspect of
ancient Near Eastern culture, its literature. Some interpreters argue that the quality of biblical literature demands formal education,[35] just as classic texts from Egypt and Mesopotamia are unthinkable apart from a system of scribal
training. No one has succeeded in demonstrating, however,
the absolute necessity to posit formal training as an explanation for the proverbial sayings that have been collected in
the Bible, and the extent of literary adaptation can be explained as the work of persons trained in a single guild. The
same applies to the Books of Job and Qoheleth; the language
and themes pertain to a sapiential community, but one that
has not isolated itself from society. Interpreters have seldom

[34] *Ibid.*, 209–11.
[35] von Rad, *Wisdom in Israel*, 17.

remarked on the obvious implication of Ben Sira's school—
that it is a private place of learning consonant with the theory of limited education by an elder statesman.[36]

CONCLUSION

The strongest evidence for the existence of schools is epigraphic. These inscriptions leave little doubt that schools
existed in Israel from about the eighth century, if not earlier,
but they do not clarify the nature of these places of learning.
Were they sponsored by the government and open to all citizens, or were the schools under the control of a few heads
of families? In all probability, a combination of these alternatives best explains the situation. A few scribal guilds existed from early times and were conscripted, probably at
their own initiative, by some monarchs to assist in propaganda, record keeping, and administrative activity. With the
collapse of the monarchy, first in the north and later in Judah, a single guild may have continued to train scribes in
exile and subsequently in Judah. A decisive shift probably
took place under Ezra, who threw his considerable weight
behind priestly scribes. Ben Sira continues this scribal tradition.[37] Presumably, however, at least one secular guild, pos-

[36] See my commentary "Sirach" (*The New Interpreter's Bible*, vol. V. Nashville:
Abingdon Press, 1997), 601–867, and "The Primacy of Listening in Ben Sira's Peda-
gogy," 172–87 in *Wisdom, You Are My Sister: Studies in Honor of Roland E. Murphy, O.
Carm., on the Occasion of His Eightieth Birthday*, ed. Michael L. Barré (CBQMS 29;
Washington, D.C.: The Catholic Biblical Association of America, 1997).

[37] But certainly not in the direct line of Ezra, whom Ben Sira considers too much
enamored of Levites.

sibly more, vied for rights to revenue from the numerous official documents of prominent merchants, as well as for the business of ordinary citizens.

Such a formulation of the matter is pure conjecture, although one based on probability. Nothing seems to require the existence of public schools, supported by taxpayers and open to everyone. Indeed, there were few incentives to attend school, but major disincentives. Exactly when this situation changed cannot be determined, but the Gospels assume that the son of a carpenter was literate, and this understanding of things accords with rabbinic tradition about the beginnings of public education.

Chapter Four

⌒

The Acquisition
of Knowledge

"Amusement does not go with learning,
for learning is a painful process."

ARISTOTLE

Modern scholars possess a staggering amount of information about ancient Near Eastern sages, thanks to
copious texts from Egypt and Mesopotamia. It has become
current knowledge that the early sages reflected on the distinct advantages of belonging to an elite class of scholars,
described in some detail the rigors associated with study, divided life's span in terms of the years devoted to education
as opposed to reaping its benefits, identified the goal of education, characterized wise persons as silent ones and their
opposites as hotheaded fools of at least six different types,
and used in-house language to define the relationships between teachers and students.

But one thing is missing in Israel's wisdom literature and
in extra-biblical texts. Where is reflection on the learning
process itself? To be sure, there is talk of pitching camp and
peering through Wisdom's windows and speculation about
pursuing Dame Wisdom like precious treasure or a bride.
But not a whisper about the acquisition of knowledge is

heard. How did learning occur, and how was it transmitted? To answer these questions, it may be useful to ponder the underlying presuppositions of perhaps the oldest riddle from the ancient world and to reflect on three fundamentally different kinds of knowledge.

A THEORY OF KNOWLEDGE

"Whoever enters it has closed eyes; whoever departs from it has eyes that are wide open. What is it?"[1] Because riddles employ cipher language that offers a clue and conceals a trap at the same time, the secret is to seize the clue without being caught in the hidden trap. It follows that riddles have more than one answer. The first impulse is to answer, "Life," for a child enters the world with closed eyes and at death the eyes must be closed for the individual. Indeed, a son is actually described as the person who closes his father's eyes at the moment of death. Alternatively, one is tempted to respond to the question "What is it?" along erotic lines, for it is widely acknowledged that love is blind. The mystery of eros certainly begins in ignorance and ends with eyes that have been opened widely. However, the intended response is "A school."

What makes the image of open and closed eyes appropriate as a description of the learning process? Because eyes mirror the soul, the symbolism is particularly apt. Just as

[1] The first part of the riddle is obscure; see Samuel Noah Kramer, *The Sumerians* (Chicago and London: University of Chicago, 1963) 236–37.

eyes are paired, so knowledge was of two kinds: systematic and gnomic. Systematic knowledge sought to order reality by means of philosophical reflection, while gnomic apperception endeavored to capture insights from experience and to clothe them in clever statements that could easily be committed to memory.

The image of closed eyes naturally connotes ignorance—whether the empty head, or the wrongly filled mind, or the one that has an illusion of knowledge. The first, ignorance, is by far the easiest to overcome, and the second, prejudice, is the next easiest, for it merely requires a sweeping away of misinformation and a substituting of accurate facts and perceptions. The illusion of knowledge is highly resistant to education, for a closed mind is subject to stagnation. This situation occurs most often where values are treasured, and that makes religion highly vulnerable.

How did teachers open their students' eyes? First, they beat them vigorously. From ancient Sumer we have a nostalgic speech that might have been given at a class reunion. Here are some of the things that this former student recalls: Arriving late, he was caned; his homework was incorrect, his teachers beat him; he whispered in class, and was whipped; he neglected to get permission to stand and was caned; his calligraphy was below standard, and they thrashed him; he loitered on the way to school and his teachers beat him.[2]

Second, teachers stimulated lively debate. Perhaps the debate over what is the strongest thing in the world exercised more imaginations than any other topic. One answer

[2] S. Kramer, *The Sumerians*, 238.

to this popular controversy appears in a history of Ethiopia from 1681.[3]

> Iron is strong, but fire tempers it.
> Fire is awesome, but water extinguishes it.
> Water is forceful, but the sun dries it.
> The sun is mighty, but a storm cloud conceals it.
> A storm cloud is explosive, but the earth subdues it.
> The earth is majestic, but humans master it.
> Humans are powerful, but grief overtakes them.
> Grief is heavy, but wine assuages it.
> Wine is powerful, but sleep renders it weak.
> Yet woman is strongest of all.
> *(Author's Translation)*

The surprising break in the *sorites* is unexpected, both in terms of style and of content.

The third means of opening eyes was the use of suggestive language. Because students almost without exception were males, wisdom was described as a beautiful bride, and folly was depicted as a harlot enticing young men to destruction. In this way language became highly explosive, and the quest for wisdom suddenly took on erotic dimensions, but teachers often stood in the way of learning, unintentionally encouraging sleep. Two features of the pedagogic method seem counterproductive, for learning was by memorization and by endless copying of texts. The result in

[3] The Latin text is printed in R. Laqueur, "Ephoros. Die Proömium," *Hermes* 46 (1911) 172.

Egypt was reproduction with no real grasp of the meaning of the text being copied.

What about those students whose eyes were opened? They encountered three obstacles to moving beyond knowledge to wisdom. Open eyes see many options, recognizing the complexity of knowledge and refusing to give simple answers; they are bombarded with light, producing the insatiable appetite of scholars, a source of permanent discontent; and they also become tired, almost jaded, hence the temptation to skepticism. Another ancient text from Mesopotamia advises a potential philanthropist to go up to the cemetery and look at the numerous skulls there and to ask which one is a malefactor and which is the benefactor.[4]

Such skepticism, nay pessimism, is a daily companion of the knowledgeable student of life. How, then, did teachers overcome these obstacles to higher wisdom? They did so by achieving focus. True wisdom, the Egyptian teachers insisted, is virtue. It consists of knowing the right word for the occasion, arguing persuasively, exercising restraint, and speaking the truth. Thus kaleidoscopic images took on recognizable patterns, and jaded eyes lit up with infinite configurations of insight shaped by dominant images.

Nevertheless, wide-open eyes blink and must close in sleep, a poignant acknowledgment that learned men sometimes act like fools. But these teachers never forgot that wisdom (hearing) was a stage beyond knowledge (teaching) and that it meant far more than the accumulation of informa-

---

[4] *The Dialogue of Pessimism*, lines 76–78; see W. G. Lambert, *Babylonian Wisdom Literature* (Oxford: Clarendon, 1960) 149.

tion. Wisdom, the capacity to use information for human good, includes virtue. By virtue these teachers meant generosity and humility. Perhaps a biblical proverb best sums up what these ancient scholars seem to have meant.

> Three things are too wonderful for me;
> four I do not understand:
> the way of an eagle in the sky,
> the way of a serpent on a rock,
> the way of a ship on the high seas,
> and the way of a man with a maiden.
> *(Prov. 30:18–19)*

Life's abundant mysteries evoke gratitude and reverence before the author of wisdom and truth.

THREE WAYS OF ACQUIRING KNOWLEDGE

1. Observation of Nature and Human Behavior

After this brief effort to formulate a theory of knowledge for the ancient world and to demonstrate an integral connection between knowledge and virtue, let us turn to an elaboration of knowledge in biblical wisdom. How was knowledge acquired? In a word, knowledge resulted from human inquiry rather than from divine initiative. Actually, this formulation of the situation is not exactly correct, for at creation the deity was said to have taken the initiative, concealing valuable truths within nature itself. From then on, however, it was left to humans to search out these lessons from nature and from human behavior. The means by which they did this was personal observation, and once an insight emerged it had to be transferred from the natural realm to the human by analogy. Some examples taken at random from the Books of Proverbs, Ecclesiastes, and Sirach should clarify this complex process of reasoning.

Gold is tested by fire/humans are tried in the furnace of affliction. *(Prov. 17:3)*

Bees produce honey/do not despise little things. *(Sir. 11:3)*

A new friend is like new wine/when it has aged you will drink it with pleasure. *(Sir. 9:10)*

A door turns on its hinges/a lazy person turns over and over in bed. *(Prov. 26:14)*

A wooden stake is wedged in a fissure between two stones/ sin is squeezed in between buying and selling. *(Sir. 27:2)*

Some clouds yield no rain/some people boast of giving and fail to do so. *(Prov. 25:14)*

A continual dripping of rain on a cold day/a nagging wife. *(Prov. 27:15)*

The crackling of thorns in a fire/the laughter of fools. *(Eccles. 7:6)*

A bird flitting from nest to nest/an adulterous old man. *(Prov. 27:8)*

Whips to control beasts/discipline for children. *(Sir. 7:22–23)*

An insatiable appetite like Sheol/a barren womb.
  (Prov. 30:15–16)

The rich inflict wrong and berate others/the poor suffer
  harm and must apologize. *(Sir. 13:3)*

The rich answer gruffly/the poor are obliged to plead.
  (Prov. 18:23)

An ox led to the slaughter/a young man enticed into the
  home of an adulteress. *(Prov. 7:22–23)*

These statements of truth(s) are the fruit of personal observation by countless sages, who then endeavored to express their insights in language that was both accurate and
memorable. In most instances the poet was content to leave
the application of the saying to others, and the teacher's task
was therefore to discern the circumstance in which a given
saying fit. The lessons had to ring true, else they were
quickly extinguished from memory, and they had to apply
generally to society regardless of time or place. Often quite
different possibilities presented themselves to sages, who
reached a decision on the basis of the situation. "Do not
answer a fool lest you be like him yourself/answer a fool lest
he be wise in his own eyes" (Prov. 26:4–5). In such circumstances one can only lose, so a choice must be made either
to remain silent and give the impression of defeat before an
incompetent, or to speak up and thus bestow dignity on the
fool's remarks.

Other observations about human behavior moved beyond simple statements of truth to explicit counsel, usually
reinforced by elaborate exhortations and warnings. These

Instructions do not leave interpretation to the student, but freely offer advice that leads to happiness and success. Here the religious dimension comes to prominence, and sexual temptation stands as a major source of human folly. Whereas sages who used statements of truth were content to describe reality and therefore to let women and men act on their own reading of the situation, those who preferred Instructions imposed parental authority on their hearers. In some instances divine authority was also invoked, especially when parental instruction and the statutes of the Mosaic Law seemed to coalesce. A good example of this commingling of the two kinds of authority occurs in Prov. 6:20–35, which juxtaposes images of two competing flames. The first is the lamp that mothers and fathers light in the hearts of children, while the second is the fire that sexual passion kindles in unbridled thoughts. The former flame, fueled by divine law, preserves one from the consuming fire.

Do these two distinct types of teaching, statements of truth and Instructions, go their separate ways, producing two different literary traditions? Not at all. By the second century Ben Sira combines both kinds of teaching, permitting the emphasis to fall on the conscious development of Instructions. As a matter of fact, he fashions the teaching into paragraph units that permit him to take up numerous topics and to examine subjects at considerable length. Nevertheless, Ben Sira retains the statements of truth as well, and some of his observations demonstrate striking intuition. Take, for example, this maxim: "Dreams give wings to fools" (Sir. 34:1). Here in a few words he has captured an important reality, and while it is true that Ben Sira goes on to apply this insight to a specific case of divination, the allusive quality of the truthful saying makes it applicable to many circumstances.

If we could only recover the sociological setting for these two kinds of teaching it would enable us to understand them far better.[5] For example, did sages use statements of truth when dealing with advanced students and colleagues, while reserving Instructions for younger learners? We do not know, but one thing seems clearer today than before: the statements of truth were just as authoritative as Instructions despite their different literary form. In at least three cases within Proverbs, larger Instructions quote statements of truth as their clinching argument. Dame Folly offers her most persuasive appeal to young men in a statement of truth: "Stolen water is sweet, and bread eaten in secret is pleasant" (Prov. 9:17). Here is the heart of her seduction, and it rests on an awareness of the incredible power of suggestion. Once the mind has been set on a track, it proceeds to fill in the picture from its store of imagination and desire.

2. Analogy: Creed and Reality

Thus far we have restricted our thoughts to the insights that come through human inquiry. The observation of nature and humans yields dividends precisely because it was believed that laws governed the universe and ensured prosperity if one lived in harmony with them. But not all truth was

---

[5] Frank Crüsemann, "The Unchangeable World: The 'Crisis of Wisdom' in Koheleth," *God of the Lowly*, eds. Willi Schottroff and Wolfgang Stegemann (Maryknoll, NY: Orbis, 1984) 57–77, is an immensely suggestive attempt to recover the sociological setting for Qoheleth's ideas, although somewhat harsh in its judgment of Qoheleth. Choon-Leong Seow, *Ecclesiastes* (AB 18C; New York: Doubleday, 1997), envisions an entirely different sociological environment for the book, the fifth-century Persian era.

the product of human inquiry. In reality, each passing generation was confronted with the accumulated tradition of statements of truth and of Instructions, which had lost the freshness of discovery. This treasury from the past came with certain claims of authority and therefore placed new generations in a context of decision. Do these statements ring true for me? they had to ask. In a sense, the legacy from the past comprised faith reports, and devotion toward parents complicated matters enormously. The tendency was to accept these faith reports at face value, even when they contradicted the personal experience of later generations. Often this inclination was strengthened by an understanding of the world as becoming progressively worse. Because the golden age lay in the past, they thought, the human intellect may have lost some of its power. It therefore followed that assent could be given to parental convictions even when present reality failed to confirm them. Naturally, dogmas arose as a result of this combination of factors, and nowhere was rigidity of beliefs as destructive as in the area of reward and punishment. The belief that sinners fared badly and virtuous persons prospered was seldom borne out in reality, but this dogma produced crises in Mesopotamia, Egypt, and Israel. When the authority of the past weighed heavily on the present, such a crisis naturally followed.

Canonical wisdom bears impressive witness to the difficulty encountered by those who tested faith reports in the light of their own experience of reality. The unknown author of Job examines this dilemma with immense pathos, finally declaring the bankruptcy of secondhand faith. Such assent to the convictions that once sustained others could not survive divine absence or hostile presence. In the end

Job confessed as much, insisting that his spiritual life had always been derivative, despite quite a different assessment of the matter by God and by the narrator in the prologue. For Job the issue was simply hearing as opposed to sight, a strange way of stating things in a community of scholars for whom a sage was best characterized as the hearing, that is, obedient one. Indeed, hearing was equivalent to acting on one's insights, and that was the supreme achievement within wisdom.

Psalm Seventy-three describes a comparable struggle between creed and reality. It opens with a confession of faith that God is truly good to the pure in heart, but the psalmist quickly admits that events render such faith vacuous, for the lion's share of goodies has fallen to wicked persons. Beset by sore temptation, this believer wrestles with doubting thoughts that are recognized as brutish, but a change occurs when the psalmist looks away from prosperous villains and enters the holy place where hearts are purified. There the doubter affirms the faith once more and soars to hitherto unachieved heights. Suddenly, a redefinition of divine goodness overwhelms the psalmist, who realizes for the first time that God's goodness has absolutely nothing to do with things that can be seen and touched, such as material prosperity. Instead, the goodness which comes to decent persons is a feeling of divine presence that bestows confidence regardless of the circumstances. Then at long last the psalmist is able to subscribe to the ancient confession, now that its real meaning has become clear.

The same kind of struggle overtook a traditionalist like Ben Sira, who recounted Israel's sacred story in a time when history gave no evidence that the deity guided the nation toward some unseen destiny. In this instance the scribe complicated matters by taking over traditional faith and linking it with wisdom's universal truths. Whereas he could easily test the latter teachings by his own experience, he could not demonstrate the reliability of claims that God had fought against Pharaoh on behalf of an oppressed people. So what did Ben Sira do in this situation—discard the sacred story? By no means. Instead, he uttered a fervent prayer that God would renew the wondrous signs witnessed by previous generations. Here we see the positive reinforcement of faith that often accompanies experiences that ordinarily render creedal affirmations suspect.

3. Encounter with the Transcendent One

So far we have observed two ways through which people arrived at truth. They observed nature, drawing conclusions by means of analogical thinking, and they listened to reports from others who claimed to have discovered valuable insights. There is yet a third way by which knowledge was thought to have reached ancient sages: immediate encounter with the Transcendent One. From one perspective, such claims do not belong in wisdom literature, where a premium is placed on verifiability. How can others test the truth of claims about encountering the deity? When the sages resort to this sort of argument, they threaten their own fundamental assumption about the capability of the intellect to secure one's existence. The ending to the Book of Job, for example, is a response that derives from traditions that are more at home in prophecy and sacred narrative than in wisdom. Here Job claims to have achieved new insight as a direct result of an encounter with the deity. The same thing seems to be implied in Psalm Seventy-three, where an experience of the deity's hand on the psalmist evokes a splendid acknowledgment that this moment alone is worthy of recollection. The result of the encounter is nothing less than a transvaluation of values, and the psalmist cherishes this sensed presence above all else. A comparable testimony to an encounter with the Holy One occurs in the speech by one of Job's friends, Eliphaz. The account describes an appearance of a numinous figure and the resulting response by a mere earthling. The physical transformation (the hair standing straight up and sense of overwhelming dread) was nothing compared with the knowledge communicated to Eliphaz. In short, the deity is said to have whispered an accusing word: "Shall mortals be more righteous than the creator?" (Job 4:17).

In these appeals to direct encounter with the Most High, a decisive step is taken that opens the door to elaborate theories about communication between creator and creature. The first impressive figure to walk through this door was a woman who identified herself as Wisdom. In many respects, this development is one of the most interesting ones to come out of sapiential thinking. The imagery seems at first to be purely metaphorical, but eventually it signifies an actual divine attribute. Egyptian influence is evident at the initial stage, Greek at the very end. Antedating creation, Wisdom assisted the creator and later came to earth in order to communicate the deity's thoughts to all creatures. In Ben Sira's adaptation of the concept, Wisdom established a dwelling in Jerusalem and infused the Mosaic Law, with which she became identical. For the author of the Greek

Wisdom of Solomon, Wisdom is a pure emanation of the deity. Therefore, whoever acquires Wisdom as a bride also possesses the personal attributes of the deity, particularly the four cardinal virtues.

What enabled such ideas to thrive within wisdom literature? An answer appears to lie in the central position that reflections about creation occupied among the sages. A theology of creation is at home in texts that speak of the High God, as opposed to patron deities, who guided the affairs of a small clan. The advantage of patron deities was their accessibility in all circumstances, their nearness to devotees. No such assumptions adhere to thoughts about the distant creator, whose task was to govern the universe. Naturally, the need was soon felt to find some means to bridge the great distance separating humans from the High God. One answer came from Hebraic tradition, another from the Hellenic world. The Spirit of God, who inspired poets, priests, and prophets, was identified with divine thought, word, and wisdom. Alternatively, the human mind was a microcopy of the divine mind. Hence the human intellect possessed a tiny spark of the divine rationality governing the universe, an idea that linked Israelite sages with Greek philosophers. These two responses to the problem of a transcendent deity implied that the human intellect was in direct touch with ultimate truth.[6]

Belief in direct encounter with transcendence constitutes a link with nonsapiential texts in the biblical canon. However, a decisive difference between the wise and others remained. Perhaps Deut. 30:1–14 comes closest to illustrating

---

[6] Two skeptical responses to such optimism are Qoheleth and Agur (Prov. 30:1–4).

this difference. For this author the divine statute is neither too difficult nor too remote, but it is very near and can be kept. The text seems to suggest that detractors were denigrating the divine word because of its accessibility, exalting insights that were acquired at great cost. The author elevates revelation over discoveries resulting from human inquiry. For Israel's sages, revelation occurred at creation, and the goal of men and women was to discover hidden truth.

PEDAGOGY[7]

So much for the learning process. Beyond using riddles and erotic language, what did Israelite teachers do to overcome students' resistance to instruction? They used a combination of persuasive techniques and rhetorical strategies. Their approach differed, depending on the speaker and the audience. A variety of speakers endeavored to communicate their teachings to innocent youngsters in the Book of Proverbs, to young men and perhaps people generally in the Book of Ecclesiastes, to a distracted victim of divine villainy in the Book of Job, and to potential scribes in Sirach, possibly also to ordinary citizens. With the exception of the Book of Job, the teachings may easily fall under parental instruction.

Perhaps the most surprising instructor appears in a tempest and offers a defiant Job a lesson in meteorology and in

---

[7] For a fuller discussion of rhetoric, see my article titled "Wisdom and Authority: Sapiential Rhetoric and its Warrants," 10–29 in *VTS Congress Volume, Vienna 1980* (Leiden: E. J. Brill, 1981), reprinted in *Urgent Advice and Probing Questions*, 326–43.

zoology, one calculated to instill in him a lasting impression about divine largesse outside the human domain. Here rhetorical questions remotely resembling a teacher's questions in *Papyrus Anastasi* function to demolish Job's pretension to knowledge. Egyptian students would have been able to answer their teacher's questions with a little effort, but God's queries went beyond human ken, making the ironical taunt, "Surely you know!" all the more caustic. This divine teacher emphasizes the huge chasm separating creature from creator and challenges Job to perform some exemplary feats that are perfunctory in God's case.

Two other extraordinary teachers make appearances in the Book of Proverbs, each a poetic personification. They represent voices of reason and folly, and hence lure students in opposite directions. The voice of reason, Wisdom, uses rhetoric steeped in prophetic tradition, filled with threats and authoritative claim. She also offers rich reward for those who heed her teachings. Her rival, Folly, relies on suggestive eloquence, a smooth line that echoes promises often associated with clandestine sexual encounters. The mystique of the foreign woman enhances her appeal, the freedom to cast off all restraint in pursuit of sensual pleasure. To offset the powerful attraction of such smooth words, Wisdom resorts to an authority just short of divine; she claims unique relationship with the creator, a status based on existence prior to the origin of the universe. In addition to claiming divine favor, she also takes credit for the sound judgment exhibited by kings like Solomon. Once such extraordinary thoughts begin to surface, there is no stopping them—and Wisdom eventually becomes a divine manifestation, the essential thought processes of the creator. She also inspires prophets, weds sages, and expresses herself in the Mosaic Law.

The usual speakers in the Book of Proverbs are parents, both father and mother. They teach their children in the privacy of the home, although the explicit audience is restricted to boys. To shape character in the youth, parents rely on insights accumulated over years of experience by the community at large. These fresh discoveries, stated in succinct form, are presented as statements demanding assent because they represent a consensus. Such sayings need not be argued or defended; they just are. Parents do not stop there, however, in their effort to transmit knowledge across the generations. They also use Instructions, or imperatives, in which they make strong demands on the young, at the same time reinforcing these directives with exhortations and warnings, promises and threats. The irony of this type of teaching lies in its apparent authority, but the accompanying motive clauses and threats undercut the illusion of authority.

In several instances within the Book of Proverbs such Instructions resort to the use of proverbial sayings to clinch the argument. For example, the Instruction in Prov. 1:6–19 appeals to a truism, "For in vain is a net spread in the sight of any bird," to get its point across, just as Prov. 6:20–35 draws on two impossible questions for its clinching argument: "Can a man carry fire in his bosom and his clothes not be burned? Or can one walk upon hot coals and his feet not be scorched?" Again, Prov. 9:13–18 quotes an astute proverbial saying to settle the argument, and it is so effective that one can hardly raise objection: "Stolen water is sweet, and bread eaten in secret is pleasant." The twice-used anecdote about indolent sons reaches a climax with the following observation: "A little sleep, a little slumber, a little folding of the hands to rest, and poverty will come upon you like a vagabond, and want like an armed man" (Prov. 6:6–11). It follows that nameless individuals also raise their voices in teaching, however indirectly, and this acknowledgment involves the larger community in teaching the young.

The teachers in the Book of Job differ from the parents in the Book of Proverbs, as do the objects of the Instruction. Job's friends offer sagacious counsel to one whom they once admired as a paragon of virtue but whose impatience forces them to reconsider this opinion. In response, Job has his own views that he wishes to reinforce through personal experience and that he hopes will change his friends' minds. Job's wife also makes a futile attempt to persuade her husband to alter his speech with respect to the deity as a means of finding relief from his unbearable misery. And the *Sāṭān*, God's Adversary, successfully entices the deity to subject a faithful servant to intolerable suffering. This instance of teaching someone through extreme adversity differs sharply from the instruction by the deity discussed earlier.

What rhetorical strategies do these teachers employ? They appeal to *ethos, pathos,* and *logos.* By *ethos* is meant the character of the speaker. In Job 8:8–10, Bildad appeals to the accumulated knowledge of past generations, to character acquired over the years. He understands this knowledge as a system of beliefs, values, and customs that had become as natural as breathing itself. Eliphaz carries such logic to its natural conclusion, insisting that age and experience, symbolized by gray hair, has the right to be heard (15:7, 10). He adds his own testimony, a kind of personal confirmation, to that of vast experience. This kind of resorting to personal experience can also become communal: "As I have seen, those who plow iniquity and sow trouble reap the same" (4:8) and "Lo, this we have searched out; it is true. Hear and know it for your good" (5:27).

This argument from ethos did not elude Job, who felt that his character, although under attack, justified such rhetoric. Naturally, he turns the argument about gray hairs on its head, insisting that God deprives elders of discernment (12:20). Job, too, has learned from experience (13:1–2), and he has broadened his insights by talking with experienced travelers, who have encountered brutal reality (12:25). The two essentials of ethos, inherited tradition and personal appropriation, underlie these observations.

Not every teaching relies on ethos for its warrant; some move beyond the speaker's character to concentrate on the audience. Such rhetoric of *pathos* makes its appeal to the emotions. A speaker uses whatever means possible to arouse the passions of the audience, thereby enhancing the chances of action born out of emotion. Some emotions, particularly fear and wonder, play into the hands of speakers. Eliphaz stuns his audience with an account of a sinister visitor, a spirit gliding past his face and awakening him with an eerie whisper. He describes his own reaction, one of dread that brought feelings of terror, particularly when accompanied by an uncanny message in the form of an interrogative accusation: "Can mortal man be more righteous than God; can a man be purer than his maker?" (4:12–17). In like manner, Elihu appeals to pathos in this gripping account of divine action on passive subjects: "For God speaks in one way, and in two, though man does not perceive it. In a dream, in a vision of the night, when deep sleep falls upon men, while they slumber on their beds, then he opens the ears of men, and terrifies them with warnings" (Job 33:14–18). This type of rhetoric aims at instilling terror, shifting the authority from the human to the divine. Occasionally, the argument combines a sense of conscience with supernatural inspiration, as when Zophar observes: "I hear censure that insults me, and out of my understanding a spirit answers me" (Job 20:3).

When a teacher relies on logical argument—the coherence of what is stated—to convince others, the rhetoric of *logos* is at work. Persuasion by the force of logic, not by appealing to personal authority or the emotions of the audience, places all the emphasis on the speech, although the hearers determine what passes as coherent and convincing argument. Given the ancient Israelites' tendency to use emotion-laden discourse, even arguments by logos may not be entirely free of pathos. The finest example of such persuasion occurs when teachers appeal to consensus and clothe it in rhetorical questions. For example, Job asks the following questions: "Does the wild ass bray when he has grass, or the ox low over his fodder?" and follows that up with a second question of the same kind (6:5–6). Bildad counters with a similar appeal to logos: "Can papyrus grow where there is no marsh? Can reeds flourish where there is no water?" (7:8–10). Zophar, too, uses this rhetorical strategy: "But a stupid man will get understanding when a wild ass's colt is born a man" (11:12).

Logos is at work in 12:7–9 when Job uses a maxim drawn from nature.

> But ask the beasts, and they will teach you;
>   the birds of the air, and they will tell you;
> or the plants of the earth, and they will teach you;
>   and the fish of the sea will declare to you.
> Who among all of these does not know
>   that the hand of the Lord has done this?

Such wisdom drawn from the study of nature, like that derived from the analysis of human beings and their interactions, reinforced arguments based on personal character and an audience's emotions. Together the three rhetorical strategies went a long way toward convincing students, professional or otherwise.

In addition to using such rhetorical strategies, Israel's parents and teachers selected a wide range of stylistic devices to get their points across to reluctant learners. Besides Instructions and maxims, already discussed above, they used existential statements that simply commented on what none could deny.

> There is a way that seems right to a man, but its end is the
>   way to death.
>   *(Prov. 14:12)*

This kind of assertion occurs often in Qoheleth's teachings, but it also finds frequent use in Sirach ("There is a man who buys much for a little, but pays for it seven times over," 20:12). This sober assessment of so-called bargains comes close to warning that one gets what one pays for, advice particularly germane in a society characterized by bartering.

Teachers also used graded numerical sayings to drive their point home: "Three things are stately in their tread; four are stately in their stride; the lion . . . the strutting cock, the he-goat, and a king striding before his people" (Prov. 30:29–31). Although both numbers in this saying are real, only the actual number is the higher one, namely four. The lower number provides balance for the higher number and heads up to it. They taught students to make evaluative judgments, especially through sayings introduced by a word of comparison ("Better is a handful of quietness than two handfuls of toil and a striving after wind," Eccles. 4:6). They appealed to personal experience in a sort of autobiographical narrative (Prov. 4:3–4), and they used poems, hymns, lists, and so much more—all in the service of communicating an important message.

This combination of rhetoric and literary devices demonstrates the care with which Israel's teachers, whether in an official capacity or not, went about their task. Their sensitivity to the demands of rhetoric suggests that they realized the extraordinary appeal of alternative lifestyles to that endorsed by their instructors. They also understood the danger posed by a life of folly, and they strongly urged young men to gain mastery over their passions.

It should not be forgotten that wisdom literature presents an ordered world quite different from the real one the sages occupied, and what they describe has a considerable amount of self-serving. The ideal world they present is the one they hope will become reality. Their rhetoric belongs to this imaginary world; if successful in its use, they will create such a society. That serious aim makes it entirely appropriate to use a riddle in characterizing a school, for in their clever way riddles combined both fun and seriousness.

Chapter Five

≈

Resistance to Learning

*"The root of education is bitter,
but the fruit is sweet."*

<small>GREEK MAXIM</small>

Scholarly discussion often has little relevance to everyday problems occupying the minds of ordinary citizens. We explain a peculiar verbal usage in light of some obscure northwest Semitic root; we clarify a textual variant by appealing to recently discovered manuscripts; we recognize strata within the Hebrew Bible by comparable levels of stories in ancient mythic traditions from Mesopotamia; we imagine pure forms and elaborate traditions by constructing artificial plots, either on the microlevel or macrolevel; we conjecture a host of sociological entities on the principle of plausibility and try to confirm the latter's validity by comparative analysis; we delve into the polyvalency of literary units from every conceivable perspective; we reconstruct history from artifacts discovered in widely separated tells and from chronologies based on randomly discovered pottery and paleography; and we concentrate on the religious views of an Amos rather than asking the fundamental question about continuity or discontinuity between ancient—or modern—theology and truth.

"Scientific dispassion," which has captured the imaginations of most researchers in modern universities, is presently under attack from various quarters as a postenlightenment bias, one not qualitatively superior to precritical assumptions about epistemology. Such radical questioning of historical-critical presuppositions opens the way for reassessing earlier modes of interpretation, usually dismissed as precritical and therefore inferior to modern categories. Dissatisfaction with prevailing norms has always lurked in the shadows, often promoted by conservative religious groups, but in a few instances enjoying respectability within academic circles. For example, the biblical theology movement seized the day and flourished in post–World War II religious interpretation, offering an alternative to the history of religions. Ironically, the strong historical emphasis of biblical theology brought about its decline precisely when enlightenment thought also became suspect. One exciting feature of the present situation is the willingness of at least two significant Jewish scholars to abandon the "safe haven" of historical philology and religious history in favor of asking theological questions.[1]

Mesopotamian scholars made their subject matter so esoteric that it eventually lost its hold on the interests of the

---

[1] Jon D. Levenson, "Why Jews Are Not Interested in Biblical Theology," *Judaic Perspectives on Ancient Israel*, ed. Jacob Neusner (Philadelphia: Fortress Press, 1987), republished in *The Hebrew Bible, the Old Testament, and Historical Criticism* (Louisville: Westminster John Knox, 1993); *Creation and the Persistence of Evil*; M. H. Goshen-Gottstein, "Tanakh Theology: The Religion of the Old Testament and the Place of Jewish Biblical Theology," *Ancient Israelite Religion*, eds. Patrick D. Miller, Jr., Paul D. Hanson, and S. Dean McBride (Philadelphia: Fortress Press, 1987) 617–44.

very people who employed the scribes. The complex language and the enormous divinatory corpus combined to make a sharp division between scribal and religious establishments, on the one hand, and the ordinary populace, on the other hand. The mixture of phonetic and logographic writing, together with the resulting bilingualism of the scribal class, made education a taxing endeavor that restricted its clientele to bureaucratic institutions able to bear the cost of training scribes—at first the royal court, afterward a merchant class.

Religious specialists were likewise removed from the ordinary life of those persons who benefited from their ritual. The actual participation of the nonspecialist may have been minimal—"some prayers—we do not know if they were even daily prayers—some oracular petitions, some apotropaic incantations, a few propitiatory offerings. The rest and the most important—providing for the god, the celebration of feasts, the observance of the rites essential to the prosperity of the country—were performed without the participation of the populace. It was the business of the specialists, and, occasionally, of the representatives of the community, that is, the king."[2]

We, too, have created a guild that communicates solely with itself; witness the small print runs of most scholarly books and the rapid escape of many publishers from such low-profit ventures. Barbara Wheeler points to an alarming trend, the subjecting of religious presses to the pressure of quick profits, and the enslavement of the same presses to

[2] Paul Garelli, "The Changing Facets of Conservative Mesopotamian Thought," *Daedalus* (Spring 1975) 53. See also A. Leo Oppenheim, "The Intellectual in Mesopotamian Society," *Daedalus* (Spring 1975) 37–46.

popular taste, which rarely exceeds the level of secondary education. A few presses have resisted buyouts and pressure to drop "scholarly" publication altogether, but the changed tax laws have resulted in lower print runs and hastened decisions to let books go out of print as soon as the initial interest in them slackens at all.

Wheeler's observations about academic deans taking a more active role in assisting faculty, while helpful in a few instances, do not appear to take into account professors' remarkable interest and knowledge about possibilities of publishing in the present marketplace. Indeed, one suspects that academic demands to "publish or perish" have caused many young scholars to rush manuscripts into print long before the thoughts have been digested and a synthesis achieved. This situation will not change appreciably until colleges and universities give equal weight to excellence in teaching as they do to scholarly publications;[3] thus, teachers will emphasize communicating with their students as much as they do impressing their colleagues.

Our strategy, like that of Mesopotamian scribes, has succeeded in keeping the ranks of scholars small, spreading the honor around, but the price of fame has been immense. We have lost our clientele.

A vast chasm separates biblical scholars from the religious populace in most ecclesiastical bodies. The dismantling of theological faculties in two of the more moderate Baptist seminaries, Southern in Louisville and Southeastern in Wake Forest, by conservative forces determined to squelch

---

[3] Barbara Wheeler, "Theological Publishing and Theological Education," *Theological Education* (Autumn 1990) 56–70.

views at odds with their own by any means possible is but one notable instance of this chasm separating scholars and the church. While a theological student at Southern, I watched a similar destruction of educational integrity when thirteen faculty members were forced to depart in a futile struggle over the exercise of power. The current battle is also essentially a conflict over power, the theological issues serving as a convenient smokescreen to cover what appear to be base tactics and questionable motives. Whatever the motives and issues, one thing is clear: theological education in Southern Baptist seminaries has suffered a stifling blow from which a full recovery will be extremely difficult, if not impossible.

Sadly, similar endeavors to capture control of seminaries have succeeded in undermining theological education in other denominations as diverse as the Missouri Synod Lutherans and the Seventh-Day Adventists. The surge in fundamentalism parallels the rise in right-wing political movements throughout the world, with the concomitant reaction by postmodernist intellectuals. Absolutism and relativism are both alive and well.

Such resistance to knowledge has a long history, and it is by no means limited to religious education, as any public school teacher knows today. The dismal performance of American students in recent tests is a national disgrace, suggesting that fresh examination of ancient discussions of reluctant learners qualifies as something more than an academic exercise. The pejorative phrase "merely academic" suggests that rigorous intellectual pursuits have no utility but serve only to satisfy curiosity. Learning for learning's

sake has had this negative fallout, and academics have com-
pounded the problem by defending a nonfunctional understanding of education in order to protect classical disciplines. The tension between cost-effective disciplines such
as medicine, business, law, and engineering, on the one
hand, and other professions like divinity and the humanities
in general merely mirrors the deep rift within higher education today. Current emphases on a system of accounting in
which every educational unit covers its own financial costs,
the principle of "Every tub on its own bottom," only widens
the division and calls into question the very concept of a
university.

THE *INSTRUCTION OF ANII*

The oldest surviving extensive reflection on resistance to
learning occurs at the conclusion of the Egyptian *Instruction
of Anii*, a difficult text dating from the Eighteenth Dynasty
(1550–1305 B.C.E.). Although this text has nothing specifically aristocratic about it, addressing its teachings to an
ordinary individual, it does assume that the reader has attended school. In fact, the reference to his mother's important role in providing food and drink for the young student,
as well as supervising his daily comings and goings, ac-
knowledges the joint parental effort lying behind the son's
education. Anii's advice that his son return the mother's favor by giving her twice the amount of food she gave him

has a religious motivation—to avoid any harsh feelings that might provoke her to pray for redress.[4]

Two new features characterize the instructions from the New Kingdom: (1) the teachings are intended for the middle class, whereas earlier instructions addressed the aristocracy; and (2) the teachers openly acknowledge that instruction may fail, even if their purpose is to refute the idea. In addition, these teachings manifest a new spirit, the fusion of reason and piety. Earlier optimism, grounded in the order of the universe, took for granted that an ordering principle existed throughout the ancient Near East. Egyptians elevated the notion of *Ma'at*, the scribes in Mesopotamia wrote enigmatically of Tablets of Destiny called *ME*, and biblical writers referred to *ṣedāqâ* and *mišpāṭ*.

Widespread debate among modern critics has centered on the nature of this supposed order, whether or not the gods were themselves thought to be subject to its power. Because religious people have always managed to hold on to contradictory ideas, one need not assume that the tension between fate and divine freedom was ever resolved. In all probability the two notions complemented one another, and individuals assumed that the gods instituted the order and maintained it for stability. One needs to recall that a competing force, anarchy or chaos, was equally real to ancients, as the oft-mentioned myth about the struggle against chaos demonstrates.

---

[4] "The papyrus known as *P. Boulaq* IV, to the contents of which Chabas gave the name *Les Maximes du scribe Anii*, has long enjoyed the unenviable reputation of being the obscurest of all Egyptian wisdom texts" (Sir Alan Gardiner, *JEA* 45 [1959] 12, quoted in Miriam Lichtheim, *Ancient Egyptian Literature*, vol. II [Berkeley, Los Angeles, London: University of California Press, 1976]).

Social reality introduced a spirit of doubt that ultimately achieves dominance during the Demotic period, if the *Instruction of Ankhsheshonqy* and *Papyrus Insinger* accurately reflect the attitude of teachers. In the final analysis it matters little whether or not the crisis within Egyptian wisdom beginning in the Middle Kingdom was a literary fiction or a historical fact. If the former, one would need to explain why so many authors depicted reality in such a negative fashion, and whatever answer one comes up with will surely imply skepticism on the part of those who wrote in such an unrealistic manner. In actuality, a literary fiction belongs to the category of history too, for the depiction of events is in itself an event.

Miriam Lichtheim correctly notes the presence of older optimism within the same texts that reflect increasing doubt, and her point surely will require tempering such extreme views as Hans Heinrich Schmid's all-embracing hypothesis of widespread crisis in Mesopotamia, Egypt, and Israel. The evidence he provides seems to prove that early optimism eventually hardened into rigid dogma, which eroded over time and generated considerable skepticism. Nevertheless, pockets of old optimism probably survived all efforts to undermine its simple trust, continuing alongside more negative sentiments.

Egyptian scribal texts confirm the thesis that a strong reluctance to learn had to be overcome. Scribal texts from *Papyrus Sallier* and *Papyrus Anastasi* IV and V illustrate this point. The first (*Papyrus Sallier* I, 6, 9–7, 9) scolds the scribe Pentawere for carousing and for preferring work in the fields. The text contrasts the hard life of a farmer with the scribe's favorable freedom from any taskmaster. *Papyrus Anastasi* V, 8, 1–9, 1 warns against idle pleasures, urging the scribe to write, to recite, and to talk with learned people. The threat of physical punishment is reinforced by assurance that one can teach apes to dance and that one tames horses. *Papyrus Anastasi* V, 9, 2–10, 2 is a prayer to Thoth for skill and accomplishment as a magistrate, for which the people will praise the god. *Papyrus Anastasi* IV, 10, 1–5 contains a fervent prayer to Amun in a period of chaos. *Papyrus Anastasi* IV, 9, 4–10, 1 seeks to dissuade the scribe Inena from the view that a soldier's life is preferable to that of a scribe. The beatings inflicted on scribes, which may have provoked Inena's comment, are said to pale in comparison with those endured by soldiers, who are beaten like papyrus.[5] The argument must have persuaded Inena, for several manuscripts are attributed to his hand.

Papyrus Lansing: A Schoolbook accuses a student as follows: "You are busy coming and going, and don't think of writing. You resist listening to me; you neglect my teachings" and adds, "But though I spend the day telling you, 'Write,' it seems like a plague to you."[6]

A Sumerian school text indicates that a similar situation existed in the land between the Euphrates and Tigris rivers. In this particular text, *A Scribe and his Perverse Son*, a father and son discuss the advantages of receiving a scribal training, and the father complains because his son entertains thoughts about choosing a different profession. The father

[5] William Kelly Simpson, *The Literature of Ancient Egypt* (New Haven and London: Yale University Press, 1973) 343–47.

[6] Miriam Lichtheim, *Ancient Egyptian Literature*, vol. II, 169.

offers numerous instructions that are intended to help his son in a "humanistic" endeavor as a scribe, and the text ends on a happy note.

Another text, which Kramer entitles *Schooldays*, takes the form of a former student reminiscing about what it was like while at school. The student seems to recall one beating after another, which did not moderate until the teachers were given some extra money for their trouble. *The Disputation between Enkimansi and Girnishag* implies that teachers had difficulty maintaining order. An older student hurls insults at a younger, who responds in kind. Both Girnishag and Enkimansi claim to be superior scribes, but the latter so infuriated a monitor that he threatened to put Enkimansi in chains. *Colloquy between a Monitor (ugula) and a Scribe* contains a long-winded speech by the *ugula* describing his own accomplishments in the *edubba* and the scribe's response, which details his faithful handling of administrative responsibilities. The text concludes on a more favorable note in which the *ugula* praises the scribe.

From these texts Kramer deduces that the head of the Sumerian school was the *ummia*, also known as the school-father, and that students were school-sons. Alongside the *ummia* was an assistant, called "big brother," and special monitors who were responsible for class attendance and discipline.[7]

Biblical texts attest the same phenomenon—students who chafe at the rigorous requirements imposed on them by well-meaning teachers. They also chafed from the pain of physical punishment, widespread in ancient Near Eastern pedagogy.

---

[7] "A Scribe and His Perverse Son." Samuel Noah Kramer, *The Sumerians*, 229–48.

Apparently teachers believed that learning traveled to students' ears by way of their backs, and a cane was the chief pedagogical instrument.

An Egyptian scribe, Wenemdiamun, confesses to his teacher as follows: "I grew into a youth at your side. You beat my back, your teaching entered my ear" (*Papyrus Lansing: A Schoolbook*). This scribal text has eleven sections united by a single theme: Be a scribe. Lichtheim analyzes the sequence as follows: (1) an address; (2–4) praise of the scribal profession and exhortations to the pupil; (5–6) the miseries of other professions; (7) additional advice and exhortations; (8) the special hardships of the soldier's life; (9–11) the pupil praises his teacher. The third section takes up the problem of a reluctant learner, one who has not yet known a woman but who has demonstrated scribal potential. The royal scribe contrasts Wenemdiamun with a great obelisk that yields to human will and with a cow and a horse, which perform their daily tasks for fear of a beating. Wenemdiamun remains unmoved by beatings, and the royal scribe admits to being at a loss for a remedy that would turn the unwilling student around.

Section 4 compares Wenemdiamun unfavorably to the mischievous goose and carefree antelope, while the seventh section accuses him of having a heart like an empty room and of surrendering to hot passion for pleasure with a whore. The concluding encomium of a teacher furnishes sharp contrast to the earlier characterization of a soldier's life. The teacher is "wise in planning, skilled in speech; far-seeing at all times; . . . succeeds . . . judge of hearts . . . the good champion of . . . people . . . one of weighty counsel who weighs his answer . . . handsome in body, gracious in manner . . . a man of choice words, who is skilled in saying them."[8]

In the *Instruction of Anii* this early reflection about obstacles confronting teachers takes the form of debate between a father and his son. Sara Denning Bolle examines the dialogic tradition in the West from Socrates to Bakhtin and traces a lively give-and-take to much earlier literature. She recognizes dialogue as a social activity and considers all dialogue to be mimetic (105), but she also insists that one can carry on a dialogue with the inner self (112). Into the latter category Bolle places *The Babylonian Theodicy*, Qoheleth, and *Dispute of a Man with his Ba*.

All of these dialogues stop short of the Platonic dialectic, which involves an ascent and a descent (to the One and back), preparation for which comes through Socratic *elenchus* (questioning to show up ignorance), and *epagoge* (inducing a universal from the particular). Socratic definition, the searching for the essence, does not seem to have formed part of dialogue in ancient Mesopotamia (100–102). The prominence of debate in sapiential literature suggests that students actively participated in the educational process, despite the heavy emphasis on passive learning.

Hearing was not the only response required of young pupils; they were also expected to answer, responding to questions with evidence of attentiveness and insight.[9] Such dialogues express thought and feeling, tracing the development of an idea from its inception in a kind of heuristic recovery.

---

[8] Lichtheim, *Ancient Egyptian Literature*, vol. II, 167–75.

[9] "Wisdom is a matter of communicating, enlightening, and instructing; dialogue is its vehicle" (Sara Denning-Bolle, *Wisdom in Akkadian Literature: Expression, Instruction, Dialogue*, 280).

"The intended effect is to bring about, through a dynamic rendering of a process of mental acquisition, the natural birth of an idea: the reader, or listener, identifies so fully with the process that the resulting conclusion is already internalized in its premises."[10]

The debate between Anii and his son Khonshotep, also a scribe,[11] rewards close analysis, for it suggests that students' resistance arose from a sense that learning stopped short unless it achieved embodiment. For the most part ancient education was functional rather than knowledge for knowledge's sake. The utilitarian nature of learning was to some extent a product of the circumstances within which it was pursued and the restricted clientele from whom students were recruited. Professional guilds assumed responsibility for training their members; knowledge therefore amounted to skill in performing requisite tasks. Moreover, educated persons filled official positions in the government, and as respected leaders they were expected to render just decisions. Extraordinary expectations among the ordinary citizenry imposed heavy burdens on these officials, who prepared themselves for office by embodying the teachings. To be sure, not everyone who acquired an education committed the knowledge to the inner self, and as a result learned rogues certainly existed then as now. For the majority of students, nevertheless, a single question achieved dominancy: What is good for men and women? The quest for knowl-

---

[10] Giorgio Buccellati, "Wisdom and Not: the Case of Mesopotamia," *JAOS* 101 (1981) 43. Buccellati considers Mesopotamian dialogues "an early moment" in the development of the Socratic dialogue. He thinks the dialogue form "emphasizes the unfolding of a thought process viewed dynamically in its becoming" (39).

[11] Perhaps Khonshotep at this stage possesses only the *potential* for becoming a scribe.

edge thus assisted the greater search for ways to cope in every circumstance. In other words, wisdom, not knowledge, was the goal of instruction.

The ancient understanding of a fool as morally corrupt rather than intellectually deficient underlies this distinction between knowledge and wisdom. A person could be both knowledgeable and foolish, but no one could be wise and foolish too. Wisdom consists of judicious use of information to enrich life. The mere gathering of information, however valuable, did not make a person wise, for the truly learned individual gave the teachings flesh and blood. Controlling the passions—anger, lust, envy, appetite—and mastering the tongue—avoiding gossip and slander, learning eloquence and timing—demanded far more discipline than merely accumulating facts and storing them in the brain.

The modern ideal of scientific objectivity, itself a bogus claim, would have found no toehold among ancient students. In their view, education aims to equip people for living; in the parlance of a later time, learning makes "gentlemen scholars."[12]

Furthermore, a desire to embody the teachings is quite a different thing from actual moral maturity. Khonshotep recognizes this disparity between volition and action. Wishing to emulate the virtues of his father, he perceives a weak-

---

[12] Jerome S. Bruner makes the same point, illustrating it with reference to the *talmud khokhen* in the shtetl of Eastern Europe, the Chinese scholar-administrator (beautiful person), and the gentleman of seventeenth-to-eighteenth-century Europe (*On Knowing* [Cambridge: The Belknap Press of Harvard University Press, 1966] 119). The biblical axiom "As a person thinks, so is the individual" has its parallel in *Papyrus Insinger*, which states that "He who thinks of the good is one who masters it" (30:3), but this same text concedes that some informed persons have not mastered the technique of applying the teaching to daily living ("There is the one who knows the instruction, yet he does not know how to live by it," 9:17).

ness on his own part against the impressive achievement of Anii. Rejecting a magical understanding of reciting the classics,[13] Khonshotep concedes that "A boy does not follow the moral instructions though the writings are on his tongue!" The centrality of ear and tongue rather than eye and writing instrument occasions no surprise in light of ancient practice. Instructors recited texts orally and placed a premium on memorization, hence the frequent summons to listen.

The oldest surviving Egyptian instruction, *Ptahhotep*, formulates the matter hypothetically: "If you listen to my sayings, all your affairs will go forward." The form of address in *Amenemope* is more direct: "Give your ears, hear the sayings, give your heart to understand them" (III, 9–10). This latter formulation resembles biblical admonitions to hear a father's teachings, an insistence that opens the initial collection proper (after the prologue in Prov. 1:1–7): "Hear, my son, your father's instruction, and reject not your mother's teaching" (1:8).

This summons to hear punctuates the teachings in this particular collection, for instance, "Hear, O sons, a father's

[13] Despite the vital role of magic in Egyptian religious ritual, it does not appear to have enjoyed wide esteem among the sages. The situation is altogether different in Mesopotamia, where wisdom and magic coalesced, leading Wilfrid G. Lambert to conclude that strictly speaking wisdom is a misnomer there (*Babylonian Wisdom Literature* [Oxford: At the Clarendon Press, 1960]). Israelite wisdom literature is remarkably free of any magical incantation, the cult playing a minimal role as well. The extent of cultic influence throughout the ancient Near East has been examined by Leo G. Perdue (*Wisdom and Cult* [SBLDS 30; Missoula: Scholars Press, 1977]). Occasional remarks by Israel's sages imply that even they accepted the validity of ritual, for example Ben Sira's comparison of the Law's trustworthiness and the reliability of inquiry by means of the sacred lots (Sir. 33:3). Modern interpreters often fail to discern the extent of human trust in the deity's freedom to act despite sacral, that is, manipulative attempts to determine the divine will. Ancient Israelites believed that the deity conveyed his will through such human means, and magic was an important way to bring the deity's intention to bear on everyday experience, one that enjoyed divine approval in the view of ancient peoples.

instruction, and be attentive that you may gain insight" (4:1); "My son, be attentive to my wisdom, incline your ear to my understanding" (5:1); "And now, O sons, listen to me, and do not depart from the words of my mouth" (5:7); "And now, O sons, listen to me, and be attentive to the words of my mouth" (7:24).

The collection in 22:17–24:22, which has several sayings in common with *Amenemope*, begins with the advice, "Incline your ear, and hear; apply your mind to my knowledge" (22:17), eliminating "the words of the wise" as the original title of this collection, a phrase that has been inserted into the present text as the object of the imperative "hear." Hans Walther Wolff has used the summons to hear as evidence for wisdom influence within prophetic literature, but his argument is seriously weakened by the probability that all segments of society used such impassioned urging to communicate values they desired to propagate.

Ptahhotep's Instruction concludes with a well-known pun on the pregnant expression for hearing: "Useful is hearing to a son who hears; if hearing enters the hearer, the hearer becomes a listener; hearing well is speaking well. Useful is hearing to one who hears; hearing is better than all else; it creates good will. How good for a son to grasp his father's words; he will reach old age through them. He who hears is beloved of god; he whom god hates does not hear. The heart makes of its owner a hearer or non-hearer. Man's heart is his life-prosperity-health. He who loves to hear is one who does what is said. How good for a son to listen to his father, how happy is he to whom it is said: 'The son, who pleases as a master of hearing'. . . ."

By contrast, the Akkadian *Counsels of Wisdom* states three

times: "In your wisdom (by virtue of your education) read in the tablet." An oral tradition of Seven Sages certainly flourished in Mesopotamia, but later sages emphasized the written tradition at the expense of the oral, or popular, one. This emphasis even produced bizarre comments about Sumerian sages who had four ears, enabling them to hear and consequently to achieve wisdom. "Four were his (Marduk's) eyes, four were his ears. When he moved his lips, fire blazed forth. Each of his four ears grew large and (his) eyes likewise, to see everything."[14]

To my knowledge, the comparable acknowledgment that eyes play an important role in education did not produce technical expressions equivalent to "the hearing one" although it did give rise to legends about sages with more than two eyes. The Sumerian riddle about the tablet house mentioned above does, however, focus attention on sight in its deeper sense. It asks: "What does one enter with closed eyes and depart with open eyes?" The full form of the riddle is as follows: "A house with a foundation like heaven, a house which like a vessel has been covered with linen, a house which like a goose stands on a (firm) base. One with eyes not opened has entered it, one with open eyes has come out of it. Its solution: the school."[15]

It is noteworthy that the eyes rather than ears symbolize learning in this Sumerian riddle, and this emphasis on seeing corresponds to the stress on consulting the tablets.

---

[14] Bolle, *Wisdom in Akkadian Literature*, 58. Here Marduk, the king of the gods in the Babylonian pantheon, is understood as a sage (similar to Solomon in the Bible). Because the ear was the seat of intelligence in ancient Mesopotamia, writing served as an aid to memory.

[15] Robert Seth Falkowitz, *The Sumerian Rhetoric Collections*, Ph.D. Dissertation, University of Pennsylvania, 1980, 91.

The riddle alone of the many genres in the rhetoric collections is marked by a siglum, "its solution."[16] Blindness caused by ignorance, prejudice, and misinformation vanishes with the arrival of knowledge, the altering of preconceived notions, and the substitution of fact for fiction. Only as knowledge becomes embodied can the eyes mirror the soul. According to Qoheleth, "A person's wisdom illumines his countenance and changes the hardness of his face" (8:1b), a conviction that was widely shared in the ancient world.

Concomitantly, the sages recognized the heavy burden borne by all who exercised their mental faculties in pursuit of knowledge, a depleting of one's energy and increasing of sorrow, which none really knew but the individual involved. Moving from the written word to its author's psychic makeup was equally hazardous, as interpreters of the *Dialogue between a Master and his Slave* have found out. Experts disagree about the nature of this dispute, whether or not it is satire or deadly serious. An author's ability to depict various personae in a literary work complicates the issue vastly. For example, does *The Babylonian Theodicy* actually constitute an inner debate within a single persona, or does it represent two separate individuals with competing views?

Khonshotep accepts the common assumption that wisdom, like good wine, requires time to establish itself. By their very nature sons are inferior to fathers, who possess the advantage of years. Judah Goldin states that "By defini-

---

[16] Despite this marker, it is difficult to distinguish riddles from difficult questions, perhaps a subgenre itself, on which see my essay entitled "Questions, dictions, et épreuves impossibles," *La Sagesse de l'Ancien Testament*, 96–111 and "Impossible Questions, Sayings, and Tasks," 19–34 in *Gnomic Wisdom*, ed. John Dominic Crossan (*Semeia* 17, 1980).

tion sons fall short."[17] His insightful discussion of moralistic discourse as paternal, experienced, threatening, and beseeching grasps the complexity inherent in the context of teaching. Individuals who have acquired long years of valuable experience wish to save younger persons from picking up the same bumps and bruises, so teachers earnestly offer the stick and the carrot, hoping to motivate youth. In every way age equips parents with insights, both positive and negative, hidden from the inexperienced. Furthermore, fathers have the advantage of having begot sons, with all that this relationship implies. At no time can the relationship change, although in time sons become fathers and acquire superiority over the next generation.

Indeed, Anii does not hesitate to assert paternal authority.[18] Thus he labels his son's thoughts as worthless and wrong, and he warns Khonshotep that such thinking has ruinous consequences. In Anii's view, education has no recognizable limits. It consists in radically reorienting the status quo.

Numerous proverbs reorient the reader or listener by way of disorientation. They state something in such a manner that the accepted understanding of reality ceases to have unquestioned status. People tend to think they have fully understood a matter until a clever formulation challenges its validity, at which point they open their minds to an entirely new insight. Because a proverb is by nature self-assertive, conveying a certainty that resembles consensus, the saying belies its hypothetical nature and demands acquiescence.

---

[17] Judah Goldin, *Studies in Midrash and Related Literature*, 196.
[18] "Turn your back to these many words, That are not worth being heard . . . You foolish heart, Do you wish to teach?" *Anii*.

Few interpreters have seen this aspect of aphorisms as clearly as James G. Williams.[19]

For this reason, the conservative nature of wisdom literature has been overplayed by many critics. To be sure, the sages wished to uphold the status quo, believing it to be ordained by God, and societal upheaval brought great consternation to well-placed teachers. Still, sages readily challenged dominant hypotheses and forced radical changes in thought and action. In the long run, however, the worldview of sages remained remarkably constant, despite powerful disorientation now and again. Just as wild beasts conquer their nature and adopt wholly new patterns of behavior, so students can change their character.

Anii mentions the wild bull, fierce lion, dog, goose, monkey, Nubian, and Syrian as examples of completely altered patterns of conduct through an educational process. The ability of Nubians and Syrians to speak Egyptian must have impressed Anii, for he includes their acquired skill alongside changes in ferocious and mischievous wild animals. *Papyrus Lansing* also uses the adaptability of cow and horse to human needs as a forceful argument on behalf of education. Anii's answer to Khonshotep's defense that nature determines one's actions amounts to a strong denial, as if father and son engage in a shouting match: "Does not!" "Does!"

An indication that wisdom had achieved its goal was a sage's mastery of passions. In their opinion, wise persons did not need to shout but only to state things factually and eloquently; fools gave vent to anger and raised their voices in vain. Nevertheless, circumstances sometimes called for pas-

---

[19] *Those Who Ponder Proverbs* (Sheffield: The Almond Press, 1981).

sionate speech, best illustrated in Egypt by *The Protests of the Eloquent Peasant* and in Israel by the Book of Job. Khonshotep avers that the masses follow their base nature, making an individualist rare. The reason, as *Papyrus Insinger* remarks, is that "Whoever raves with the crowd is not regarded as a fool." Conformity has always had amazing appeal, as this popular aphorism indicates. Naturally, going along with the crowd insulated one from its fickle fury; such persons can take comfort in the belief that conformity is not always a bad thing. Popular opinion occasionally gets things right, but *Papyrus Insinger* implies that the actions of the crowd are less than praiseworthy. Hiding among the masses, obtaining anonymity through numbers may be a safe policy, but sages are expected to stand up for truth and virtue rather than lope along the path of least resistance. This path of least resistance, which Khonshotep also mentions while urging his father to slacken the curricular requirements, has extraordinary attraction. Having attained advanced standing on the moral plain, Anii resists any lowering of educational standards to benefit lazy students.

Each disputant appeals to human development, Khonshotep to defend a lighter load and Anii to justify strenuous requirements. They start from the fact that infants eat different food from the fare prepared for adults. Like the Apostle Paul, Anii insists that this argument supports his position that the educational curriculum should be a rigorous one. Having conceded the desirability of a solid education, Khonshotep feels obliged to ask for assistance from a higher power, although he apparently thinks such a request would be more successful coming from his virtuous father. Astonishingly, this curious expression of human need includes Anii, whose wisdom is attributed to a gift from the god.

The later *Papyrus Insinger* concludes various sections with a refrain crediting the god with everything that befalls human beings ("The fate and fortune that come, it is the god that sends them"). The twenty-fourth instruction comprises an encomium of the god who created appropriate things for every occasion. This lavish praise does not overlook mystery, the hidden work of the god who "created the breath in the egg though there is no access to it" (32, 7), to which one may compare Qoheleth's observation, "Just as you do not know what is the way of the life-breath in the bones in a pregnant womb, so you do not know the work of God, who does everything" (11:5).

Qoheleth uses the notion of "divine gift" in a manner similar to *Papyrus Insinger*'s refrain about fate and fortune, for no individual can control either the nature of God's gift or its timing. It comes in the same arbitrary way as fate, and Qoheleth almost introduces such a concept, although chance for him remains an act of God. In this way reason and piety come together to place a cloud over human effort. "When wisdom has become God's wisdom rather than that of man, more than two millennia of sapiential thinking have come to an end."[20] This comment applies not to Anii but to the culmination of such thinking as his, *The Teachings of Silvanus*, a Christian moral treatise.

Balancing human effort and divine assistance has not been easy for interpreters of wisdom literature, some critics insisting that the unsavory features of early wisdom, nicely

---

[20] Lichtheim, *Late Egyptian Wisdom Literature in the International Context*, 192.

portrayed in the story of Adam and Eve, led to a distancing
of YHWH from wisdom until quite late. No such disasso-
ciating of deities and wisdom occurred in Mesopotamia,
where certain gods are credited with exceptional wisdom.
One can scarcely imagine any culture boasting that its god
lacked wisdom, despite the fact that shrewdness was one aspect of it.

The debate concludes on a positive note emphasizing the
iron will of teachers, who mold reluctant students into para-
gons of virtue. Anii uses an analogy from carpentry: neither
a straight stick nor a crooked one retains its shape in the
skillful hands of a carpenter. Anii's message is therefore
plain: resisting my teaching will fail in the end. Still, he introduces a disturbing thought—that his son may have been
corrupted. "Do you wish us to teach, or have you been corrupted?"[21]

Only one other Instruction may conclude with a son's response—the so-called *Counsels of Sube'awilum.* This multi-
lingual Akkadian text, fragments of which were discovered
at Ras Shamra and at Emar, implies an even more advanced
degree of "corruption" on the son's part, than does Anii. His
reaction to the father's advice has been interpreted as heavily
pessimistic, like biblical Qoheleth. Indeed, the emphasis on
the futility of striving to acquire wealth and death's certainty
resemble this later biblical sage.

Biblical wisdom gives the impression of vulnerability to
rival claims, particularly those issuing from youthful rebels
who promise freedom from want and from external authority. In regard to Prov. 1:10–19 Carol Newsom writes: "The

---

[21] Anii, in Lichtheim, *Ancient Egyptian Literature*, 145.

rival discourse against which the father argues can be made visible in its general outlines: it is one with a horizontal rather than a vertical structure of authority, based not on patriarchal family affiliation but on common enterprise, and one that offers young men immediate access to wealth rather than the deferred wealth of inheritance. What lurks beneath the surface is the generational chasm, the division of power between older and younger men in patriarchal society."[22] As late as the first century B.C.E. wisdom teachers continued to struggle against corrupting influences from "ungodly men" who seek to capture every pleasure before it vanishes from sight (Wisd. of Sol. 1:16–2:24).

Scribal texts confirm that a similar temptation also enticed youthful sages in Egypt and Mesopotamia. The sages' worldview always stood in danger of being overthrown by rival understandings. Perhaps interpreters have erred in thinking that a single, unified worldview existed among the sages, for considerable differences characterize the several literary genres. Within the Bible these differences stand out, for the Book of Job submits optimistic wisdom, especially that enunciated in Proverbs, to scathing review, and Qoheleth denies the very premises on which wisdom ordinarily took its stand. Ben Sira reaffirms traditional optimism, reinforcing it with sacred tradition and a myth that identifies the Mosaic Torah with wisdom.

Nevertheless, this literature has enough consistency to justify talk about a common understanding, and the crisis it confronted only underscores this fact. This real threat gave

---

[22] "Women and the Discourse of Patriarchal Wisdom," *Gender and Difference in Ancient Israel,* ed. Peggy L. Day (Minneapolis: Fortress Press, 1989) 144.

a sense of urgency to paternal instruction, for a single generation could bring a halt to everything the father held sacred. That is why emotional language flows freely in the Instructions, the wringing of feelings from exhortation and admonition to warning and rebuke. Thus a wronged father, Ahiqar, writes: "My eyes which I lifted up upon you, and my heart which I gave you in wisdom [you have despised and] have brought my name into disrepute" (no. 76). Only two sayings of *Ahiqar*, numbers 50 and 76, have any direct bearing on the son's infamous treatment of his benefactor. The wronged father, brought down by his son's false testimony against him, did not follow the advice of the gentler teachings within ancient wisdom to exercise forgiveness when wronged, but brought about Nadin's destruction.

Ahiqar did, however, acknowledge his own responsibility for what Nadin did. Had Ahiqar not adopted the boy, the sanctity of the family would not have been disturbed by the false testimony against the father. The story naturally abounds in references to Nadin's ingratitude, for example, "My son, thou hast been like the man who saw his companion shivering from cold, and took a pitcher of water and threw it over him."

PAPYRUS INSINGER

More than a millennium later than Anii, the unknown teacher whose Instruction has been preserved on *Papyrus Insinger* devotes an entire chapter, the tenth, to the important task of instructing one's son. The first five chapters are missing from *Papyrus Insinger*, which probably dates from the late Ptolemaic period. The sixteenth Instruction divides life's span as follows: ten years as a child before understanding death and life, ten years training for an occupation, ten years acquiring possessions, ten years maturing, after which one has sixty years. Presumably, instruction took place during the first two decades of life.

Assenting to popular belief that an uninstructed son resembles a statue of stone, a variant of which occurs in *Ankhsheshonqy* ("Better is a statue of stone than a foolish son"), *Papyrus Insinger* advances a theory that goes to the very heart and soul of learning. In a word, instruction cannot succeed where there is dislike, resentment, or blame.[23] The precise meaning of this statement remains unclear, for it may refer to a teacher's contempt for students, or for the pedagogical task and its subject matter; alternatively it may allude to a student's dislike for the teacher or for the topic under consideration and the process of learning itself.

Papyrus Insinger recognizes at least two factors contributing to students' less-than-enthusiastic embracing of learning. The first concerns the sacrifices demanded of those who embody the moral lessons transmitted from one generation to another. Control of the belly and the phallus is no easy matter, although absolutely essential. He writes: "The evil that befalls the fool, his belly and his phallus bring it." In another context *Papyrus Insinger* encourages readers to show superiority over a beautiful woman; he does not say how,

---

[23] Lichtheim notes that the word translated "dislike" has all three senses, as well as that of "fault, wrong" (*Ancient Egyptian Literature*, vol. III, 214, n. 28).

but the larger setting implies that a wise person will be able to resist her lure. Like Qoheleth, *Papyrus Insinger* believed woman's heart to be an unyielding mystery ("One does not ever discover the heart of a woman anymore than [one knows] the sky"). This observation about woman contrasts with other mysteries he mentions in that they all become clear through some particular course of action. Unlike these temporary mysteries, the hiddenness of a woman's heart is reckoned to be an absolute.

Excessive eating and illicit sexual behavior must have been highly desirable to ancient students (as they appear to be to modern students), if the frequent warnings against such activity accurately reflect reality. *Papyrus Lansing*, an Egyptian scribal text, reveals a father's frustration over a disappointing son who prefers visiting a harlot to studying.[24] The second thing that hindered love for learning has already been mentioned, the punishment associated with instruction. *Papyrus Insinger* grounds this harsh practice in the divine will, claiming that the deity Thoth created the stick for the purpose of whipping lazy students. Like biblical teachers, the author of *Papyrus Insinger* thinks physical punishment should be used only on fools.

An entirely different instrument, a sense of shame, was given to the wise as a prophylactic against sin. The impor-

[24] The powerful attraction between the sexes finds expression in the Egyptian *Harper's Songs* and in the biblical Song of Songs, on both of which Michael V. Fox, *The Song of Songs and the Ancient Egyptian Love Songs* (Madison: The University of Wisconsin, 1985), throws dazzling light. His commentaries, informed by modern literary theory and traditional philology, should be supplemented by Ann W. Astell's *The Song of Songs in the Middle Ages* (Ithaca and London: Cornell University Press, 1990) and by Marcia Falk's fresh translation, with "commentary" (*The Song of Songs* [San Francisco: Harper San Francisco, 1990]).

tance of the notion of shame, "not previously found in Egyptian wisdom,"[25] has not been examined adequately in modern scholarship. The idea surfaces frequently in Sirach also. The basis for the concept was the sages' high estimation of personal reputation, loss of which induced shame in the presence of one's peers. Avoidance of such reduced standing in the eyes of persons who mattered provided a powerful motive for conduct that would enhance one's reputation and for avoiding behavior of a demeaning sort. A refined conscience and remorse over the possibility of moral failure distinguished the instructed from the uninstructed.

To judge from widespread comments regarding a son's ability to survive physical punishment, the blows must have been especially forceful. The author of *Insinger* remarks that a son does not die from paternal thrashing, and comparable observations occur in the eighth-century Aramaic *Sayings of Ahiqar* and in the early second-century Sirach.[26] The Syriac version of *Ahiqar* puts it nicely: "My son, withhold not thy son from stripes; for the beating of a boy is like manure to the garden, and like rope to an ass (or any other beast) and like tether on the foot of an ass." The Armenian version (no. 14) has "Son, spare not the rod to thy son, for the rod is to children as the dung in the garden; and as the tie and seal fastening the packet, and as the tether on the foot of the ass, so is the rod profitable to the child." The

---

[25] Lichtheim, *Late Egyptian Wisdom Literature in the International Context,* 159.

[26] James M. Lindenberger, *The Aramaic Proverbs of Ahiqar* (Baltimore and London: The Johns Hopkins University Press, 1983) 17, thinks that the proverbs antedate the narrative. Perhaps the differences in language between the sayings and the story owe more to their genre than to their relative age, for poetry usually employs different (more traditional and archaic) vocabulary and syntax than prose. Lindenberger dates the manuscript to the fifth century on the basis of its paleography (19).

saying proceeds to encourage one to whip a child rather than abstaining from discipline, which results in the son's misconduct and possible execution, together with the father's deep remorse.[27]

An astonishing remark in *Papyrus Insinger* indicates the seriousness with which the teacher took the learning process: genealogical descent counts less than willingness to learn. "Better the son of another than a son who is an accursed fool." This questioning of lineal descent as the primary consideration is attributed to Jesus in Mk. 3:31–35, where the teacher insists that one who has the same values as he is a true brother or sister. The Hellenistic Wisdom of Solomon pushes this idea a step further, insisting that childlessness with virtue is preferable to sinful progeny. The difference between this idea of barrenness with virtue and the ancient suspicion of barren women as sinners because of their inability to have children is noteworthy. The sympathetic treatment of eunuchs in Wisd. of Sol. 3:14 indicates a changed ethos; Ben Sira's wry observation about a eunuch's frustrated sexual desire participates more in the old ethos than in the new (30:20, cf. 20:4).

Papyrus Insinger customarily closes a chapter with a set of paradoxes and two concluding thoughts. The first paradox introduces the idea that intuitive intelligence exists, a kind of recognition without benefit of instruction. As early as *Ptahhotep* the existence of natural eloquence among untaught maidens was acknowledged: "Good speech is more hidden than greenstone, yet may be found among maids at the grindstones." The attribution of exceptional eloquence

[27] Lindenberger, *The Aramaic Proverbs of Ahiqar*, 49.

to a peasant shows that some people possessed native gifts
that caught the eyes of persons who studied arduously to
acquire such qualities. Native intelligence finds a way of
manifesting itself regardless of personal circumstances.

The second paradox concedes that even learned scoun-
drels exist, for a sinister aspect lurks deeply within all wisdom.[28] Not all people who know the teachings actually embody them. The author of *Papyrus Insinger* does not accuse
such persons of faulty knowledge, which would provide a
facile explanation for this unpleasant reality. Still, a considerable chasm separates *Papyrus Insinger* from the earlier
Anii, who links virtue and knowledge inseparably. Closer to
Papyrus Insinger is Ahiqar, who experienced personal calamity as a result of an ungrateful son whom Ahiqar had
adopted and trained to succeed him at the royal court. Ahiqar is said to have served as vizier to Sennacherib and Esar-
haddon in the Assyrian court, although the several versions
confuse the historical sequence of the two rulers.[29]

The idea that instruction does not always produce virtuous living also underlies the common sentiment that anyone
who taught women provided poison for vipers[30] or that the
effort was just as futile as pouring sand into a sack with a
hole in it.[31] Unfortunately, such attitudes seem to have pre-

[28] George Mendenhall, "The Shady Side of Wisdom: The Date and Purpose of
Genesis 3," 319–34, in *A Light unto My Path*, eds. H. N. Bream, and R. D. Heim, and
C. A. Moore (Philadelphia: Temple University Press, 1974).

[29] Lindenberger reports that only the Elephantine Aramaic and one late Syriac
manuscript get the sequence right (*The Aramaic Proverbs of Ahiqar*, 28, n. 1).

[30] The citation of Menander's observation about women is taken from William V.
Harris, *Ancient Literacy*, 108.

[31] "Instructing a woman is like having a sack of sand whose side is split open"
(*Ankhsheshonqy* 13, 20).

vailed throughout the ancient world,[32] despite rare exceptions of learned women in aristocratic circles. See the discussion (pp. 14–15), which provides examples of women with wisdom.[33]

Papyrus Insinger reaffirms the two paradoxes when drawing final conclusions about instructing sons, although the emphasis changes somewhat. Presumably the first concluding observation implies that a teacher's true son is the person who hears and obeys rather than one identified through biological descent. The second remark introduces a religious dimension, for it attributes the disposition to learn, the resulting virtue, and indeed the life of students to the kindness of the god. This pious remark is *Papyrus Insinger's* way of dealing with the puzzling recalcitrance among some boys and the avid hunger for knowledge on the part of others. In the final analysis, he argues, the teacher's effort, however valiant, cannot overcome dislike if the god placed it in the student's heart.

SIRACH (BEN SIRA)

Ben Sira's remarks about adverse circumstances surrounding the pursuit of wisdom further demonstrate the extent of

---

[32] Charles E. Carlston, "Proverbs, Maxims, and the Historical Jesus," *JBL* 99 (1980) 87–105, examines, among other things, the hostility toward women as expressed in proverbial sayings in the Greco-Roman world and in rabbinic literature.

[33] "The Female 'Sage' in Mesopotamian Literature (with an Appendix on Egypt)" 3–17 in *The Sage in Israel and the Ancient Near East.*

ideas shared by Israelite and Egyptian sages.[34] In one textual unit, 6:18–37, he ponders this educational dilemma and offers his own perspective, a rich understanding that surfaces elsewhere more than once. Ben Sira's first point denies the usual distinction between teacher and student, implying that learning continues into the twilight years. In this way wisdom becomes a manner of life, a habit, established in early years and lasting throughout one's life. This manner of seeing things lessens the revered distinction between brash youth and learned elders. To be sure, the familiar address "my son" reasserts the existence of a gulf between the instructor and those who receive instruction.[35] All are learners pursuing wisdom, although not all individuals attain the same educational level. In another context Ben Sira asserts paternal authority and encourages fathers who love their sons to whip them often (30:1).

The second point in this discussion of reluctant learners focuses on the irksome aspects of scholarship, which Qoheleth's epilogist summed up as succinctly as anyone: "My son, beware of anything beyond these. Of composing many written texts there is no end, and much study is a weariness of the flesh" (12:12). Elsewhere Qoheleth speaks of a positive correlation between knowledge and sorrow, a view that Ben Sira seems to share ("The mark of a happy heart is a cheerful face, but to devise proverbs requires painful thinking," 13:26). Ben Sira adopts images from agriculture, urging students to plow and harvest, submitting to a brief stint of ar-

---

[34] Jack T. Sanders, *Ben Sira and Demotic Wisdom* (SBLMS 28; Chico: Scholars Press, 1983), argues that the Israelite sage knew Egyptian wisdom literature and drew on it for specific ideas.

[35] The Hebrew text lacks "my son" in 6:18 (only the last two words in the verse have survived) and in 6:23.

duous labor, all the while eagerly anticipating a bountiful harvest. In this regard Ben Sira resorts to the useful sapiential distinction between appearance and reality. Study only seems to be difficult and unpleasant, but such adversity functions to hone intellectual acumen.

Ben Sira personifies the object of research, describing her as testing students with a heavy stone, which the unworthy hastily drop, and as a harsh path that renders progress both slow and uncomfortable. The descriptive adjective modifying the word "path" occurs in the Masoretic Text only once, Isa. 40:4, and refers to the leveling of hilly terrain. The Syriac specifies wisdom, as does the Vulgate, rather than the indefinite pronoun. The technical phrase "the one lacking heart" alludes to moral deprivation.

A third observation plays on the meaning of the word for discipline, which Ben Sira substitutes for *ḥokmâ*. He writes: "For wisdom is like her name: she is not readily perceived by many" (6:22). The most likely reading of this enigmatic expression depends on a pun between the noun *mûsār* and a participle *môsēr*,[36] discipline and bond, or *mûsār* in two senses, discipline and withdrawn.[37] Like so many etymologies in ancient literature, this one owes more to the author's ingenuity than to actual philology. The hint of esotericism conflicts with Ben Sira's general appeal for eager students to

[36] John G. Snaith, *Ecclesiasticus* (CBC; Cambridge: Cambridge University Press, 1974) 39 ("More probably some kind of play on words is intended—perhaps *mûsār* ['discipline, training'] and *môsēr* ['bond, halter'], thus providing a link with the 'fetters' of verse 24. But such a pun is not very apparent in the Hebrew—let alone the Greek translation").

[37] "In v. 22 Ben Sira plays on the word *mûsār*, 'discipline,' making it mean also 'withdrawn' (*mûsār* being the *hopʿal* masculine singular participle of the verb *sûr*, which means 'to turn aside, depart, withdraw'); cf. 51:23" (Patrick W. Skehan and Alexander A. Di Lella, *The Wisdom of Ben Sira* [AB 39; New York: Doubleday, 1987] 193).

enroll in his academy, although the cost of doing so certainly limited his clientele. Perhaps the real intention of this elitism was to rationalize an unhealthy situation in which youngsters spurned the invitation to follow the path of instruction. Qoheleth was certainly not the only teacher who thought wisdom resided beyond human comprehension. As is well known, such sentiment crops up in unexpected places as disparate as aphorisms in the Book of Proverbs and in Job.[38] Ben Sira therefore continues a venerable tradition, despite his theory of Wisdom's residence in Zion and her identification with the divine will as expressed in the Torah, an entity readily accessible to everyone.

Developing the image of Knowledge as something harsh, at least on the surface, Ben Sira encourages students to submit to her fetters and to wear her yoke like oxen used by farmers to plow fields. The imagery appears to derive from hunting or from warfare. Lindenberger writes that "from very early times in the ancient Near East, woodblocks were used for immobilizing prisoners of war and fugitives, and Arabic and Greek sources evidence the use in later periods of an iron plate called a 'brick' (Arabic *tuba tun*) to increase the weight of a fetter."[39]

At this point Ben Sira democratizes the royal search that, according to Prov. 25:2, focalizes a fundamental difference between deity and king. Whereas God's glory consists in

---

[38] The concept of wisdom's remoteness has been studied by Paul Fiddes, *The Hiddenness of Wisdom* (D. Phil. Dissertation, Oxford, 1981); Samuel Balentine, *The Hiddenness of God* (Oxford: Oxford University Press, 1983), has examined the broader concept, along with the terminology for concealment.

[39] (Nöldeke, T. H., "Zum Achiqar,"*ZDMG* 67 [1913], 766); as referred to by Lindenberger, *The Aramaic Proverbs of Ahiqar*, 48.

concealing something unspecified, a king achieves renown through searching out whatever is hidden and making it manifest.[40] Ben Sira expects everyone to hunt for Wisdom, and having found her, to hold on for dear life. He uses three different verbs in 6:27 to reinforce the necessity for individuals to search tenaciously for Wisdom—*dāraš, ḥāqar, bāqaš*—(cf. Prov. 4:13 and the threefold imperatives in Mt. 7:7). Although he belonged to the ranks of the fortunate scribal class, he undoubtedly understood workers' longing for rest after a day of backbreaking toil.

That this grasp of what it meant to be a laborer is not foreign to Ben Sira must surely follow from his knowledgeable description of various types of work, which was probably a topos in the Hellenistic world—if Ben Sira does not consciously adapt the earlier Egyptian *Instruction of Khety.* Differences between the two texts and the centuries separating them in composition render any claim of literary dependence on Khety's advice to his son highly uncertain. One could still argue for Ben Sira's use of the Egyptian text by recognizing the freedom with which such borrowing occurred.[41] Ancient laborers in fields also looked for abundant harvest, a time associated with joyous festivity. In Ben Sira's view, this too will come to those who persevere in their pursuit of knowledge. Temporal expressions unite the brevity of forced labor (a little while) and the ultimate reward (at

[40] Leonidas Kalugila, *The Wise King* (CBOTS 15; Lund: CWK Gleerup, 1980), and my essay, "A Mother's Instruction to Her Son (Proverbs 31:1–9)," 9–22 in *Perspectives on the Hebrew Bible,* ed. James L. Crenshaw (Macon: Mercer University Press, 1988).

[41] See the discussion by Glendon E. Bryce, *A Legacy of Wisdom* (Lewisburg: Bucknell University Press, 1979), in which he uses the adjectives "adaptive," "assimilative," and "integrative" to describe the different stages of dependence.

last). The word *me'at* probably implies quantity and time (a little effort, a short endeavor), and *'aharît* has a temporal sense ("finally"). Ben Sira now attributes royal renown to ordinary students. Their fetters are transformed into articles of security, their collar into a beautiful robe, their yoke into a golden ornament, and their bonds into a blue cord. Donning the robe like a king, the faithful student will wear wisdom like a crown. Such flirting with the royal implications of knowledge also occurs in Wis. of Sol. 6:17–20.[42]

Like his Egyptian predecessors who ventured to examine students' reluctance to learn, Ben Sira now explores the paradoxical relationship between freedom and determinism. Insisting that volition is absolutely essential to the educational process, he also allows for a prominent role of the deity. Ben Sira's emphasis on students' desire to learn leads him to offer unselfish advice, even though he may secretly hope they will choose to learn at his feet. In any event, he counsels them to select astute companions, for in listening to their reflections and studying their metaphors students will mature into wise men. The vocabulary in 8:6–9 includes meditation, riddles or maxims, and discourses. The priority of listening is noteworthy in both texts, 8:6–9 and 6:33–37. Ben Sira urges potential sages to listen to musing (the Greek has "divine musing") and maxims.

Here for the first time in these discussions the importance of one's associates enters the picture, but the idea was

---

[42] On this example of *sorites*, see the discussions in James M. Reese, *Hellenistic Influence on the Book of Wisdom and its Consequences* (An Bib 41; Rome: Biblical Institute Press, 1970), and David Winston, *The Wisdom of Solomon* (AB 43; Garden City: Doubleday & Company, Inc., 1979) 154–56.

definitely integral to the earliest wisdom in Egypt and elsewhere. Nowhere has this notion found better expression
than in the rabbinic dictum: "Much have I learned from my
masters [teachers], more from my colleagues, but from my
disciples most of all."[43] Ben Sira probably did not place the
emphasis on what teachers learned from their students, but
he most assuredly recognizes the educational contribution
of exemplary role models. As for the other half of the paradox, Ben Sira encourages religious meditation because, in
his view, God is the giver of all knowledge. Once again a
sage's probing of resistance to learning ends in acknowledgment that all wisdom derives from God.

Ben Sira's remarks about education extend beyond the
unit under consideration, and some of them introduce exciting concepts not encountered thus far. For instance, in the
context of paternal admonition he imagines an ancestral
chain of tradition (8:9), a way of expressing continuity between past and present that receives definitive expression
in *Pirke Aboth:* "Moses received Torah from Sinai and delivered it to Joshua, and Joshua to the Elders, and the Elders to the Prophets, and the Prophets delivered it to the
Men of the Great Synagogue.[44] Because keepers of ancient
tradition valued the intellectual heritage of the past and believed that sages of a remote era surpassed those of their
own time, later teachers felt obliged to link up with the
past. Mesopotamian myths refer to seven *apkallûs*, sages of

---

[43] B. T. Makkot 102 and 11; quoted from Goldin, *Studies in Midrash and Related Literature*, 11.

[44] *The Ethics of the Talmud: Sayings of the Fathers*, ed. R. Travers Herford (New York: Schocken Books, 1962).

primordial times, and Israelite apocalyptic literature invested great wisdom in certain antediluvian heroes, particularly Enoch.[45] One way of achieving that worthy goal was for a father to communicate his insights to sons, who in turn passed down his teachings to their sons. Still, this transmission did not merely consist of faithful communication of what past generations had learned. Ben Sira mentions an additive factor resulting from each generation's assessment of the *traditum* in light of new circumstances (21:15).

Although the sages did not value originality in quite the same way modern scholars do, preferring instead those truths that had stood the test of time, they did appreciate novelty so long as the new insights did not contradict what they understood as "givens." *The Complaints of Khakheperre-sonb* speaks eloquently for previously unknown words and phrases that would effectively banish troublous times, ancient ritualistic texts having failed to do so. Khakheperre-sonb writes: "Had I unknown phrases, sayings that are strange, novel, untried words, free of repetition; not transmitted sayings, spoken by the ancestors! . . . Ancestors' words are nothing to boast of; they are found by those who come after."[46] Every "text" possessed multiple meanings, every answer opening up at least two new questions, as a Yiddish proverb expresses the matter.[47]

---

[45] James C. VanderKam, *Enoch and the Growth of an Apocalyptic Tradition* (CBQMS 16; Washington: The Catholic Biblical Association of America, 1984) and John J. Collins, *The Apocalyptic Imagination* (New York: Crossroad, 1984). As is well known, Solomon enjoyed a reputation among Israelite sages as the sage par excellence.

[46] Lichtheim, *Ancient Egyptian Literature*, vol. I, 146.

[47] "Ojf itlechn terez ken men gefinen a naje kaschje (Aus jeglicher Antwort entsteht eine neue Frage"—from every answer emerges a new question). This proverb is taken from *Jiddische Sprichwörter* (Insel-Bücherei Nr. 828; Frankfurt am Main: Im Insel-

In fact, Ben Sira actually mentions the value of beliefs that function to anchor thought almost like absolutes in modern philosophical debate (22:16–17). He distinguishes in this setting between those things that anchor the mind and others that only adorn it, just as we speak of constitutive and ornamental features. (Similarly, the *Instruction of Amenemope* calls the teachings a mooring post for the tongue.) This ancillary aesthetic dimension ought not be downplayed, for it enhanced teachings and contributed mightily to their retention in students' memories.[48] An epilogist who commented on Qoheleth's work does not overlook the importance of crafting sayings in a pleasing manner (Eccles. 12:10). Furthermore, Ben Sira believes in a positive correlation between clarity of expression and mental capacity (27:6).

The near obsession with eloquence among ancient sages[49] cannot be explained simply in terms of suasion, however important the task of convincing others in the court may have been. In a very real sense speech revealed the quality of a mind; more than this, speech also pointed to one's inner character. The following sayings from Prov. 14:10 and 13 show how thoroughly in touch with their feelings the authors were: "The heart knows its own bitterness, and no stranger shares its joy" and "Even in laughter the heart is sad, and the end of joy is grief." Ben Sira thinks of

Verlag, 1965) 50. One may also compare "A kluger farschtejt fun ejn wort zwej (Ein Weiser hört ein Wort, versteht aber zwei"—A wise person hears one word but understands two, 43).

[48] The most thorough study of aesthetics in the book of Proverbs, Hans-Jürgen Hermisson, *Studien zur israelitischen Spruchweisheit,* suffers from the low esteem in which the author holds popular maxims relative to literary, or learned, sayings.

[49] Walter Bühlmann, *Von rechten Reden und Schweigen* (OBO 12; Göttingen: Vandenhoeck & Ruprecht, 1976).

knowledge as a sort of conscience alerting people to imminent danger (37:14). In a rare moment of self-conscious assessment of his own vocation, he claims to be a teacher for others (33:17), transcending the oft-heralded motto "What is good for a person?" that has given sages the undeserved reputation of selfish individualists.[50]

In light of frequent interpretations of ancient sages as members of the upper-class strata in society,[51] Ben Sira's remarks about improving one's social standing through education merit attention (10:30). Perhaps he does not really imply any enhancement of status but thinks instead of attaining honor irrespective of social class. In all probability the doors to the academy were more often than not closed to those who had no means of supporting their studies. In the ancient Near Eastern world, sages enjoyed wide respect and modest remuneration for services rendered, so that poor persons could improve their lot by joining their ranks, whatever the personal sacrifice.[52] This literary topos was ap-

[50] Walther Zimmerli, "Concerning the Structure of Old Testament Wisdom," 175–207 in *Studies in Ancient Israelite Wisdom*, ed. James L. Crenshaw (New York: Ktav Publishing House, Inc., 1976), states the case for using the question sages asked, What is good/profitable for a person? to determine the very structure of their thought. Contemporary interpreters qualify the eudaemonism attributed to sages, largely as a result of studies by Egyptologists who perceived the ethical basis for the sages' conduct.

[51] Robert Gordis, "The Social Background of Wisdom Literature," *HUCA* 18 (1943/44) 77–118, championed the hypothesis that sages enjoyed privileged social status, although the evidence for this interpretation of the data was meager. Gordis's understanding of the sages as members of the upper class has been adopted by many critics, e.g. by Gerhard von Rad, *Wisdom in Israel*, 17 and passim, and by R. N. Whybray, *The Intellectual Tradition in the Old Testament*, 15–54. The low level of literacy in the ancient Near East lends plausibility to Gordis's hypothesis, for the average citizen in Israel and Judah would probably have been unable to read and write. Much instruction, however, occurred orally, particularly during the early stages of wisdom, and possibly much later as well.

[52] The most thorough study of sages, the anthology entitled *The Sage in Israel and the Ancient Near East*, edited by John G. Gammie and Leo G. Perdue (Winona Lake: Eisenbrauns, 1990), lacks an adequate definition of the profession being described (see Loren Mack-Fisher's ludicrous remarks in this regard [115] and the editors' references

plied to the famous rabbinic teacher Akiba as encourage-
ment to all,[53] possibly also as a means of shaming those individuals who refused studies on the basis of their poverty. In
contrast, the aristocracy in ancient Greece held schoolteachers in contempt, and the social advantages of education
were minimal.[54] Within rabbinic circles the schools of
Shammai and Hillel held opposite views about candidates
for admission, the former preferring talented and meek
children from rich families with distinguished ancestry and
the latter opting for a more democratic clientele, with the exception that girls were excluded from the ranks of students.[55]

Another feature of Ben Sira's teaching about education
has immense evocative power inasmuch as it appeals to a
fundamental human drive. I refer to the erotic dimension of
knowledge (15:2), which achieves lavish expression in Prov.
1–9 and in the Wisdom of Solomon.[56] For some unexplained reason, Egyptian and Mesopotamian sages overlook
this fascinating interplay between the one who pursues
knowledge and the object of that search itself.[57] The Israelite harnessing of sexual energy for intellectual ends has
generated powerful erotic poetry in which lover and beloved play out love's drama, one that includes a femme
fatale. Egyptian *Papyrus Chester Beatty* IV (British Museum

---

to Ezra as a sage and to Deuteronomy as wisdom). Unfortunately, cross-cultural com-
parisons often lack cogency because of different functions of sages in Iran and in Israel,
for example. The essays on biblical material demonstrate the difficulty of assuming
uniformity even in a single culture, for some authors seem to be grasping at a straw
when discussing sages (Frymer-Kemsky, McCarter, and others).

[53] Goldin, *Studies in Midrash and Related Literature*, 114.

[54] Harris, *Ancient Literacy*, 19, 98, 135.

[55] Goldin, *Studies in Midrash and Related Literature*, 101.

[56] Samuel Terrien, *Till the Heart Sings* (Philadelphia: Fortress Press, 1985).

[57] The materials for such erotic thinking about wisdom were certainly present, especially the association of *Ma'at* with right order.

10684) calls the scribe's books his heirs, the instructions his tomb, the reed pen his children, and the stone writing surface his wife. This symbolism falls far short of the dynamic imagery in biblical wisdom, where love's reciprocity issues in conjugal bliss. Religious constraints prevent this eroticism from running rampant, however, and love seems always to be directed toward a family setting.[58] Greek philosophers also perceived the uncanny connection between knowledge and the erotic, and *sophia* corresponds to *ḥokmâ* as the feminine subject of scholarly desire.[59] Who can remain a reluctant learner when faced with the prospects of a passionate lover? It thus appears that Israel's sages discovered a convincing response to the dilemma presented by resistance to their teachings, except that the answer was readily subject to distortion. The forces of ignorance also recognize the power eros wields over young minds.[60]

CONCLUSION

The religious sentiment concluding all three discussions of recalcitrant students calls for further reflection. Has each

---

[58] Claus Westermann, *Wurzeln der Weisheit* (Göttingen: Vandenhoeck & Ruprecht, 1990), emphasizes the importance of the family in the composition of wisdom literature, a point that has been obscured by excessive emphasis on bureaucratic wisdom.

[59] Burton L. Mack, *Logos und Sophia: Untersuchungen zur Weisheitstheologie im hellenistischen Judentum* (Göttingen: Vandenhoeck & Ruprecht, 1973).

[60] Lennart Boström, *The God of the Sages* (CBOTS 29; Stockholm: Almqvist and Wiksell International, 1990) 56, n. 52, raises the possibility that folly was personified before the personification of wisdom occurred. He bases this view on the prominence of warnings against seductive women.

teacher played an ace until this moment kept hidden up a sleeve? On the surface, the argument that God gives all knowledge seems thoroughly convincing, so much so that one would expect students to abandon their resistance to learning and to take advantage of an easy mode of acquiring an education. "Ask and you shall receive" makes their earlier conduct appear ludicrous. Yet that is precisely the point that each text under discussion makes: God gives wisdom to those who pray for it. In a word all knowledge is sacred[61] and can be wrested from its source only through religious devotion. The humility of prayer has intruded on the restraints of reason,[62] claiming equal time. Here one encounters a remarkable phenomenon, geniuses who acknowledge their fundamental ignorance and saints who confess their sinfulness.

This minor key can be heard in texts other than Anii, *Papyrus Insinger*, and Sirach. Within canonical wisdom it balances a more somber note, one that placed the stress on human achievement. The opening collection within Proverbs boldly asserts that the Lord gives wisdom (2:6), and the Wisdom of Solomon associates prayer with the gift of *sophia* (7:7). The myth about *ḥokmâ* in Prov. 1 and 8–9, as well as its variant in Sir. 1 and 24, emphasizes the divine source of knowledge and the gracious act of its dispersal within the

---

[61] Seyyed Hossein Nasr, *Knowledge and the Sacred* (Albany: State University of New York, 1989), laments the depleting of knowledge's sacred character resulting from the Enlightenment. He asks an interesting question: "How can a mind totally depleted of the sense of the sacred grasp the significance of the sacred as sacred?" (16).

[62] I have borrowed this marvelous phrase from Lichtheim, *Ancient Egyptian Literature*, vol. I, 131 ("As a corpus, the *Coffin Texts* are far less coherent than the *Pyramid Texts*, for they lack a unifying point of view. Inspired by a reliance on magic, they lack the humility of prayer and the restraints of reason").

cosmos.[63] Faithful adherence to the Commandments, prayer in action (cf. Sir. 38:34),[64] moves God to supply wisdom, according to Sir. 1:26. In this connection *testimonia* increase the force of the argument, each teacher confiding that intellectual achievement alone cannot explain success in the pursuit of knowledge. Sirach's comments in this vein include several interesting features: prayer for Wisdom during youth, but intended persistence to old age; taking delight in her developing stages and following her steps; grappling with Wisdom and exercising self-discipline; and gratitude issuing in praise of her (51:13–30). The erotic dimension that throbs vibrantly in a comparable testimony within the Wisdom of Solomon has made only a fleeting impression on Ben Sira, despite his counsel[65] elsewhere to pitch one's tent alongside Wisdom's dwelling (14:20–27).

Instead, he offers a realistic means of attaining an education, specifically by enrolling in his school. In the midst of this invitation he boldly contrasts the imbalance between expended effort and acquired rest, surely aimed at curbing objections that education is hardly cost-effective. Ben Sira ends with a flourish, distinguishing between human and di-

---

[63] Bernhard Lang, *Wisdom and the Book of Proverbs* (New York: Pilgrim Press, 1986), moves one step further, arguing that the myth of wisdom is grounded in polytheism, specifically in an Israelite goddess.

[64] For the role of prayer in wisdom literature, see my article, "The Restraint of Reason, the Humility of Prayer," 206–21 in *Urgent Advice and Probing Questions*. In addition, several scholars have shown renewed interest in the general problem of prayer in the Old Testament (Ronald E. Clements, *In Spirit and Truth* [Atlanta: John Knox, 1985], Moshe Greenberg, *Biblical Prose Prayer* [Berkeley, Los Angeles, London: University of California Press, 1983], and Samuel E. Balentine, *Prayer in the Hebrew Bible* [Minneapolis: Fortress Press, 1993]).

[65] The form of this advice merits consideration, inasmuch as macarisms occur rather frequently in Psalms.

vine time. He seems to say that wisdom may come as a result of prayer, but not without considerable sweat also. In any event, he links individual effort with a divine reward, suggesting that knowledge is a gift for meritorious conduct.

The absence in Deut. 30:11–14 of any tension between individual effort and divine gift makes it difficult to accept the hypothesis that this book derives from the sages of Israel.[66] Nevertheless, the unknown author seems intent on answering those who insist that anything valuable must surely come at great cost.[67] Quite the contrary, the author asserts, God's commandment requires no extraordinary search and retrieval, for it already resides within and can therefore be put into practice. This view sounds like Jeremiah 31; the language is prophetic rather than sapiential.

Scholars often characterize ancient wisdom as a kind of meritocracy wherein individuals received precisely what they deserved, with rare exceptions.[68] These anomalies evoked classic challenges to the general consensus (Job, Qoheleth, and comparable texts). Where does the concept of divine gift fit into this worldview according to which persons possessed the capacity to generate weal or woe through

[66] Moshe Weinfeld, *Deuteronomy and the Deuteronomic School* (Oxford: The Clarendon Press, 1972).

[67] Such a view must surely underlie Agur's pressing questions in Prov. 30:1–14, on which see my "Clanging Symbols," 51–64 in *Justice and the Holy*, eds. Douglas A. Knight and Peter J. Paris (Atlanta: Scholars Press, 1989).

[68] Klaus Koch, "Is There a Doctrine of Retribution in the Old Testament?" 57–87 in *Theodicy in the Old Testament*, ed. James L. Crenshaw (IRT 4; Philadelphia and London: Fortress Press and SPCK, 1983, originally published in *ZThK* 52 [1955], 1–42), has put forth a radical hypothesis, which many interpreters accept in modified form. He thinks the Israelites believed that actions automatically set into motion certain consequences, and that Yahweh served only as a sort of midwife in bringing evil effects on the guilty and rewards to good people. The principle of deed and consequence is sovereign here, not Yahweh.

acts of self-control or passion?[69] Perhaps there is more here than humble acknowledgment that intellectual capacity is determined at birth. Even one's ability to exercise this wondrous potential comes as culture's gift to its citizens.

We confront controls on every hand: deliberate ones in the many laws and norms imposed by society, latent controls that influence decisions unconsciously and when least expected, cognitive controls that we administer to keep things in check, and coercive or seductive controls that others enforce and thereby limit our free expression.[70] How do these controls work? The language we use shapes our discourse and determines our thoughts; the myths we fabricate become the script in which we read the drama of our lives and the truth to which we ultimately submit; the groups to which we belong, and those to which we do not, impose hidden pressure on us in subtle and not so subtle ways; our anticipation of rejection and isolation issues in a particular code of conduct; the level of access or availability of a given choice enters heavily into our decisions; and the expected compensation for an action determines to some degree whether or not the reward or punishment justifies it.[71]

All these and more combine to assist us in recognizing the familiar, but how do we achieve the shock of recognition when intuition arrives at insight about something wholly unfamiliar, something entirely new? Here is a paradox of learning for which culture has not prepared its citizens! How can someone recognize the unheard of, the radically

---

[69] My own analysis of this problem appeared in a memorial volume to John G. Gammie as "The Concept of God in Old Testament Wisdom" (*In Search of Wisdom*, 1–18).

[70] Bruner, *On Knowing*, 132–37.

[71] *Ibid.*, 137.

unfamiliar, unless through a gift of intuitive insight? Yet both types of knowledge are real, both the familiar and the effective surprise. The first type yields to self-disciplined research, the second comes upon us as if bestowed by a generous but mysterious Teacher. I believe this phenomenon, all the more awesome in a society that venerated the ancient *traditum* far more than any *novum*, assists in understanding the combined humility of prayer and restraints of reason in ancient discussions of the teaching enterprise. Our post-enlightenment celebration of reason has brought commendable results, which I for one do not wish to question.[72] I do wish this sure gain had not come at the price of humility, a sense that all knowledge has an ultimate source beyond the human mind and that insights sometimes come as sheer grace. This I think Anii, *Papyrus Insinger,* and Ben Sira saw with amazing clarity, and for that insight they deserve our undying gratitude.

---

[72] The danger of absolutism, however, is very real. Perhaps that threat partially explains the passionate defense of certain postmodern approaches to knowledge and the equally passionate championing of pre-Enlightenment understandings. Nasr, *Knowledge and the Sacred,* provides a useful critique of the presuppositions that govern Western thought. Current literary theory accomplishes the same thing from a quite different perspective.

≈

Chapter Six

The Missing Voice

A paternal voice reverberates throughout the initial collection in the Book of Proverbs—berating, warning, pleading, instructing, admonishing. The son, ever-present as addressee, never assumes the position of respondent. His well-being occupies the thought from first to last, but not one utterance escapes his lips. At best, the father ventures into ventriloquism long enough to attribute an expression of regret to a son whose sexual appetite has led him into deep trouble (5:12–14).

Silence reigns throughout wisdom literature insofar as the son as speaker is concerned. That absence of a youthful voice occasions little surprise in folk wisdom, where the voice of experience expresses itself succinctly in an artful manner. Two recent publications by Claus Westermann and Friedemann W. Golka have strengthened the understanding of early Israelite wisdom as the product of popular reflection, thus undermining the view that the Book of Proverbs was written by teachers for students in temple schools. Westermann emphasizes the rural context reflected in the sayings, their concentration on the family and small towns, comparing their language and interests with those of simple African tribes. Similarly, Golka draws on African proverbs to show that the same concerns in biblical sayings indicate a setting other than the royal court or school. For him, the minimal role of politics, war, and cult points to ordinary people, as does the emphasis on the interaction among brothers, cousins, spouses, old people, and youth.[1] Instructions, however, differ in their concentration on the pedagogic situation, which naturally involves young boys. The genre Instruction has a long history. The *Instruction of Šuruppak* and the several Egyptian Instructions (e.g., *Ptahhotep, Amenemope, Anii*) indicate that both advanced cultures, Mesopotamian and Egyptian, valued the transmission of teachings from an authority figure to his probable successor. In this context a father advised his son about the responsibilities of office and endeavored to prepare him for successful performance of duties. Eventually, the giving of advice became the prerogative of professional teachers, but they retained the earlier language implying an address by a father to his son. Whereas, with a single exception, Egyptian Instructions restrict the direct address "my son" to the introductory section, Mesopotamian and biblical Instructions regularly insert these references in the body of the Instructions. One therefore expects interaction between teacher and student in the extant Instructions within canonical wis-

---

[1] *Wurzeln der Weisheit* [ET, *Roots of Wisdom*] (Louisville, KY: Westminster John Knox Press, 1995) and *The Leopard's Spots*.

dom, Prov. 1–9, 22:17–24:22, and 31:1–9. Instead, the student's voice is drowned out by the steady drone of a teacher bent on passing along what he has learned over the years.

In one instance the maternal voice vies with the dominant, paternal tradition, advising her young prince in an equally authoritative manner (Prov. 31:1–9). The combination of rhetoric and passion gives her counsel exceptional power, as if her gender qualifies the queen mother for providing instruction concerning the dangers posed by women, perhaps also by the strong drink that often accompanied an evening of sexual pleasure. Curiously, Lemuel's mother urges him to speak up—but not on his own behalf. She reminds her son of the royal obligation[2] to attend to the needs of marginalized subjects, those who cannot speak for themselves, the perishing, the poor and needy.[3]

A case has recently been made for enlarging the scope of advice placed in feminine mouths within the Book of Proverbs. Jack Miles has attributed the memorable description of a young man being seduced to utter ruin (Prov. 7:6–23) and the accompanying urgent warning (Prov. 7:24–27) to a woman. He does so on the basis of virtual consistency in the

---

[2] Leonidas Kalugila, *The Wise King*, discusses royal ideology in the ancient world, the expectation that the king would look after the rights of disenfranchised citizens of the community, particularly widows, orphans, and the needy (cf. also F. C. Fensham, "Widow, Orphan and the Poor in the Ancient Near Eastern Legal and Wisdom Literature," *JNES* 21 [1962] 129–39, and Norbert Lohfink, "Poverty in the Laws of the Ancient Near East and of the Bible," *TS* 52 [1991] 34–50). This idealization of kingship occurs in early legal material, for example, in the prologue to the Code of Hammurabi, as well as in wisdom literature, and may provide the roots of later Messianic speculation in Israel.

[3] For discussion of Prov. 31:1–9, see my article titled "A Mother's Instruction to her Son (Proverbs 31:1–9)," 9–22 in *Perspectives on the Hebrew Bible*. Although this maternal instruction is unique in the Bible and the ancient Near East, the association of mothers with fathers in the Book of Proverbs suggests that within the family both spouses shared the responsibility for teaching the young. The commandment to honor father and mother may reflect the role of both parents in giving instruction to children.

Old Testament when depicting someone looking through a (latticed) window as a woman (the mother of Sisera in Judg. 5:28, Michal in 2 Sam. 6:16, and Jezebel in 2 Kgs. 9:30; the exception—Abimelech in Gen. 26:8), as well as the positive attitude toward female sexual arousal. On the saying about the mystery of sex and its problematic outcome, Miles writes: "This is, as the saying goes, splitting the arrow, a bull's eye followed by another bull's eye, eloquence about the wonder of sexual love followed by superb bluntness about what it can sometimes become. There is no reason whatsoever why 'my son' might not have seen both arrows shot by his mother."[4] Moreover, the advice to observe the ant as a caution against laziness (Prov. 6:6–11),[5] the numerical saying about the mystery of sex and its abuse (Prov. 30:18–20),[6] and the description of a good wife (Prov. 31:10–31)[7] have also been claimed for feminine teaching. (Similarly, the well-known poem about a time for everything in Eccles. 3:2–8 has been interpreted as one about desire, sex, and gender relations, possibly masculine love lyrics aimed at feminine recipients.[8]) Because women can be just as critical of other women as men can, overt attacks against women and even statements that appear to be androcentric may reflect feminine acquiescence when confronting masculine

---

[4] Jack Miles, *God: A Biography* (New York: Vintage Books, 1995) 298–99, 300.

[5] *Ibid.*, 300.

[6] *Ibid.*

[7] Athalya Brenner, "Some Observations on the Figurations of Woman in Wisdom Literature," *A Feminist Companion to Wisdom Literature*, ed. A. Brenner (Sheffield: Sheffield Academic Press, 1995) 54.

[8] Brenner, "Some Observations on the Figurations of Woman in Wisdom Literature," 60–61, also in *On Gendering Texts: Female and Male Voices in the Hebrew Bible*, 133–53.

cultural values and perspectives.[9] As a check on such broadening of feminine authorship, Carole R. Fontaine writes: "Certainly, if women had written many of the proverbs found in that book, we would expect to see far more about drunken, violent husbands, and less emphasis on the 'nagging wife' as the sole scapegoat for domestic discord (cf. Prov. 21:9, 19; 25:24; 27:15)."[10]

Neither the Book of Job nor Ecclesiastes permits students to become vocal, although Elihu belongs to the awkward stage between youth and adult. What he says thus falls into the category of a self-defensive pique characterized by excessive heat. Such lack of control over the passions identifies him as one who has not yet achieved wisdom. The metaphor for a fool in Egypt, "the heated man," stresses his inability to govern the passions, perhaps the most difficult battle confronting human beings, if the unusual observation is correct that one who conquers the passions is superior to the person who takes a city in battle (cf. Prov. 16:32). Nili Shupak argues that eight biblical expressions from wisdom literature are similar to Egyptian expressions (the heated person, chambers of the belly, a well-constructed saying [*taḥbulôt*], one who weighs the heart, cool-tempered, slow to anger, short-tempered) and indicate a linguistic relationship, either direct or indirect.[11] The closest Qoheleth comes to letting a student express himself amounts to an existential sigh in the face of the aging process (cf. Sir. 38:22). Actually, the

[9] Brenner, "Some Observations on the Figurations of Woman in Wisdom Literature," 53, 55–56.

[10] "The Social Roles of Women in the World of Wisdom," in *A Feminist Companion to Wisdom Literature*, 38.

[11] Nili Shupak, *Where can Wisdom be found?* 339.

poignant denial of finding any pleasure in the darkening
days of old age belongs to everyone, and hence cannot be
attributed to students at their tender age. The actual audience for these biblical books has yet to be determined.
Rainer Albertz's hypothesis of three different audiences for
the Book of Job—a selfish upper class, a compassionate upper class, and a lower class—does not necessarily follow
from the different attitudes to the poor expressed in the
book.[12]

Ben Sira's manner of expression gives the appearance of
elevating students' voices to the same level as that of teachers, but the formula of debate, introduced by *'al tō'mar* ("do
not say") actually disguises his own voice of instruction.[13]
What follows the introductory formula consists of imagined
speech, none of it very flattering to the supposed speakers.
Such speeches resemble that of the fool in Ps. 14:1 (=53:1),
who denies God's existence, and those of prophetic opponents who conveniently vocalize objectionable views. The
author of the Wisdom of Solomon carries this unflattering
strategy to new heights (1:16–2:20), but this hedonism is
more widespread than mere student unrest. The ideas being
combated in this section resemble those of Qoheleth to

---

[12] "Der sozialgeschichtliche Hintergrund des Hiobbuches und der 'Babylonischen
Theodizee'," 349–72 in *Die Botschaft und die Boten: Festschrift H. W. Wolff*, eds. Jörg
Jeremias and Lothar Perlitt (Neukirchen-Vluyn: Neukirchener Verlag, 1981). Like-
wise, Qoheleth's actual attitude toward the marginalized citizens of his own day is
more complex than Franz Crüsemann's theory suggests ("Die unveränderbare Welt.
Überlegungen zur 'Krisis der Weisheit' beim Prediger [Kohelet]," 80–104, ET, *The
God of the Lowly* [Maryknoll, NY: Orbis, 1984]).

[13] For analysis of the ancient formula of debate, see James L. Crenshaw, "The Problem of Theodicy in Sirach: On Human Bondage," *JBL* 94 (1975) 47–64. Although
Ben Sira formulates the challenge to traditional teaching, he probably imitates actual
language among the youth who, for whatever reason, found ancestral views no longer
sufficient for the new situation in a Hellenized culture.

some degree, especially the emphasis on enjoying one's youth, the portion granted everyone, the role of chance, the finality of death, the extinction of one's name, the bleak character of reality, and the image of life as a shadow—but the concluding remarks about oppressing the weak have no parallel in Qoheleth's thought. Michael Kolarcik argues that the author uses three distinct yet related perceptions of death: mortality, physical death as punishment, and ultimate death. In Kolarcik's view, the author thinks that evil results from refusing to accept limits implied in mortality and this injustice "brings on the ultimate death in the apocalyptic judgment according to the scheme of the trial." [14]

This cry on behalf of instant gratification recalls a powerfully seductive appeal in Prov. 1:11–14, the invitation to join a band of highway robbers in a scheme to get rich quickly at the expense of weak, vulnerable travelers. The attractiveness of this alternative to inaction awaiting a parental legacy many years in the future made this appeal particularly dangerous, especially when combined with an exaggerated sense of camaraderie and adventure. The dominance of the father's voice in this section and the problem presented by the long delay in receiving an inheritance would have troubled impatient young men (cf. the impatience of David's son Absalom in 2 Sam. 15:1–6). Perhaps an even greater source for concern was the meager prospect of inherited property before money income became the societal norm. [15]

---

[14] Michael Kolarcik, *The Ambiguity of Death in the Book of Wisdom 1–6* (Roma: Editrice Pontificio Istituto Biblico, 1991) 163, 174.

[15] Carol A. Newsom, "Woman and the Discourse of Patriarchal Wisdom: A Study of Proverbs 1–9," 142–60 in *Gender and Difference in Ancient Israel.*

Imaginary speeches, attributed to unsavory characters, do exist, but not in any large number. The pitiable drunk described in Prov. 23:29–35 recalls physical abuse that made no lasting impression because of his drunken stupor and then vows to take another drink. An adulterer convinces himself that secrecy surrounds his lecherous conduct: "Who can see me? Darkness surrounds me, the walls hide me, and no one sees me. Why should I worry? The Most High will not remember sins" (Sir. 23:18). Similarly, an adulteress persuades herself that her behavior is perfectly appropriate; after eating and wiping her mouth, she observes nonchalantly: "I have done no wrong" (Prov. 30:20). A person bent on revenge vows to retaliate in exact measure as he had received evil (Prov. 24:29). According to Prov. 30:15–16, an insatiable creature, often translated "a leech," cries, "Give, give," in the same way Sheol, a barren womb, earth, and fire are never content to the point of saying, "Enough." In Prov. 20:14 the endless posturing of buyer and seller in an economy characterized by a lively process of bargaining issues in a humorous imagined speech: "Bad, bad," says the buyer, then he goes away and boasts.

Not every instance of imagined speech in wisdom literature has been assessed here. One could also cite Sir. 29:26–28, where a guest must listen while a host orders him around and even removes him entirely from the premises to make room for someone else. Other examples exist, but the ones noted here indicate the essential character of such speech. On the question of whether to consider these speeches authentic, Moshe Greenberg's approach to prayer as literary fiction is applicable here. Just as prayer in the Bible is modeled on real prayers, so these imagined speeches reflect views prevalent in the community.[16] Within the profound prayer recorded in Prov. 30:8–9, an imaginary speech lays bare the dangers lurking in the shadows for persons in dire straits and for others rolling in wealth. The former, people of action, proceed to steal as a way out of poverty, whereas the latter intellectualize their situation with a question, "Who is the Lord?" The LXX offers an interesting variant that approximates the Hebrew text orthographically (*me hora*, "who sees me?"), but this notion of sinners thinking that they escape detection may result from its common use elsewhere, especially in the Psalter. The Hebrew text has the more compelling sentiment, for it strikes at the essence of deity, whereas the Greek text merely expresses skepticism about God's visibility, and by extension, punishment of sin. In Prov. 31:29 a husband praises an exceptional wife, who may recall personified Wisdom.

The proverbial fool who thinks that a bountiful supply of worldly goods assures well-being also comes in for censure. The hollow boast, "I have found rest, and now I shall feast on my goods!" does not take into account an unknown factor, the hour of death (Sir. 11:19). The well-known parable of the rich fool in Luke 12:13–21 brings the same teaching into the context of dominical sayings. The fool considers everyone else an enemy, consuming his bread without gratitude (Sir. 20:16); he lacks the mental capacity to comprehend simple narratives, sleepily asking about the point of a story (Sir. 22:10); or he makes rash vows, only to reconsider the action when it is too late (Prov. 20:25).

[16] *Biblical Prose Prayer.*

All the more astonishing, therefore, is the lavish attention within Prov. 1–9 given to imagined speeches by two
rivals, Wisdom and Folly, here personified in poetic fiction.
Nothing in the first speech by Wisdom (1:20–33) moves
beyond similar personifications in prophetic literature—
of the two kingdoms Israel and Judah, or of the city Zion/
Jerusalem—and linguistic affinities support this relationship. The language for pouring out one's thoughts, re-
fusal to listen, stretching out the hand, laughing at calamity, calling on someone but to no avail, seeking but not
finding, eating the fruit of one's deeds—all this fits well
in prophetic discourse on behalf of YHWH. The teacher
in this description is surely modeled after a prophet.
Here Wisdom is depicted as one who combines prophetic and divine characteristics in the same manner prophets move from first-person speech to third person when representing the deity before Israel. In Prov. 8, however, the
imagery incorporates extrabiblical concepts more at home
in hymns celebrating the virtues of the Mesopotamian goddess Ishtar and her Egyptian equivalent, Isis, as well as in
descriptions associated with the Egyptian goddess of order,
Ma'at.

Decisive differences prevent a simple equation of Wisdom with either of these figures. The primary difference,
that Wisdom praises YHWH, accords with her subject status, whereas both Isis and *Ma'at* are goddesses. Moreover,
Ma'at never utters a hymn of self-praise. Nevertheless, the
language that Wisdom uses comes very close to divine self-
praise, particularly in Deutero-Isaiah, for she appears as an
authoritative figure in YHWH's presence, one "acquired" in

the beginning.[17] The most one can legitimately conclude is that the Israelite author of Prov. 8:22–31 probably knew about similar hymns honoring other deities, especially Isis and *Ma'at*.

The juxtaposition of Wisdom and Folly in Prov. 9, never again attempted in extant sapiential literature, features two hostesses who issue invitations to banquets. Asymmetry characterizes the banquet fare, with Wisdom promising meat as well as wine and bread.[18] Folly offers a simple meal of bread and water, but this ordinary staple, bread and water, becomes a culinary feast precisely because of its furtive circumstances, appealing to the sense of adventure and to a desire to taste forbidden fruit. "Stolen water is sweet, and bread eaten in secret is pleasant" (Prov. 9:17). One suspects that her words persisted long after the teacher's warning about the consequences of eating and drinking with her had faded from memory. More abiding, perhaps, than this warning is that projected on an imaginary victim of the strange woman in Prov. 5:11–14 (". . . and at the end of your life you will groan, when your flesh and body are consumed, and you say, 'Oh, how I hated discipline, and my heart despised reproof! I did not listen to the voice of my teachers or incline my ear to my instructors. Now I am at the point of utter ruin in the public assembly.'" The sole national refer-

---

[17] R. N. Whybray, *Proverbs* (NCB, Grand Rapids: William B. Eerdmans, 1995) 121, thinks Prov. 8:22–31 "can be regarded as a kind of baroque development of the simple statement made in 3:19 that 'The Lord by wisdom founded the earth.'" Wisdom is thus understood both as a divine quality ("acumen") and as the foremost of God's coworkers, a female presence in heaven.

[18] Lennart Boström, *The God of the Sages*, 56, raises the possibility that the figure of Folly is primary, arising from the constant emphasis on seductive women, and that personified Wisdom came later as a contrast and foil to Folly.

ence in Proverbs ("in the midst of the congregation") has a hendiadys, *betôk qāhāl we'ēdâ*. The adulterer is disgraced but not utterly destroyed, for he confesses that he was almost ruined (*kime'aṭ*) in public. There is not a single account of the execution of an adulterer in the Bible or the Apocrypha, despite the strong threats in prophetic books such as Hosea and Ezekiel. Even in the story of David's adulterous act, coupled with murder of Bathsheba's husband, Uriah the Hittite, God does not require the death penalty of David.

Shame, resulting from loss of honor, teamed up with odious physical disease, possibly sexually transmitted, to evoke a rare admission of inattention, the exact opposite of what teachers desired ("The mind of the intelligent appreciates proverbs, and an attentive ear is the desire of the wise," Sir. 3:20). The same emphasis occurs in the motif of the hearing one in Egyptian wisdom, accentuated in the conclusion to the *Instruction of Ptahhotep*, and in Mesopotamian lore about sages—and exceptional gods like Marduk—with four ears, a way of emphasizing their capacity for hearing.

Extracanonical wisdom literature set the precedent for silencing students under a barrage of authoritative counsel. Exceptions do occur, but their paucity only heightens the point. The Sumerian text, *Schooldays*, has a graduate of the *edubba* (academy or tablet house) reflect on his earlier days as a student when seemingly everything he did provoked harsh beatings from those in charge of various tasks. *The Disputation between Enkimansi and Girnishag* reflects a rivalry between two accomplished scribes, and *Colloquy between a Monitor (ugula) and a Scribe* deals either with a graduate of the school or with an advanced student. An interesting feature of this text is the teacher's appeal to a time when he was a student, a phenomenon also present in Prov. 4:3–9. Here the Israelite instructor recalls an earlier period when his own father taught him. By using this fiction of speech from a bygone era, the teacher allows the teaching to span three generations. In this way, the continuity of the instruction comes to the fore. The text entitled *A Scribe and his Perverse Son* consists of a dialogue between teacher and student, one in which the son demonstrates his worth by repeating verbatim what his father has said to him.[19]

As we have seen, the only surviving Egyptian Instruction that allows a student to vocalize his point of view concludes with a brief dialogue between Anii and his son Khonshotep. Recognizing the disparity between volition and action, the boy feels incapable of reaching the moral heights that his father has attained. Merely reciting classical texts does not serve as a magic stone, enabling him to live up to admittedly worthy goals. Believing that wisdom, like good wine, required time to establish itself, Khonshotep concedes that sons are by nature inferior to their fathers (cf. Sir. 3:2). In his view, nature determines one's conduct, making an individualist rare. *Papyrus Insinger* makes the point tellingly: "Whoever raves with the crowd is not regarded as a fool." The path of least resistance, conformity, prompts Khonshotep to urge his father to weaken the requirements—as a concession to persons of less discipline than that possessed by the demanding teacher. Khonshotep appeals to parental practice in adapting to the taste and ability of infants, implying that a similar laxness should be followed in educa-

---

[19] Samuel Noah Kramer, *The Sumerians*, 237–48. Learning consisted primarily of repetition, not original thinking.

tion. The Apostle Paul uses the same analogy in correspondence with the Christians at Corinth; he reminds them that
as a concession to their spiritual immaturity he fed them
with milk rather than solid food (1 Cor. 3:1–3).

Anii asserts paternal authority from the outset, warning
his son of the ruinous consequences of such reasoning. For
the father, education has no recognizable limits.[20] It consists
in radically reorienting the status quo. The nature of wild
beasts can be changed; wild bulls can be domesticated, fierce
lions tamed, wild dogs, geese, and monkeys subdued. Even
Nubians and Syrians can be taught to speak Egyptian. Having subjected himself to the rigorous curriculum of the sages
and moved beyond knowledge to wisdom, Anii resists the
suggestion that the demands are unrealistic. The analogy
with human development persuades him that adults ought
to consume hearty fare, not a weakened substitute for
pabulum.

The debate ends positively, Khonshotep raising a voice
to heaven for divine assistance[21] and Anii appealing to the
iron will of teachers who mold reluctant students into para-
gons of virtue. In the skilled hands of a carpenter, neither a

---

[20] Gerhard von Rad, *Wisdom in Israel*, 97–110 and James L. Crenshaw, "Wisdom
and the Sage: On Knowing and Not Knowing," 137–44 in *Proceedings of the Eleventh
World Congress of Jewish Studies*, Division A (Jerusalem: World Union of Jewish Studies, 1994).

[21] The overtly religious character of Egyptian wisdom beginning with the Middle
Kingdom has been well documented, although its explanation remains in doubt.
Whether the result of a social crisis or not, this growing emphasis on piety persists
from Anii onward, finally eventuating in resignation to divine fate, a constant refrain in
Papyrus Insinger. Miriam Lichtheim, *Maat in Egyptian Autobiographies and Related Studies*
(OBO 120, Freiburg & Göttingen: Universitätsverlag and Vandenhoeck & Ruprecht,
1992) 99, challenges the view that in the New Kingdom piety completely replaced
Ma'at. In *Late Egyptian Wisdom Literature in the International Context*, 63, she rejects
the idea that Egyptian wisdom underwent a crisis similar to that in Israel. Stuart
Weeks, *Early Israelite Wisdom*, 57–73, combats the notion that Israelite wisdom originated as a secular phenomenon.

straight stick nor a crooked one retains its original shape. The message comes across clearly: resisting my teaching will ultimately fail. The only disturbing possibility concerns corruption, a perverting of the son's cognitive processes. That is why poignantly emotional language sometimes occurs: this real threat gives paternal teaching its urgency, for a single generation can bring to a halt the entire sapiential enterprise. The importance of an unbroken chain of tradition surfaces in the rabbinic tractate, *Pirke Aboth*. A Christian parallel can be seen in the emphasis on the role of the Twelve Disciples and Paul's insistence on a place in this chain of tradition, one granted him by special revelation.

The urgency of such appeals from teacher to student, father/mother to son assumes new importance in light of the popular story of Ahiqar, where one reads: "My son, thou hast been like the man who saw his companion shivering from cold, and took a pitcher of water and threw it over him." Imagined speech occurs in saying 109 of *Ahiqar* ("Let not the rich man say, 'In my riches I am glorious'").[22]

What do these imagined speeches from ancient teachers convey to modern interpreters? Their fictional character does not mask a central concern among those responsible for composing wisdom Instructions, and in that sense the speeches communicate authentic reality. By studying the sentiments attributed by Israelite prophets to the populace in general, one arrives at concepts that an Amos or an Isaiah wished to eradicate.[23] Similarly, the imagined speeches within wisdom literature give voice to ideas currently in

---

[22] James M. Lindenberger, *The Aramaic Proverbs of Ahiqar*, 4.

[23] James L. Crenshaw, *Prophetic Conflict* (BZAW 124; Berlin and New York: Walter de Gruyter, 1971).

vogue that the teachers considered a threat to their world-view. Like the popular voice ridiculed in prophetic literature, this collective voice in wisdom literature serves as a negative example, introducing us to the inner world of the composers of these imagined speeches, their secret fears.

When later sages finally take the step toward providing positive exemplars, they attribute the ideas to themselves and eventually relate them to an erotic quest for knowledge. The fascination with erotic language in regard to wisdom cannot simply be explained as teachers' attempts to capture the interest of young boys. The endless quest for knowledge, the excitement over discovering new insights, the seductive lure and secretive hiding of truth—all this resembles an amorous adventure where lovers come together and bask in each other's arms. Every disclosure opens up new possibilities, and this excitement characterizes all genuine pursuit of the unknown. That excitement fills the paternal advice in Prov. 7:4 that the son address wisdom lovingly as "my sister," the normal expression for a lover in ancient Egypt. The author of Song of Songs uses this language of brother/sister to designate lovers, and the marriage of brothers and sisters was allowed at one time, but the laws governing Israel forbade the practice. The picture is complicated, however, for Tamar implies that she could become her brother Amnon's wife (2 Sam. 13:13).

An internalization of speech, creating a monologue,[24] comes to the fore in Qoheleth, surfaces occasionally in Sirach, and reaches its peak in the self-reflections of the un-

---

[24] Sara Denning Bolle, *Wisdom in Akkadian Literature: Expression, Instruction, Dialogue*, discusses the relationship between monologue and dialogue in Akkadian texts, using the perspective of Mikael Bakhtin as a heuristic tool.

known author of the Wisdom of Solomon. The literary fiction of Solomonic authorship permits the author of this late Hellenistic work to describe in great detail his successful courtship of Wisdom and thus to serve as a model for everyone who values her. In the view of ancient sages, children should be seen but not heard.

The harsh treatment of children in the ancient world carried over into the schools of Mesopotamia and Egypt, as demonstrated by frequent references. The saying from *Ahiqar* comparing the whipping of children to putting manure on gardens implies that the infliction of pain resulted in growth toward maturity, a theory that has been taken over by modern sports enthusiasts ("No pain, no gain"). Modern educators differ with one another about corporal punishment as an incentive to learning, and at least one contemporary government, Singapore, has reinstated caning as punishment for juvenile delinquency.

Chapter Seven

᷈

Language for
Intellectual Achievement

*"One must grasp that a long and a short discourse
aim at the same thing."*

Epicurus

Although the sages never quite drew up a compendium of terms relating to learning, they did occasionally reflect on the pursuit of knowledge in ways that draw attention to specific verbs and nouns having to do with the intellectual process. In a few instances these teachers actually gather together several verbs that cover the entire scope of learning, and at other times they seem to discourage certain types of speculation. An examination of this vocabulary for intellectual achievement throws additional light on the larger problem under review, the nature of ancient Israelite education.[1]

[1] This section was written before the publication of Nili Shupak's analysis of the linguistic affinities between Egyptian and Hebraic vocabulary for learning. Her interest is much broader than mine, which adhere closely to the biblical canon. In a sense, however, my investigation covers far more than vocabulary, probing the very nature of the intellectual task and the relationship between knowledge and transcendence.

VOCABULARY FOR TEACHER

Two expressions in Gen. 12:6 and Judg. 7:1 seem to reflect a period when Israel endeavored, through the assistance of trained technicians, to ascertain the divine plan for the future by means of divination. The teachers' terebinth near Shechem (*'ēlôn môreh*) and hill of instruction (*gibʿat hammôreh*) respectively allude to the places where access to divine secrets took place. Belief in God as teacher occurs in several texts, but Job 35:11 and Isa. 28:26 and 30:20 stand out as particularly significant manifestations of this notion. Elihu describes Eloah as "one who gives songs during the night, who teaches us [*mallepēnû* with missing ʾ; the root is *ʾlp* and one expects *mᵉʾallepēnû*] more than the beasts of the earth and bestows more wisdom than the birds of the sky." The comparison appears to be between experiential observation, the basis of conclusions about reality in the sayings within the Book of Proverbs, and revelation.

The two approaches to learning, the one horizontal, the other vertical, come together in Isa. 28:23–29, for the farmer observes a certain rhythm in planting and sowing, but Isaiah insists that God also instructs him rightly, indeed that YHWH of hosts, the one who works wonders in counsel (*hiplîʾ ʿēṣâ*) and excels in perspicacity, oversees this natural rhythm. The other text from the Book of Isaiah, probably postexilic, concedes that YHWH will afflict Judah sorely, bestowing "bread of affliction and water of adversity," but promises that its teacher (*môreykā*) will no longer hide, enabling eyes to behold the divine Instructor (*môreykā*) and ears to discern a word from behind: "This is the way; walk in it," when the people veer either to the right or to the left. The divine enclosure of Judah, front and rear, is a noteworthy theological concept. In a text from the same general period, a personal name in 1 Chr. 5:13, *yôray*, may be a short form of *yôreyyâ*, with the probable meaning "whom YHWH teaches." Elihu sums up this theological conviction in the following words: "Look, El is sovereign in power; who is a teacher (*môreh*) like him?" This religious conviction manifests its power in the Psalter (e.g., 94:12 with the Piel of *ysr* and *lmd*, 119:108 with *lammedēnî*) and in a hymnic text in Sirach (51:17, with *melammedēnî*; cf. also 11QPsa). This religious ideology shows signs of encountering skepticism over the effectiveness of divine instruction, given recalcitrant human nature. Accordingly, a text in Jer. 32:33 places blame squarely on human shoulders. Even persistent effort on God's part, expressed by an infinitive absolute of *lāmad*, failed to overcome resistance.

Abstract qualities were also thought to possess the potential for instruction, not always for good. In Job 15:5 Eliphaz contends that Job's wickedness dictates his speech (*ye'allēp 'awōnekā pîkā*) with the result that his tongue chooses crafty retorts. Ben Sira notes that a person's mind (Greek *psyche*) informs him (*yaggîd*) more reliably than seven watchmen (37:14), a viewpoint at odds with the observation in Prov. 28:26 that a fool relies on his own insights (*lēb*) but the person who walks in wisdom will survive. Even the dead continue to function as teachers, according to Bildad, who in Job 8:8, 10 urges Job to inquire about the reasoned conclusions they have bequeathed to society (*ḥēqer*). This resorting to ancestral teaching is his way of compensating for life's ephemerality. Our remote ancestors teach us (*yrh*) across the centuries by reasoned utterances (*millibbām*).

A list of living teachers within Israelite society would include virtually everyone, inasmuch as instruction is both positive and negative, intentional and unintentional. Sages, priests, parents, prophets, specialists of all kinds taught others both in word and in deed. Not always successfully, as a student confesses in Prov. 5:13 ("I did not obey my teacher [*môrāy*], did not incline my ear to my instructor [*limlamme-day*]"). Teachers did not necessarily escape a certain amount of pride in their ability to communicate effectively. Thus Elihu promises to teach Job rationality ("Be quiet, and I shall teach you wisdom" [*haḥarēš waʾăʾallepkā*], Job 33:33b).

From these texts one can discern the broad semantic range in Hebrew for teaching. The more frequently used verbs include Piel (intensive) forms of *ʾlp*, *lmd*, and *ysr*; Hiphil (causative) forms of *bîn*, *śkl*, and *yrh*, but various circumlocutions enrich this vocabulary (e.g., *yōsîp leqaḥ*). A measure of reproof often characterized ancient instruction, graphically indicated in the Egyptian symbol for a teacher as a strong arm poised to strike with a cane. This predilection to punish uncooperative and dull students was given a theological basis in Prov. 3:11–12 ("YHWH's discipline [*mûsār*], my son, do not reject, nor loathe his teaching; for whom YHWH loves he instructs [*yôkîaḥ*] and afflicts [reading *weyakʾib* with LXX] the son in whom he delights"). This understanding of corrective discipline led to the use of the verb *ykḥ* in the sense of "to teach" and to circumlocutions such as "to receive *tôkaḥ̂ôt*."

VOCABULARY FOR STUDENTS AND THEIR ACTIVITY

The considerably richer vocabulary designating students and their activity indicates the focus of countless aphorisms and Instructions. The familiar form of address "my son" (Hebrew *benî*) occurs throughout the ancient Near East in Instructions; as noted earlier, with a single exception, Egyptian Instructions limit this direct address of father to son to the prologue, whereas Mesopotamian and Israelite texts intersperse it throughout the Instruction. Initially, this language actually indicated blood relationship, although it eventually came to signify a student, at least in Mesopotamia. Similarly, *father* (Hebrew *'āb*) at first referred to the head of a household; subsequently it may have taken on the extended meaning of "teacher." The word *limmûdîm* ("those who are taught") connotes an acquired response that has become habitual—in animals as well as among human beings. One embarking on the task of acquiring such ingrained behavior bore the title *talmîd* ("pupil") in a late text, 1 Chr. 25:8 ("Both small and large, teacher and pupil" [*mēbîn 'im-talmîd*, assuming chiasm in the parallelism]).

The primary responsibility of students was to observe and listen, eye and ear uniting to convey knowledge to the mind for storage in the belly until released through the mouth. Such corporal imagery underlined the belief that the act of cognition involved more than the mental faculty, the heart (*lēb*). Curiously, writing does not play a significant role in canonical wisdom literature. The verb *ktb* occurs only five times (Prov. 3:3, 7:3; Job 13:26, 19:23; Qoh. 12:10). The two occurrences in the Book of Proverbs may echo Deuteronomic influence, the symbolic etching of divine teaching on the tablets of the heart (*kātebēn ʿal lûaḥ libbekā*). The two occurrences in the Book of Job mark emotional peaks in the struggle to maintain Job's integrity. In the first, he accuses God of writing bitter things about him, bringing to mind youthful indiscretions. The idea of God keeping a ledger is familiar from various texts in the Bible, as is the notion of YHWH writing on tablets of stone or on a wall. This idea, too, finds symbolic expression in Jer. 31:33 (". . . my teaching I will put within them, and I will write it on their hearts"). In the second text from the Book of Job, the victim of God and friends expresses the wish that his words be written down, indeed inscribed in stone with an iron pen and lead as a perpetual testimony to his innocence, like the exploits of Darius recorded on the Behistun Rock.

The only use of *ktb* in Qoheleth occurs in the First Epilogue and presents a textual difficulty. The verb should be pointed as an infinitive absolute, *wekātôb*, in accord with Qoheleth's linguistic usage.[2] The words *wekātûb yōšer dibrê ʾemet* conclude an enumeration of activities that Qoheleth is said to have performed: "he wrote the most reliable words." This reluctance to use the verb *ktb* continues in Sirach, despite the obvious engagement of Ben Sira in literary activity (39:32). Nevertheless, he urges students to associate with

---

[2] Despite the passive rendering in the Septuagint, strong textual evidence supports an active verb. One could object to an argument based on Qoheleth's linguistic practice, for the Epilogue derives from someone other than the author of the rest of the book.

learned people and to listen to their discourse. Nowhere does he tell them to read and write texts, but he assumes that they will become thoroughly familiar with traditional literature, possibly viewed as sacred by his time (cf. 48:10; 44:5). He does urge the keeping of careful records of income and expenses (42:7), and he refers to engraved gem stones and jewelry (45:11).

The learning process began with observation. One looked carefully (*rā'â, ḥāzâ, śākal*), exploring thoroughly (*tûr, dāraś, bāqaš, ḥāqar*), assessing data by arranging them in an orderly way (*tāqan*). Listening supplemented ocular discovery (*'āzan, šāma', nātan lēb*). Reflecting on something and talking about it followed (*śît lēb* and *sāpar*). The actual discovery of an insight was expressed by verbs for finding and knowing, *māṣā', yāda'*; attaining a full grasp of an idea, by *bîn, lāqaḥ mûsār, qānâ,* and *kûn*. Once an individual had acquired knowledge, he was obligated to hold on to it (*ḥā-zaq*), guard it (*šāmar, nāṣar*), love it (*'āhab*), not abandon it (*'āzab*), or neglect it (*pāra'*), or despise it (*bāzâ, śānā'*), or let it drop (*rāpâ*). The end product of this quest for learning went by many names, but one word, *ḥokmâ*, served as a supernym for all the rest (*da'at, mûsār, tôrâ, bînâ, tebûnâ, 'ormâ, tušiyyâ, tôḥaḥat, nābôn, 'ārûm, kišrôn*). For Qoheleth that word *ḥokmâ* combined with the preposition *b* designated rational inquiry, and *ḥešbôn* stood for the process of thinking and its result.[3] The person who possessed such knowledge was *ḥākām*, a sage.

---

[3] Peter Machinist, "Fate, *miqreh*, and Reason: Some Reflections on Qohelet and Biblical Thought," 159–75 in *Solving Riddles and Untying Knots: Biblical, Epigraphic, and*

The verbs for investigating the nature of things sometimes appear in clusters, probably in additive fashion, although the exact relationship in poetic parallelism cannot easily be determined. In Eccles. 7:25, a context explosive with reflection about the nature of rational calculation, one finds the following sequence: *tûr, bāqaš, yādā‛,* and *māṣā’,* together with the result of this inquiry into things—*ḥokmâ* and *ḥešbôn* as the general conclusion, with specific manifestations involving the evil nature of folly and madness, and a certain type of woman, a femme fatale. Qoheleth refers to the process of drawing conclusions and associating them with one another to reach a total assessment of things ("one to one to find the sum [*ḥešbôn*], 7:27b), regrettably acknowledging that, despite all his effort, he has not found it (7:28a). He admits to having discovered one man among a thousand but not a woman, and also that God made humans morally upright but they have sought out numerous contrivances.[4] Perhaps this suggests that they have replaced the single absolute, the *ḥešbôn,* with multiple alternatives, *ḥiššebōnôt.*

Qoheleth's use of the infinitive *lātûr* with abstract qualities, wisdom and the sum of things, represents a shift from its usual application to tangible qualities like the land that

---

Semitic Studies in Honor of Jonas C. Greenfield, eds. Ziony Zevit, Seymour Gitin, and Michael Sokoloff (Winona Lake: Eisenbrauns, 1995) argues that Qoheleth moves toward a more explicit conceptualization and abstraction than earlier understandings of fate. He finds this tendency in three expressions for patterned time, *ḥešbôn, ma‛aśeh,* and *‛ōlām,* as well as in *miqreh.* He writes: "Put another way, what is significant in Qohelet is not simply the concern with the subject matter on which human reason focuses and the conclusions it yields, but an awareness of, a reflection on the reasoning process itself" (173).

[4] Some interpreters have endeavored to rid Qoheleth of the charge that he disliked women. The most notable attempt of this kind is that of Norbert Lohfink, "War Kohelet ein Frauenfeind?" 259–87 in *La Sagesse de l'Ancien Testament.* He thinks that Qoheleth quotes a popular saying in order to refute its claim.

spies explored. His modest findings are introduced by a concession in 7:23b that wisdom always retains its essence, which was so profound as to remain permanently hidden ("Far off . . . and deep, deep, who can find it?," 7:24). This admission that none can unravel life's mystery recurs in 8:1, often taken as a later gloss.[5] It reads: "Who is like the sage, and who knows the interpretation (*pēšer*) of a thing?" Usage demands that the rhetorical question be taken as a denial: "nobody knows the meaning of a matter" (*dābār*).[6]

The epilogist who evaluated Qoheleth's contribution to society (*hāʿam*) as sage and teacher used a total of six verbs to characterize his intellectual approach (12:9–10). Qoheleth listened (*weʾizzēn*), probed deeply (*wehiqqēr*), and arranged (*tiqqēn*) numerous sayings; he sought (*biqqēš*) to discover (*limṣōʾ*) pleasing expressions, and he wrote (*wekātōb*) reliable things. The verb "he listened" implies that people constituted the "texts" that he studied. The absence of a verb for reading at this late date, probably mid-third century, is noteworthy, although its effect is weakened by the further reference to writing. Presumably, Qoheleth expected someone to read his observations and to appreciate their form and substance.

An unusual verse in Sirach also juxtaposes six verbs to indicate the goal of students (6:27). Ben Sira urges them to seek (*drš*), probe deeply (*ḥqr*), hunt for (*bqš*), discover (*mṣʾ*), and having found the answer, to grasp it firmly (*ḥzq*) and not

---

[5] The unusual word for interpretation, *pēšer*, may be an audial pun on the previous *yāšār*. It would then indicate the meaning of searching for the sum of things, hence the verse would not be intrusive.

[6] The rhetorical question "Who knows?" implies that no one does, on which see my article entitled "The Expression *mî yôdēaʿ* in the Hebrew Bible," *VT* 36 (1986) 274–88.

to let it fall (*rph*). The second half of the verse echoes Prov. 4:13, "Hold on to instruction; do not let it fall" (*haḥazēq bammûsār 'al terep*).

The thoroughness implied in the verb *ḥāqar* made it particularly appropriate as a description for divine exploration of human thoughts. In Ps. 139:1–3 the Psalmist confesses that as a result of YHWH's penetrating search nothing lies hidden in a dark corner of the divine mind: "YHWH, you have searched me (*ḥaqartanî*) and known me (*wattēdā'*); you know my sitting and rising, you comprehend (*bantâ*) my musings from afar; you measure (*zērîtâ*) my path and couch; you are familiar with (*hiskantâ*) all my ways." The same knowledge extends to speech prior to its utterance (v. 4). The psalmist's invitation to further divine scrutiny may resemble Cleanthes' famous prayer, "Teach me to do your will, O Zeus, for whether I want to do so or not I will do it," but the excitement over YHWH's extraordinary knowledge seems boundless. "Search me (*ḥāqrēnî*), God, and know my mind (*weda' lebābî*), test me (*beḥānēnî*) and ascertain (*weda'*) my anxious thoughts. See (*ûre'ēh*) if any harmful way exists within me" (Ps. 139:23–24).

An angry Job resented God's relentless searching for his sins despite the prior knowledge of his innocence ("that you seek [*tebāqqēš*] my sins and search for [*tidrôš*] my transgressions," Job 10:6). Such inquiry on God's part placed the deity on the dubious level of humans, who by nature are of short duration. For modern readers there is something shocking about depicting God as having to search diligently to discover Job's wrongdoing, but the biblical YHWH cared about good and evil, and lacking omniscience, searched the human heart. This qualification explains why verbs for seeking were usually restricted to human subjects. Prov. 18:15 is no real exception, for the human ear, the subject of the verb *tebāqqēš*, functions as *pars pro toto*. Seeking belongs to the essence of humankind, according to Eccles. 3:6 (*'et lebaqqēš*), along with its opposite, losing (*we'et le'abbēd*), possibly through a lapse of memory, or perhaps as a consequence of negligence and inattention. In one notoriously difficult text, Qoheleth characterizes God's activity as chasing the past (*yebaqqēš 'et nirdāp*), as if God attends to events that are present to human beings but were previously present reality to the deity (cf. Sir. 5:3).

In contrast to God's full knowledge as celebrated by the author of Ps. 139, human discovery invariably came up against a teacher's tight fist, the restriction of knowledge. Qoheleth makes this point in opposition to anyone who insists that he has actually found knowledge, apparently of divine activity (8:17). The diligent toiling and seeking notwithstanding, one result follows—even a sage will be unable to discover that rare thing called knowledge. In 3:11 Qoheleth makes a similar point, at the same time granting that the deity created things beautiful and implanted something positive in the human mind. This unknown quality (*hā'ōlām* in the MT, but it probably should be pointed *ha'elem*)[7] bestows a sense of the unknown and unknowable on all intellectual inquiry. Here, as well as in his notion of time, death, and rational inquiry, Qoheleth gives voice to his belief that all human endeavor comes up against absolute limits that affect the very nature of thought itself.

[7] I examine this difficult verse at length in "The Eternal Gospel (Ecclesiastes 3:11)," 23–55 in *Essays in Old Testament Ethics*, eds. J. L. Crenshaw and John T. Willis (New York: Ktav Publishing Company, 1974).

When negated, the Niph'al (passive) form of the root *ḥā-qar* regularly connotes the unfathomable and immeasurable. Matitiahu Tsevat reads only one positive use in twelve Niph'al forms of *ḥāqar*.[8] Seven have a negative particle, either *'en* or *lō'* (Job 5:9, 9:10, 34:24, 36:26; Ps. 145:3; Prov. 25:3; Isa. 40:28), two are objects of rhetorical questions and therefore negated (Job 11:7, 38:16), one appears in a corrupt text (Prov. 25:27), and one is uncertain. The sole positive assertion occurs in Job 8:8 (". . . and consider what their ancestors discovered"), unless Prov. 25:27 also belongs to this usage ("nor the discovery of their honor, honorable"). The unfathomable usually refers to God's ways and deeds, although it can apply to extraordinary human beings such as kings (Prov. 25:3, "the minds of kings are unsearchable").

The unfathomable nature of *ḥokmâ* comes to expression in the remarkable poem comprising the twenty-eighth chapter in the Book of Job. Against the backdrop celebrating the extraordinary accomplishments of human beings in exploring the bowels of the earth in search of precious stones, the author remarks that even such ingenious effort cannot make a dent in the barrier separating humans from wisdom. The most anyone can do, even mythical Sheol and Abaddon, is eavesdrop on a rumor. Here these two locations for the realm of the dead are personified. Job will later discover how terribly unsatisfactory secondhand knowledge really is—when he comes face to face with the one who rebukes him from a whirlwind, prompting him to say: "By the hearing of an ear I heard about you, but now my eye sees

[8] "*ḥāqar, ḥēqer; meḥqār,*" *Theological Dictionary of the Old Testament*, vol. 5, eds. G. Johannes Botterweck and Helmer Ringgren (Grand Rapids: William B. Eerdmans Publishing Company, 1986) 150.

you. . . ." Of God's knowledge of Wisdom the poet says, "God sees her way and knows her place, for he looks to the ends of the earth and sees under all the heavens" (28:23). The sovereign of wind and ocean, rain and lightening, saw Wisdom, discussed it, established it, and probed it deeply (28:27).

This verse covers four distinct stages in the intellectual process. The first, observation, engages the eyes as they examine an observable phenomenon. It connotes immediate knowledge, firsthand experience, thus intimate knowledge. The second, discussion, involves the organ of speech as the agency through which an individual endeavors to articulate whatever conclusion he has reached in a way that communicates with others. This discussion also entails hearing with discernment. In this way private insights become public commodity, and the collective knowledge of a given community makes its contribution to private knowledge. The third stage, establishing hypotheses and reaching provisional conclusions, functions within the mind, for the discoverer ultimately bears sole responsibility for any new insight. The final stage, analytic assessment by exploring every facet of an idea, returns to the earlier image of probing the recesses of earth in search of precious gems, then examining them for possible flaws. The four verbs—*rāʾâ*, *sāpar*, *kûn*, and *ḥāqar*—nicely describe the cognitive analytic process as the poet understood it.

Ben Sira proceeds even farther than the author of Job 28 toward limiting intellectual inquiry. Whereas the poet responsible for the above description of indefatigable energy in the pursuit of the unknown grudgingly conceded that this effort was ultimately aborted when wisdom was its object,

Ben Sira considers some kinds of curiosity not only futile but also inappropriate. He writes:

> 3¹⁷My son, when prosperous comport yourself humbly and you will be appreciated more than those who are generous with gifts. ¹⁸Defer before the great ones of society and you will discover favor with God, ²⁰for God's compassion is vast, and he reveals his secret thoughts to the lowly. ²¹Seek not unfathomable wonders, nor probe into things concealed from you. ²²Attend to what is entrusted to you; hidden things are not your business. ²³Do not talk about what exceeds your grasp, for more than you [understand] has been shown to you. ²⁴Indeed, human speculations are numerous, and evil conjectures lead one astray (Sir. 3:17–24).[9]

One naturally thinks of Am. 3:7, "Surely the Lord YHWH does not do anything without revealing his secret counsel to his servants the prophets," but Ben Sira extends this divine generosity to the humble. Having said that, he stresses the sufficiency of such revelation. Not willing to let readers draw their own conclusions on the basis of this principle of disclosure, he presses the point that some sorts of rational inquiry have perverse consequences, echoing a similar viewpoint in Deut. 29:29 (MT 28), "The secret things belong to YHWH our God, but the revealed things belong to us and to our posterity. . . ." This attack on the very essence of rational inquiry, the desire to penetrate the unknown and

---

[9] Author's translation. Some authorities add v. 19 (The exalted and esteemed are numerous, but he reveals his plan to the humble).

make it comprehensible, does not automatically follow from humble acknowledgment that the intellect can never explain the mystery of life. The necessities of polemic have forced Ben Sira into an untenable position: some things are not subject to cognitive analysis. Regardless of whether this restriction of knowledge refers to Greek astrological and cosmological speculations or to Jewish variations of such efforts to control one's fate, it clearly expresses the view that certain types of intellectual endeavors bode ill for those with a curious mind.

By reading *tōʾmar* for the meaningless *tōmar* in v. 23, one brings this discussion into line with a significant thrust in Ben Sira's apologetic. The formula of debate, introduced by *ʾal tōʾmar*, normally appears in contexts dealing with theodicy.[10] He may reject certain kinds of speculation about divine justice within society, and in doing so he insists that Israel's wonder-worker, alluded to in v. 21, has conveyed sufficient information to enable those buffeted by life's waves to trust confidently in divine goodness.

[10] James L. Crenshaw, "The Problem of Theodicy in Sirach: On Human Bondage," *JBL* 94 (1975) 49–64.

Chapter Eight

≈

A Literary Canon

*"Look to these thirty chapters. They inform, they educate,
they are the foremost of all books, they make the ignorant wise."*

Amenemope

If schools actually existed in ancient Israel, teachers and
students would have needed convenient texts for copying,
particularly at a more advanced level of instruction than the
mere learning of basic skills pertaining to reading and writing. In Mesopotamia, *Atrakhasis*, the *Gilgamesh Epic*, and
Enuma elish functioned in this capacity, students acquiring
knowledge about myths relating to the Flood, the origins of
life, and human destiny at the same time they honed their
skills at writing. Similarly, Egyptian scribes copied the *Book
of Kemit*, the *Instruction of Khety*, and other classical Instructions, as well as numerous scribal texts that modern scholars
identify as Miscellanies. In this way scribes acknowledged
their ancestors' worth and kept their memory alive, to them
a form of immortality.

Frequent use of certain texts, and the resulting familiarity
with them, gave them privileged status over the many other
texts circulating among the literati. While the term "canon"

is a product of a later era,[1] the word comes close to describing the oft-copied texts, which seem to have served as a norm for thought and expression. Among Israel's intellectuals, the Books of Job and Qoheleth may have functioned similarly. Perhaps Ben Sira hoped to add his own contribution to this elite twosome; he certainly goes far enough to claim divine inspiration for his teachings.

THE BOOK OF JOB

The modern tendency to admire rebels who shake their fists at a corrupt system, political or philosophical, tends to mislead interpreters of the Book of Job. For this reason, they often fail to ask who actually speaks for the author. Can one really imagine anyone in sixth- or fifth-century Judah attributing ultimate truth to a human being in the same literary work that has the deity soundly rebuke that individual?[2] By juxtaposing the troubling depiction of the Lord in the prologue and the overbearing harangue in the divine

---

[1] Its original meaning is that of a rule or norm, and by extension a body of literature that offers a standard for life and thought. A novelty in the ancient world when applied to sacred writings, the concept was first applied to a group of writings attributed to Moses but in some sense transmitted to him from the deity. Similarly, prophetic literature was thought to have derived from the divine commissioner of these sometimes troubling, sometimes consoling voices.

[2] Several critics have imagined just this, but they understand the book as irony. Edwin M. Good, *In Turns of Tempest: A Reading of Job* (Stanford: Stanford University Press, 1990), defends this view and offers scintillating interpretations of numerous texts. Similarly, Yair Hoffman, *A Blemished Perfection: The Book of Job in Context* (JSOT SS 213; Sheffield: Sheffield Academic Press, 1996), views irony as one of many rhetorical strategies within the book. For him, the response of Job to the divine speeches teems with irony. Carol Newsom, "The Book of Job," *The New Interpreter's Bible*, vol. IV (Nashville: Abingdon, 1966), 319–687, emphasizes the religious profundity within literary devices such as irony.

speeches, one can hazard the guess that a bold poet challenges the dominant notion of a benevolent deity, who watches over the universe in order to implement a policy of reward for the virtuous and punishment for the villainous.[3] On this reading, the divine restoration of Job that takes place in the epilogue becomes the epitome of irony. Comparable texts from Egypt and Mesopotamia confirm the existence of radical poets willing to question what others found disturbing but not serious enough to dismantle a worldview.

This extraordinary text may have served as a model for quite different kinds of intellectuals, those for whom the motto "The fear of the Lord is the beginning/first principle of knowledge" served notice that true wisdom involves the sacred dimension. Like the Babylonian prototype *I Will Praise the Lord of Wisdom*, its Jewish counterpart offers a way to respond to undeserved suffering. The bowed knee and total submission represented by Job's final remarks in 42:5–6

"I had heard of you by the
    hearing of the ear,
but now my eye sees you;
therefore I despise myself,
    and repent in dust and ashes"[4]

---

[3] Bruce Zuckerman, *Job the Silent: A Study in Historical Counterpoint* (New York: Oxford University Press, 1991), draws on Y. L. Perets's "Bontsye Shvayg" to demonstrate the way historical events can radically alter an author's original intention.

[4] The decisive verb '*em'as* lacks an object, and the other verb, *weniḥamtî*, is followed by the preposition '*al*. Does the first verb imply obstinacy ("I reject [something]") or subjection, a melting away in submissive obedience? Does the second suggest repentance or finding comfort in Job's firm resolve in spite of everything? Scholars have debated these and other issues from every conceivable angle, but the several linguistic possibilities leave the matter open.

indicates that the complainant has at last found reconcilia-
tion. To be sure, the ambiguity in the decisive verse 6 leaves
open the possibility that Job remained unrepentant to the
end.[5] Even the earlier vituperation on Job's part does not
necessarily negate the above reading of his final words as
humble submission, for they may represent the healing
function of honest expression. The author of the later Testament of Job did not understand Job's behavior as unbecom-
ing, but rather sought to embellish the devotion this unfor-
tunate victim of Satan's evil machinations gave to the Lord.

Yet a third way the Book of Job may have functioned
among the sages takes its cue from *The Babylonian Theodicy*,
which offers in dialogic form various responses to the problem of evil. The book presents a series of answers, none of
which can make an exclusive claim to solving the difficult
dilemma of unjust suffering in a good universe. The three
friends speak for traditionalists, insisting that hidden sin
must be flushed out and that humble confession will change
things dramatically. The youthful Elihu reiterates many of
their arguments and demonstrates much less patience with
them and with Job. The divine viewpoint, expressed in the
tempest, focuses almost exclusively on the realm that humans cannot, or do not, occupy. The narrator's understanding of the proper response to suffering forces one to pay
close attention to speech, as if insisting that what one says
makes all the difference when innocent suffering strikes.[6]

---

[5] Interpreters frequently communicate more about themselves than the text when
addressing a book like Job. Some literary critics think all interpretation is shaped by
what readers bring to a text more than by words on the page.

[6] Gustavo Gutiérrez, *On Job: God Talk and the Suffering of the Innocent* (Maryknoll,
NY: Orbis Books, 1987), stresses the importance to the author of speaking properly
about suffering.

A fourth way this book may have served its readers results from heeding the narrator's remark that Job's three friends came for the purpose of consoling their friend. The insightful manner by which a sufferer assuages grief and the ensuing pained speech can provide valuable assistance to all who must come to terms with extreme discomfort. The emotional roller-coaster that Job finds himself strapped into permits him to plumb both the depths and the heights,[7] at the same time allowing him to entertain notions of the wildest and boldest proportions, such as a divine champion and, however tenuous, the remote possibility of an onslaught against death itself. This use of the book, or the several uses discussed above, may explain the later willingness to include it in a collection of normative sacred writings, despite its potential to be misunderstood. Such mind-expanding dialogue, coupled with innocent-appearing prose, would have assisted in training young scholars.

THE BOOK OF ECCLESIASTES

At least one student of Qoheleth, and probably two, appended an endorsement of his teachings and at the same time sought to influence the way the book would be understood.[8] The first epilogist locates Qoheleth in the commu-

---

[7] Jack H. Kahn, *Job's Illness: Loss, Grief, and Integration: A Psychological Interpretation* (Oxford: Pergamon Press, 1975), emphasizes the appropriateness of the various stages of grief through which Job passes in reintegrating his personality.

[8] Michael Fox has offered an alternative reading of the Epilogues, which he views in the light of another persona employed by the author of the book in the same way writers like Joel Chandler Harris used this literary device (*Qohelet and his Contradictions*, 311–29). The epilogist is, in Fox's view, the frame narrator.

nity as a teacher of the general populace (*hāʿām*) and concedes that his collected sayings have a sting built into them, despite their elegance. In his view, Qoheleth declared the truth, which does not always issue in warm feelings—particularly when the subject extends to existential matters such as life's true meaning and the unpleasant implications of human finitude. The second epilogist warns that students need not consult anything other than the complete corpus of Qoheleth's sayings, implying that these writings contain all students can handle at this stage of their education, or that they really need. The rationale for this strange restriction of curiosity follows, specifically that the making of written texts is endless, and studying them all exhausts mind and body.

The second epilogist addresses the reader in the language of the family ("my son"), something that Qoheleth never did. In light of the fact that the first admirer of Qoheleth identified him as a professional sage, a *hākām*, the reference to "my son" probably has its later symbolic sense, "student." Whether or not this second epilogist has in mind the wider collection of wisdom literature, Proverbs in particular, cannot be determined.[9] In any event, he thinks of the entire body of proverbial sayings to which he refers as the product of a single shepherd, by which he may mean the putative royal author or the deity. In the ancient Near East, the metaphor of shepherd was used of both the earthly monarch and the heavenly ruler.[10]

---

[9] Gerald T. Sheppard, "The Epilogue to Qoheleth as Theological Commentary," *CBQ* 39 (1977) 182–89 and *Wisdom as a Hermeneutical Construct* (BZAW 151; Berlin and New York, 1980).

[10] D. Müller, "Der gute Hirte: Ein Beitrag zur Geschichte ägyptischer Bildrede," *ZÄS* 86 (1961) 126–44; Leonidas Kalugila, *The Wise King: Studies in Royal Wisdom as*

The epilogist then comments on the adequacy of Qoheleth's teachings, insisting that the time has come for closure
(Eccles. 12:13–14). He thinks everything has been heard, a
sentiment approximating that in verse twelve ("beware of
anything beyond these"). An astonishing remark follows as
summation of human obligation: "fear God and observe his
commandments." The threat of a final judgment follows,
one orchestrated by God in order to expose every deed, momentarily hidden, whether from guilt or humility.

One may well wonder how faithfully the second epilogist
represented Qoheleth's own teachings, given the vast distance between the latter's radical questioning of everything
and the annotator's cautious traditionalism. True, Qoheleth
admitted the necessity for fearing God, one grounded in an
awareness of a far-off and unpredictable despot,[11] but he
never urged listeners to keep the Torah. Had Qoheleth really believed that all injustice would be corrected at some
moment in the future, he would have had no grounds for
concluding that everything was empty, indeed futile.[12]

For the subject under discussion, it matters little whether
or not the second epilogist—or even the first—misrepre-
sented Qoheleth's teachings. The remarks, however they are
taken, indicate that the collected sayings of a radical teacher
commend themselves for study. No clue is provided as to

Divine Revelation in the Old Testament and Its Environment; and Lennart Boström, *The
God of the Sages: The Portrayal of God in the Book of Proverbs.*

[11] Egon Pfeiffer, "Die Gottesfurcht im Buche Kohelet," 133–58 in *Gottes Wort und
Gottes Land: F.S. H. W. Hertzberg* (Göttingen: Vandenhoeck & Ruprecht, 1965).

[12] This is the flaw in R. N. Whybray's positive reading of Qoheleth ("Qoheleth,
Preacher of Joy," *JSOT* 23 [1982] 87–98; cf. also Graham Ogden, *Qoheleth* [Sheffield:
JSOT Press, 1987]).

where and by whom this close reading would take place, except the possible vocabulary identifying sages and students. Still, the nature of the book suggests the likelihood that readers were advanced students engaged in examining the nature of reality and wrestling with complex philosophical (and theological) problems.

SIRACH

The author of the Book of Sirach, whom modern interpreters designate by a short form of his name, Ben Sira, offers ambiguous evidence about the existence of a literary canon in his day, the first two decades of the second century B.C.E. On the one hand, he frequently alludes to incidents and names from the literature that eventually found its way into a sacred canon. In addition, within his praise of worthy ancestors, Ben Sira uses language that implies a closed canon of the Torah and Prophets, plus some more sacred texts. On the other hand, when he encourages listeners (readers?) to expand their knowledge he tells them to seek out intelligent people and discuss matters with them. Never does he invite these learners to read any text, unless that meaning can be read into his invitation to visit his "house of instruction." According to this understanding of the expression, "house of instruction," Ben Sira describes his own writing as a place where education occurs.[13]

Such a reading of this invitation is not the most natural

---

[13] Fox, "The Social Location of the Book of Proverbs," 236.

one. By its use, Ben Sira may advertise his own educational enterprise, which could explain his readiness to discuss the touchy matter of cost. He uses a defense of the high cost of study under his tutelage that has become almost universal in modern higher education, namely that it is cost effective. A pupil easily recovers all expenditures; the yield in gold far outweighs the investment in silver. Despite the echoes of presumably symbolic language in the Book of Proverbs, this appeal readily lends itself to serving as a rationale for charging tuition.

If the latter interpretation be accepted, that still does not exclude the possibility that Ben Sira expected to use his own literary achievement (perhaps along with Proverbs) as a textbook. His conscious promotion of the written work as a product of inspiration that far exceeded its original intent easily accords with such use. So do the frequent vocatives "my son" or "my sons," interspersed throughout much of the text, although this usage may comprise a literary conceit derived from the Book of Proverbs.

Ben Sira had an admirer just as Qoheleth did, and this individual, the grandson of Ben Sira, wrote an elegant prologue in Greek as a defense for translating the book from Hebrew into Greek so that Alexandrians could read it in their own language. The grandson remembers his grandfather as a student of sacred writings, now collected into two distinct entities, the Torah and the Prophets, along with a third group loosely called "the other writings." Clearly, a concept of a sacred canon lies behind these comments, but this does not necessarily mean that the emerging canon functioned as textbooks in a school, although such use cannot be ruled out. More likely, the sacred writings were read aloud in worship centers (synagogues) by persons who had acquired advanced training, either in a school associated with the Temple cult in Jerusalem or in a secular school at Alexandria.

THE BOOK OF PROVERBS

In some respects the Book of Proverbs gives the impression of random collections of folk sayings, with little attempt to achieve either thematic unity or comprehensive coverage of the moral life. For this reason, one is hard pressed to argue that the book served as a text in schools. The nature of the sayings and the haphazard arrangement, with a few notable exceptions, suggest that the book grew out of parental instruction. The aphorisms and proverbial sayings in general served to form character, and that restricted use explains their limited subject matter. Like the Decalogue or the several other legal codes, Deuteronomy 12–26, for example, the book was suggestive, pointing the way without attempting to be exhaustive on any particular subject.[14]

Nevertheless, the book does display evidence of editorial arrangement and literary adaptation, and these features are consonant with use in educational establishments. One must be cautious in drawing the conclusion that signs of literary elegance require a learned setting, for eloquence is not

[14] R. N. Whybray, *Proverbs* (Grand Rapids: Eerdmans, 1994) 24, emphasizes the selective character of Instructions.

the exclusive property of the highly educated.[15] Moreover, the intentional arrangement of proverbial sayings into ten speeches[16] or in small units with various linking devices[17] may function as an aid to memory, and the quest for a workable mnemonic device occupied poets who had no connection with schools. The authors of Lamentations and acrostic Psalms indicate the wide distribution of this aid to memory.

Another argument for the use of Proverbs in schools can be mounted on the basis of foreign material, particularly the excerpts corresponding to the *Instruction of Amenemope* and to *Ahiqar*, but also the sayings of Agur in Prov. 30:1–14 and the Instruction attributed to Prince Lemuel's mother in Prov. 31:1–9.[18] None of this material absolutely demands a school setting, but some of it seems more appropriate to the training of future clerks in governmental office. Furthermore, the presence of this material from foreign sages may be explained as popular teachings transmitted by traveling merchants, but a more probable explanation points to the activity of scribes at an advanced stage in their education.

The hypothesis that the Book of Proverbs functioned as a textbook for schools may go too far; perhaps this use applies only to a small portion of the book. If one opts for this minimal version of the theory, it becomes necessary to explain how material with such disparate functions eventu-

---

[15] "Good speech is more hidden than greenstone, yet may be found among maids at the grindstones" (*Ptahhotep*; translation by Miriam Lichtheim in *Ancient Egyptian Literature*, vol. I, 63).

[16] Whybray, *Proverbs*, 23–149.

[17] Ted Hildebrandt, "Proverbial Pairs: Compositional Units in Proverbs 10–29," *JBL* 107 (1988) 207–24; Raymond C. van Leeuwen, *Context and Meaning in Proverbs 25–27* (SBLDS 96; Atlanta: Scholars Press, 1988).

[18] James L. Crenshaw, "A Mother's Instruction to Her Son (Proverbs 31:1–9)" 9–22 in *Perspectives on the Hebrew Bible*.

ally came to rest in the same book. Who gathered the separate collections into a single anthology despite their quite
different origins and uses? Certainly not Hezekiah's men,
although they may have added the sayings from foreign
teachers. Some of the collections originated much later than
the eighth century, possibly as late as the Hellenistic era.[19]
Given this late date, one must express surprise at the meager
evidence within the book for use in schools.

Judging from Egyptian school texts, one expects a greater
indication in Proverbs of scribal elitism, something that surfaces in Sirach but not in earlier canonical wisdom. References to teachers also do not occur in Proverbs, with a
single possible exception (5:7–14). These verses may refer
to parental guidance like all the other texts that specify a
teaching activity. Furthermore, the absence of onomastica,
or lists of nouns that constitute a sort of experimental encyclopedia, within the Book of Proverbs weakens the case for
understanding Proverbs as a text compiled for use in
schools. The content of the vast majority of proverbial sayings tends toward the banal, hardly commending themselves
as worthy of careful study by serious students. The failure of
archaeologists and others to unearth any ostraca containing
children's exercises from school settings, along with corrections by teachers, may not deal a decisive blow to the hypothesis under consideration, but this missing piece of the
puzzle definitely lessens its attractiveness.

The problem of determining the setting and function of

---

[19] The possible bilingual pun in Prov. 31:27 (*ṣôpiyyâ* with the Greek word for wisdom, *sophia*) may be an editorial alteration and therefore indicate nothing about the
actual date of composition for the larger unit (cf. A. Wolters, "*Ṣôpiyyâ* [Prov. 31:27] as
Hymnic Participle and Play on *Sophia*," *JBL* 104 [1982] 58–66).

a collection of proverbs can be illustrated by an unusual saying in *Ahiqar*, in line 117 (#34): "There is no lion in the sea; therefore the sea-snake is called *labbu*." To understand this sophisticated pun on the similarities between the Akkadian words for lion and sea-dragon, one would have to be bilingual.[20] This requirement implies an erudite audience, one that grasps the point of an Aramaic proverb against mythic tradition in the Akkadian language. This saying is the only one in *Ahiqar* that points to a learned audience—and to a Mesopotamian context. Nothing like this exists in the Book of Proverbs, where a saying's meaning is always accessible to ordinary Israelites.

LITERATURE OTHER THAN WISDOM

It has been argued that Israel's scribes practiced their skills on various literary genres, including narrative, legal, historical, oracular, and apocalyptic literature. The Book of Deuteronomy undoubtedly influenced a group of "historians" who stamped their particular imprint on the recording of sacred events. Although the extent of this influence has been exaggerated, probably because of a failure to distinguish between the literary style of the author of Deuteronomy and common liturgical usage in the sixth century, it does appear that some prophetic books, especially Amos and Zechariah,[21] have been subjected to an editing process by a person

[20] Lindenberger, *The Aramaic Proverbs of Ahiqar*, 105–7.
[21] W. H. Schmidt, "Die deuteronomistische Redaktion des Amosbuches," *ZAW* 77 (1965) 168–93 and Raymond F. Person, *Second Zechariah and the Deuteronomic School* (JSOT SS 167; Sheffield: JSOT Press, 1993).

or persons wishing to place a particular slant on historical events.

This retouching of a prophetic book does not necessarily mean, however, that Deuteronomy functioned as a textbook for these editors or that they regularly copied it in school. Moshe Weinfeld's elaborate hypothesis concerning Deuteronomy's origin among Israel's sages rests on highly dubious presuppositions.[22] The linguistic variations in the few possible connections between Deuteronomy and Proverbs give greater force to the many differences between the two books, and retribution, the fundamental theme shared between the Books of Job and Deuteronomy, was central to virtually the entire Bible.

The numerous affinities between the great historical narratives in the Bible—the Deuteronomistic history and the Chronicler's work, as well as the Yahwistic and Priestly accounts of Israel's origins—do not obscure the special interests of each. In the case of the Priestly narrative, everything points to a guild of priests; similarly, the Book of Deuteronomy and the history inspired by it seem to have originated among Levites or their champions, as did the subsequent revision, Chronicles, which endeavors, among other things, to reinstate these priests, who have fallen on hard times.

The superficial similarities between certain narratives and wisdom pale when the differences come into consideration. The beautiful story of Ruth, like the narrative about Joseph in the Book of Genesis, describes divine providence in a sophisticated way, far removed from that of miraculous

---

[22] *The Book of Deuteronomy and Wisdom.*

intervention. God acts quietly and behind the scenes, completely unobserved and at crucial junctures unmentioned. So far this understanding of the world coincides with the much more relaxed teaching of the sages, but the genealogical ending to the Book of Ruth departs completely from their interests.[23] The Book of Jonah also has points of contact with the sages' worldview, although the central concerns of this prophetic satire belong to another context, one inhabited by prophets like Jeremiah and Habakkuk.[24] Other sacred legends reflect the peculiar problems facing religious Jews, whether Hellenistic imperialism as in Judith and Daniel 1–6 or religious syncretism as in Bel and the Dragon, or even judicial corruption, as in Susanna.[25] The exquisite contest in 1 Esdras 3–4 about the greatest thing in the world rises to noble heights in its praise of the God of truth, but nothing else in wisdom literature resembles this material.

Who wrote these gripping stories and other powerful explorations of philosophical issues such as those pursued in 2 Esdras? One could argue, on analogy with Egyptian and Mesopotamian literature, that scribes in Israel busied themselves with all kinds of written genres. As the sole guardians of literature and also the only persons capable of writing anything of literary merit, the scribes were responsible for mundane tasks such as copying business transactions, together with composing and transmitting great literary

---

[23] Two highly suggestive readings of the Book of Ruth are Phyllis Trible, *God and the Rhetoric of Sexuality* (Philadelphia: Fortress Press, 1978) 166–99 and Danna Nolan Fewell and David Miller Gunn, *Compromising Redemption: Relating Characters in the Book of Ruth* (Louisville: Westminster/John Knox Press, 1990).

[24] Jack Sasson, *Jonah* (AB; 24b; New York: Doubleday, 1990), opens up many new insights into this prophetic satire.

[25] Marti Steussy, *Gardens in Babylon: Narrative and Faith in the Greek Legends of Daniel* (SBLDS 141; Atlanta: Scholars Press, 1993).

works to future generations. Such a hypothesis does not rule out an oral origin for many of these narratives; the scribes would in this instance merely function as transmitters of the traditions they consider worthy of preserving.

One can object to this broad understanding of literary activity by insisting on the linguistic and thematic unity of wisdom literature.[26] Can one really believe that the same people who composed the Books of Proverbs, Job, Qoheleth, and Sirach occupied themselves with literature of such varied nature as legal texts, histories, devotional legends, prophetic satires, and so forth?

CONCLUSION

Advanced students in Mesopotamia and Egypt copied specific classical texts over and over, thereby mastering the scribal art and improving their minds by becoming thoroughly familiar with the crowning literary achievements of their predecessors. In their view such reciting of the names of remote ancestors guaranteed immortality to individuals in Egypt who had resigned themselves to virtual marriage to rush brush (or at a later time, reed pen), palette, ink, and papyrus, or in Mesopotamia to stylus and clay. To those for whom, in the words of a Sumerian proverb, "the scribal art was the mother of speakers and the father of scholars," this demanding activity brought rewards in more ways than mere financial security and social prestige. Their lives were

[26] Buccellati, "Wisdom and Not: The Case of Mesopotamia," and Crenshaw, *Old Testament Wisdom.*

enriched by constant attention to original thoughts and eloquent expression located in literary works that had demonstrated their staying power. However tedious their subsequent work may have been, these scribes could take comfort in knowing that they had at one time totally immersed themselves in the thoughts of inspired minds.

This conclusion rests on abundant evidence that ancient scribes copied the masterpieces of their ancestors. No such confirmation exists for Israelite scribal activity prior to Qumran, where the copying of diverse texts flourished as early as the second and first centuries B.C.E. This sectarian preoccupation with the production of manuscripts and the copying of all sorts of texts has less to do with the activity of students under the supervision of teachers than with the work of scribal guilds. Even if books such as Job, Ecclesiastes, and Sirach achieved such standing among sages as to invite frequent copying, this would have occurred among a select group of people who belonged to a guild of scholars. It is unlikely that widespread copying of such books took place in educational establishments.

The same judgment applies to the larger canon of biblical literature. These books were transmitted from generation to generation by rememberers and by specialized guilds of trained scribes. These specialists probably received their education at the hands of certain families who zealously guarded their scribal art. The literati had their own canon, but it did not always coincide with that of the general populace. Even here conjecture is at work, as so often in this investigation of education in ancient Israel.

Chapter Nine

⬦

Knowledge as Human Discovery and as Divine Gift

"No heavenly interference is allowed in the Academy."
RABBI JOSHUA

D o biblical sages think of knowledge as personal achievement or as a divine gift? That is the question to be pursued in this chapter, one so simple that it seems foolish to ask it. Did not modern interpreters isolate wisdom literature from the rest of the Hebrew Bible primarily because of its experiential basis?[1] That is, they called attention to the manner in which this literature establishes its arguments by observation, testing insights by looking closely at the natural world and watching how people behave. The absence of divine oracles, together with revelation through dreams or other means, seems to confirm this reasoning, and the one major exception, the divine speeches within the Book of Job, was taken as an intrusion from an-

---

[1] For example, Orvid S. Rankin, *Israel's Wisdom Literature* (Edinburgh: T. & T. Clark, 1936), and R.B.Y. Scott, *The Way of Wisdom in the Old Testament* (New York: Macmillan, 1971). Virtually everyone who studied biblical wisdom concurred in this judgment, some even considering this experiential foundation cause for embarrassment because it omitted the theological theme that was considered to be central to the Bible: YHWH's mighty acts of deliverance in historical events.

other genre.[2] Similarly, the mantic wisdom underlying the stories in the apocalyptic Book of Daniel was rightly compared with Mesopotamian wisdom,[3] which placed magic at its very center.

The reasons for viewing wisdom literature as an alien body within the Bible were overdrawn,[4] but its distinctiveness remains, regardless of how one answers the question posed above. This conclusion does not rest on the belief that early biblical wisdom was purely secular, although some proverbial sayings fall into this category. Even religious instructions and proverbial sayings emphasize personal observation as the means of acquiring knowledge. The moral legacy that parents pass along to children resulted from long experience, and behind each new insight lay a history of bumps and bruises as individuals learned valuable lessons the hard way. To learn industry and to prepare for adversity, young boys and girls looked to ants as they busily laid provisions in store for future need. To see the perils of wanton living, young people watched a seduction unfold and followed it to its disastrous consequences. To recognize the dangers presented by excessive drinking of wine, they spied on a drunkard whose irrational conduct invited brutal

---

[2] Claus Westermann, *Roots of Wisdom*, 106 ("The portions of the text of Job that allude to wisdom do not justify our classifying the book of Job as wisdom literature"). Westermann views the book as a lament. The genre of the Book of Job remains the subject of much debate; its kinship with the Mesopotamian text titled *I will Praise the Lord of Wisdom* suggests that it may be a paradigm of an answered lament, but similarities with *The Babylonian Theodicy* point to dialogue. Only in Job among wisdom texts does one find a theophany.

[3] Hans-Peter Müller, "Magisch-mantische Weisheit und die Gestalt Daniels," *UF* 1 (1969) 79–94.

[4] Franz-Josef Steiert, *Die Weisheit Israels—ein Fremdkörper im Alten Testament? Eine Untersuchung zum Buch der Sprüche auf dem Hintergrund der ägyptischen Weisheitslehren* (FthSt; Freiburg im Breisgau: Herder, 1990), responds with a decisive no to this theory.

beatings. To acquaint themselves with the undesirable consequences of laziness, they watched unmotivated persons
sleep while their fields became unproductive. In short, if
these young people wished to learn how to cope with every
eventuality, they studied their environment and society at
large—rather than, like prophets, listening for a voice from
the deity.

Perhaps the difference between sages and prophets is
largely one of semantics.[5] Prophets also studied historical
events and the actions of individuals, especially powerful
members of society, before drawing conclusions about the
nature of the message they wished to proclaim. The difference, however, lies in their insistence that this word originated in divine speech. Precisely how that transcendent
message was mediated to prophets remains a mystery, unless
the claim of divine speech is a literary conceit entered into
for the purpose of legitimating the message. In that case,
the prophetic word originated in human concern and took
different forms depending on the prophet's disposition,
whether consoling or threatening.

The most extreme example of knowledge through strict
observation occurs in Ecclesiastes, where formulas for looking, observing, contemplating, concluding, and the like
pepper the book.[6] It appears that Qoheleth examined everything under the sun in the same objective manner, asking
what it actually contributed to human happiness and dis-
missing it as utterly futile. Nothing escaped his critical eye,

---

[5] I develop this idea in *Prophetic Conflict: Its Effect upon Israelite Religion* (BZAW 124;
Berlin and New York: Walter de Gruyter, 1971) 116–23.

[6] See especially my commentary, *Ecclesiastes*, and Michael V. Fox, *Qohelet and his
Contradictions* (JSOT SS 71; Sheffield: Almond Press, 1989) 79–96.

whether friendship or religious duty, and the threat of death rendered every conceivable bonus in life utterly meaningless.[7] At the same time, he spoke often of divine gifts, by which he seems to mean fate. Whatever befalls an individual does so as divine gift, and that bounty from above may be either desirable or undesirable. Moreover, its character, whether welcome or unwelcome, has no relationship to one's virtue or lack of it. This approach to knowledge led Qoheleth to profound skepticism, the doubting of everything.

This epistemological stance issued in a denial that anyone could attain the high prize of wisdom. Knowledge, yes, but not wisdom. This desirable entity was remote and deep, beyond human reach. Presumably, that judgment includes Qoheleth; in any event, he does not hesitate to challenge wise men who boldly claim to have discovered wisdom. Qoheleth does not mince words here; he simply denies the accuracy of the professional sage's boast. The fault lies with the human intellect, somehow flawed as a result of devious schemes (evil machinations). Refrains punctuate the skeptical teachings at their climactic moment; they assert that one "cannot know" or "find out" the truth. It necessarily follows that Qoheleth's assessments of reality also fall short of wisdom, although he must have thought that they constitute a resounding assault on a locked door.

In assessing Qoheleth's epistemology, Michael Fox reaches similar conclusions, although insisting that the author of Job 28, whom he takes to be Zophar, adopts an even more

---

[7] I discuss the impact of death on Qoheleth's thinking in "The Shadow of Death in Qoheleth," 205–16 in *Israelite Wisdom: Theological and Literary Essays in Honor of Samuel Terrien*, eds. John G. Gammie et al. (Missoula: Scholars Press, 1978).

radical stance toward the limits of reason. In his view, the problem of knowledge is central to the Book of Ecclesiastes, and *ḥokma* has two senses: (1) the human faculty of reasoning and (2) the content of knowledge itself. Qoheleth's epistemology is essentially empirical; he tries various things as a means of answering a philosophical question. Fox considers this seeking out experience as a path to insight a revolutionary procedure, and he observes that Qoheleth never invokes prior insight. Moreover, Qoheleth resorts to testimony as a type of argument, allowing rhetoric to enhance credibility. His use of experience as validation is, in Fox's words, "unique in Wisdom Literature."[8]

Fox claims that wisdom literature differs in this regard from Qoheleth. His argument that the sages are not appealing to experience when they invite others to observe ants and seductions in progress overlooks one important thing: the earlier stage when the teacher discovered knowledge in these happenings and recognized their value for communicating insights. Observable facts do teach a lesson; they functioned that way in the past for the teachers who now appeal indirectly to their own experience.

An important aspect of Qoheleth's epistemology is the role of the ego. Fox recognizes this introspective tendency on Qoheleth's part and comments on how it works in his teaching. Curiously, Fox notes, Qoheleth only occasionally concerns himself with the thoughts of others. Fox also believes that Qoheleth stopped short of suspecting all knowledge, especially his own, for he arrives at new insights—

---

[8] *Qohelet and his Contradictions,* 79–120. My view of Qoheleth's epistemology, "Qoheleth's Understanding of Intellectual Inquiry," is scheduled to be published in the volume devoted to the Biblical Colloquium at Leuwen, July 30–August 1, 1997.

e.g., that all is absurd. Fox understands this discovery to be wisdom as knowledge rather than wisdom as reason. Nevertheless, Fox thinks Qoheleth had self-doubts, unlike other sages. Qoheleth did not believe in an external wisdom; for him, wisdom was a matter of sight, whereas other sages understood wisdom as a matter of hearing. Fox writes that Qoheleth thought he could observe patterns of an unfolding future, but human ignorance was inevitable. The limits of reason are rooted in the nature of the world. In Qoheleth's view, speculation, although legitimate, is futile. An element of arrogance accompanies Qoheleth's readiness to judge all of reality.

At the other extreme, the author of Proverbs 8 believed that Wisdom existed as a separate entity, participating neither in the divine nature nor in the human. Nevertheless, its coexistence with the creator and its presence at that crucial juncture removes Wisdom from the human realm and places it alongside the divine. As one who informs the creator's design of the universe—or merely brings pleasure to the deity—Wisdom relates to the creator erotically, dancing in sublime presence. Likewise, she turns toward humans and woos them with both ardor and eloquence.

This symbolic language for the mutual quest for knowledge suggests that the author of this hymn believed that Wisdom actually took the initiative, pouring herself out to willing learners. Far from merely lying out there waiting to be discovered through human effort, Wisdom actively invites the young to participate in a feast of knowledge.

The matter was not quite so simple, however, for a rival vied with Wisdom for the minds of vulnerable youth, according to the sequel in Proverbs 9. Equally passionate and eloquent, this champion of Folly wreaks havoc among the young. Such abstraction of virtues and vices, and the accompanying personification of both, implies that the search for wisdom demanded more than mere observation and the resulting empirical verification. The claim that one is loved and pursued by a powerful paramour shifts the playing field from one of objective validation to subjective belief.

One possible way to accommodate both theories of knowledge seems to have occurred to the sages, who believed that the creator infused the universe with particles of wisdom and endowed human beings with an innate curiosity (Eccles. 3:11). The quest for knowledge thus became a kind of game, one characterized by "hide and seek." According to this understanding of the intellectual task, Wisdom yields to human inquiry, although divine initiative made this discovery possible.

Not everyone viewed this talk about an external wisdom in a positive manner. The author of the poem in Job 28 understood wisdom as an unknown and unknowable factor, in the same way Qoheleth emphasized its remoteness and profundity (ch. 7). A wisdom that obscures its essence so effectively that even mythic entities such as Sheol and Abaddon can only sniff out a rumor of its whereabouts offers no promise to desperate humans. What does it matter that God can see through the darkness engulfing wisdom, unless the deity communicates this secret to humankind? The editor who added verse 28 understood this fact and endeavored to undercut its cogency by defining wisdom as religious devotion, but in doing so robbed the entire poem of its point.

Perhaps that susceptibility to misuse motivated Qoheleth to remain silent about an entity called Wisdom existing apart from observable reality. Better still, his view of the creator as indifferent to human affairs naturally implied a corollary, that no heavenly courtesan openly yearned for human companionship. Qoheleth's tendency to be a loner had clear implications for his epistemology; in searching for the truth, he would rely on his own eyes and ability to reason things out without help from outside.

That approach to the pursuit of knowledge did not appeal to Ben Sira, who sought to resurrect the idea of an external reason. In doing so, he drew on mythic themes relating to the ancient story of the first human beings in the Garden of Eden, as well as those pertaining to the experience in the wilderness when the divine presence was thought to have taken the form of a pillar of cloud. The first of these themes recalls the mist that watered the arid ground and enabled YHWH to form life from the damp clay. The universal implications of this story lend themselves well to Ben Sira's intentions; he claims that divine reason settled like mist over all nations, imparting to them a capacity for intelligent discourse. Nevertheless, Ben Sira's generosity has limits; he insists that YHWH commanded Wisdom to take up permanent residence among the Israelites. Moreover, he asserts that this eternal intelligence ministered in the Temple at Jerusalem, and hence has priestly attributes.

As if responding to skeptical charges that Israel's intellectual heritage fell short of the rich Hellenistic legacy confronting youth in Ben Sira's day, this teacher waxes eloquent about the flourishing garden of delights that Wisdom makes available to the hungry. This remarkable source of delectable fruits and pleasing aromas is characterized as addictive; those who taste its abundance will hunger for more. Knowledge, that is, inevitably lures the intellectually curious into further pursuit.

Here, as in the poem about Wisdom's hiddenness in Job 28, an astonishing conclusion focuses all eyes on a convenient means of acquiring the desired quality. Ben Sira boldly identifies Wisdom with the Law of Moses, the product of divine presence in the wilderness. For the author of Job 28:28, Wisdom comes to those who faithfully serve YHWH; Ben Sira concurs in this sentiment, although he defines the means of demonstrating obedience much more fully. It consists of adhering to the teachings contained in a book. With this bold stroke of the pen, Ben Sira has pronounced closure on the intellectual quest.

Thus when the author of the third chapter of Baruch takes up this theme of a hidden Wisdom that took on palpable form for the benefit of Israelites, the overwhelming impression on readers comes close to déjà vu. This author plays all the familiar notes, adding little other than embellishments. The long duration of the Exile is attributed to the people's forsaking of the fountain of Wisdom, which then provides an occasion to stress her hidden nature—to former princes who now reside in Sheol; to young men, still ignorant but old enough to have children; to foreigners who are renowned for intellectual accomplishments; to giants of old; to anyone wishing to retrieve her from heaven or beyond the sea, offering gold in exchange for knowledge—and to insist that the creator alone has access to her, generously sharing her with Israel. Before identifying Wisdom with the Mosaic Law, the author introduces the curious notion that

Wisdom subsequently appeared on earth and dwelt among people, a statement evoking among later church fathers the idea of the incarnation.

This learned speculation about Wisdom did not reach a dead end with Ben Sira or the unknown author of Baruch, for it sets out in new directions once the language of discourse changes from Hebrew to Greek. The poet responsible for composing Wisdom of Solomon 7 attributes the educational curriculum to divine guidance through her intermediation. This extraordinary figure participates in the divine nature so fully that she is an emanation of divine glory. This poet does not hesitate to assert that Wisdom possesses all power, enabling her to pour herself out to holy persons and prophets. This claim amounts to saying that Wisdom and the spirit of inspiration are identical. Having gone that far, the author takes readers one step farther and insists that Wisdom consents to be the bride of special people, in the fiction of the book, King Solomon.

The externalization of divine reason in a written book has given way to subjective disposition. No longer does Wisdom exist outside the human mind; it has taken up permanent residence within humans. The corollary of such thinking exists in Stoic philosophy,[9] the external Logos having a counterpart in the human logos. The rational principle of the universe and human rationality relate to each other in

---

[9] David Winston, "Theodicy in Ben Sira and Stoic Philosophy," 239–49 in *Of Scholars, Savants, and their Texts*, ed. Ruth Link-Salinger (New York/Bern/Frankfurt am Main/Paris: Peter Lang, 1989), finds minimal influence of Stoicism on Ben Sira. Even when Ben Sira uses a Stoic expression, "He is the All," it does not presuppose the pantheon but an exclusive deity, YHWH. On the thorough embeddedness of The Wisdom of Solomon in Hellenism, see Winston, *The Wisdom of Solomon* (Garden City: Doubleday, 1979).

the deepest possible way. The aptest metaphor for their relationship is that of marriage, as the author of the Wisdom
of Solomon recognized.

This dynamic epistemology within the sapiential corpus
has a parallel in its attitude to the achievement of virtue.
Believing in the wise ordering of the universe by a benevolent creator, sages assumed that they possessed the capacity
to determine their destiny to a great degree. In this scheme
of things, deserving people received their rewards and unde-
serving persons paid the price for folly. After the inevitable
collapse of such optimism, the sages began to emphasize divine compassion for humankind because of its inability to
cope with life's crippling blows.[10] Once more individual initiative, however salutary, was judged inadequate in the face
of monumental hardship. The resulting piety, best seen in
Ben Sira, brought the sages closer to traditional Yahwism
than before.[11]

This rendering of the conflicts within canonical wisdom
may be overly temporal, for these tensions undoubtedly existed at all times. Scholarly depiction of the sages in terms
of an initial period of oral assessments of reality in family
settings, followed by professional tutelage at the royal court,
and finally consolidating its teachings in a scribal religious
setting may be accurate, but such a description hardly accounts for the openness to more than one way of viewing
things typical of the Books of Job and Ecclesiastes. According to Job, wisdom is restricted to deity, and religious

[10] Crenshaw, "The Concept of God in Old Testament Wisdom."

[11] Current emphases on personal piety in Egypt are matched by studies in biblical
religion. I have examined the growing emphasis on prayer in late wisdom ("The Restraint of Reason, the Humility of Prayer," 206–21 in *Urgent Advice and Probing Questions*).

people tap into its resources; moreover, human beings get what they deserve, but they must rely on divine compassion. For Qoheleth, the source of wisdom remains inaccessible, and human beings encounter an indifferent deity.

The resulting dispute over ancient epistemology should surprise no one today. To reiterate, did the sages believe that all knowledge derived from experience or did they presuppose some sort of revelation as the basis of all insight? Refusing to choose between the two options, they gathered evidence pointing to both kinds of knowledge. Through analogy they arrived at fundamental insights linking nature and society. In this important pursuit of the reason underlying the universe, the eyes and ears held sway, justifying the symbolic use of both organs of sight and sound. Nevertheless, some things refused to yield before persistent inquiry, for, like its vessel, reason is finite. Furthermore, every resourceful student knows moments of affective surprise when insights burst forth with dazzling brilliance like a gift from the unknown. That reality, too, needed to be acknowledged. By affirming the necessity for a predisposition to knowledge, an openness to mystery, the sages sought to overcome the restraints on reason.

The specifics on which this analysis rests reach considerably beyond the texts discussed thus far. The numerous proverbial sayings (*mešālîm*) extolling the ability of the intellect and the will contrast with the exquisite poem in Job 28 relegating *ḥokmâ* to its creator and the puzzling declaration that one can assess it through religious commitment. The pious acquiescence in Job 28:28 and possibly in Prov. 30:1–14 stand over against the denial in Ecclesiastes 7 that anyone really uncovers the mystery surrounding us all. Ben Sira's

warning against unbridled thoughts (3:21–23) finds a natural sequel in the more restrictive proscription against doubt
in the Wisdom of Solomon. The richness and diversity of
the sages' reflections on the intellectual task complicate every modern attempt to systematize their thought.

The proverbial sayings hold individuals accountable for
their actions as if volition naturally guarantees success, and
yet they introduce notable exceptions. Elohim's glory is to
conceal; a king's glory is to search out hidden matters, presumably in juridical contexts such as Solomon's supreme test
with an infant's life in the balance (Prov. 25:2). Searching for
wisdom like treasure will succeed, but only because YHWH
bestows it freely on worthy persons (Prov. 2:1–6). Moreover, those who rely on their intellectual capacity are fools,
for one's own insight often deceives (Prov. 3:5; 28:28). External advisers are even less reliable than it, with a single
exception, whom one ought to invoke through prayer (Sir.
37:13–14). Because the paths our feet tread are determined
by YHWH, no one can understand the deity's plan (Prov.
20:24).

One can reach farther afield to clarify the dynamic under
discussion, for religious leaders other than the sages also
came up against a similar phenomenon. Those who introduced the Mosaic statutes and urged Israelites to live by
them succeeded in emphasizing their accessibility without
detracting from divine authority. By distinguishing between
concealed truth (*hannistārōt*) and revelatory insights (*han-
niglōt*) they managed to restrict a body of knowledge while
at the same time claiming that specific legislation was available to everyone (Deut. 29:28). To discourage those who
reasoned that such priceless teaching was too wondrous

(*niplē't*) and remote (*reḥōqâ*), they insisted that the commandment (*miṣwâ*) was readily available, requiring no acts of heroism to bring it near (Deut. 30:11–14). The vocabulary differs from that employed by sages, specifically "word" (*dābār*) rather than "wisdom" (*ḥokmâ*), the verbs "to observe, keep" (*šāmar*) and "to do" ('*āsâ*) instead of "to find" (*māṣā'*), making it unlikely that this polemic belongs within the sapiential canon.[12] Similarly, prohibitions in Deuteronomy employ different language from that of parallel texts in the Book of Proverbs.[13]

An obvious explanation for the persistent reminder that the search for knowledge always encounters closed doors is human finitude, but more than that seems implied here. Modern interpreters usually suggest that the caveats were directed at speculation about the mysteries of the universe and certain magical means of using such information. Even this interpretation of the facts may point in several different directions, depending on whether one understands the secret things as mantic wisdom, apocalyptic speculation about heavenly journeys and angelic revelations, or philosophical probings within Hellenism.

One thing seems clearer today than in earlier studies: the use of experiential wisdom as the norm for interpreting sapiential texts is flawed, for both reason and revelation occupied important places in their thought—and not just within theological wisdom, with its elevation of religious obedi-

---

[12] Moshe Weinfeld, *Deuteronomy and the Deuteronomic School* (Oxford: Oxford University Press, 1972), has argued vigorously, although unsuccessfully, for an origin of Deuteronomy among the sages.

[13] I have examined the language for prohibitions in wisdom literature and pointed out these differences ("Prohibitions in Proverbs and Qoheleth," 115–24 in *Priests, Prophets, and Scribes*, eds. Eugene Ulrich et al. [Sheffield: JSOT Press, 1992]).

ence (*yir'at YHWH*) and mediatorial *ḥokmâ*. Older Egyptian Instructions, particularly *Anii*, and later maxims such as those in *Papyrus Insinger*, as well as *mešālîm* in Sirach acknowledge that a divine gift of understanding supplements human effort. Furthermore, they insist, true wisdom is attained only through embodiment of virtue, for which divine assistance is required. In short, a sage needed a gift from the deity to grasp the full meaning of information processed by arduous intellectual effort and to put knowledge to effective use.

Chapter Ten

⁓

Probing the Unknown:
Knowledge and the Sacred

"Study is one of the highest forms of worship, if not the highest."

TALMUD TEACHERS

An element of teasing characterizes some of the more interesting proverbial sayings in the Bible. That is certainly true of Prov. 25:2: "God's glory—to conceal something, but king's glory—to search out something." The plural *'elōhîm* refers to divine beings and nicely balances *melākîm*. The saying thus contrasts heavenly and earthly matters as they relate to the inhabitants of the two realms. Succumbing to this laconic teaser, the author of the aphorism in verse 3 endeavors to interpret the text but succeeds only in deepening the mystery: "The heavens for height, the earth for depth, and the mind of kings—unsearchable." We can only imagine the feelings associated with such assertions, whether reverential awe or resentful resignation. Context seldom illuminates ancient aphorisms, recent efforts to demonstrate the opposite notwithstanding.[1] The

[1] Hildebrandt, "Proverbial Pairs: Compositional Units in Proverbs 10–29," and Leeuwen, *Context and Meaning in Proverbs 25–27.*

principle of associated words, however, comes into play here in the immediate sequel of sayings about royalty (4–7). The first of these likens the removal of dross from silver to the eradication of wickedness from a king's presence; in both instances something valuable results, either a useful vessel or a throne founded on just dealings tinged with compassion. The second, couched in the form of an Instruction, advises against frequenting the royal court. The reason, expressed in a "this is better than that" formula, counsels a policy of "wait and see" in anticipation of an invitation to a place of honor rather than, having taken the initiative, being told in the presence of a prince to step down to a lesser seat.

If one understands the king's exploration of something in the light of juridical responsibility, the comparison between refining ore and removing injustice does throw light on the original aphorism extolling royal glory. Precisely by shifting through conflicting testimonies and arriving at the facts, monarchs earned a reputation for intelligence and were therefore honored by their subjects. Solomon's astute decision when confronted with rival claims to the sole surviving infant son of a prostitute dramatically illustrates this point.[2] Similarly, the additional acknowledgment of the unsearchable character of imperial minds necessitates caution when endeavoring to bask in royal prestige. The references to height and depth thus take on emotional tonalities for exaltedness and debasement. Because the king's mind defies knowing, prudent subjects wait for clear signals as to his disposition. The humiliation of demotion within a society

---

[2] Stuart Lasine, "The Riddle of Solomon's Judgment and the Riddle of Human Nature in the Hebrew Bible," *JSOT* 45 (1989) 61–86 understands this episode as a "law-court riddle."

characterized by honor and shame later gave rise to advice attributed to Jesus about the hazards of seeking the most honored seat in the house.

A juridical reading of the reference to rulers' searching out the unknown may not lead to its original sense. Once more the legends about Solomon come into play, this time his much-heralded search for vital insight about the world concealed within flora and fauna. Assuming that God's special honor consists in hiding information within the natural order, earthly rulers like Solomon devote their energy to discovering hidden norms by which to live. According to this understanding of reality, divine revelation presents itself in veiled form, becoming actualized as a result of effort by men and women. This synergy of transcendent concealment and creaturely discerning enables sages to adhere to a dialogic view of knowledge, as opposed to a one-sided emphasis on divine disclosure. In this view, the deity's hiding is calculated to generate human participation, personified in a royal search.

What did the sages think God concealed? Attention to the language of this aphorism about the different sources of honor enjoyed by God and kings indicates the ambiguity inherent in this text. The Hebrew word *dābār* occurs in each instance as object of infinitives denoting hiding and probing the depths. It can mean both "thing" and "word"; a homonym, *deber*, has a hostile meaning and denotes a plague. According to Psalm 19, the whole universe chants God's glory, but this hymnic praise proceeds without resort to audible words. Does the proverbial saying imply a similar worldview, a divine word awaiting human discovery and bringing honor to one, glory to another? Even a neutral

translation of *dābār* as "thing" cannot entirely escape this
sense of "word," for anything that removes the veil en-
shrouding transcendence has communicative power. Although the universe declares God's glory, it is mute for
those lacking a listening ear. Ancient sages in Israel and in
Egypt believed that attentive listening depended on syner-
gistic interplay between divine initiative and human response.

THE INTELLECTUAL POTENTIAL

The unknown author of the poem in Job 28 reflects on the
initiative from below, the unending—and in his view futile—search for wisdom. Success at locating precious gems
in the depths of the earth contrasts with utter failure to find
a treasure far more valuable, wisdom itself. Concealed from
human eyes and hidden from creatures of flight, wisdom is
known to the underworld only by word of mouth. God
alone has access to this treasure. Suddenly the text explodes
with the vocabulary of intellectual pursuit: God observed it,
discussed it, drew conclusions, and searched out its farthest
limits (v. 27). The ease with which God penetrates the mystery of the unknown contrasts with the difficulty encountered by all creatures, human and mythical. This point is
lost on the individual who added a consoling word: "He said
to humankind, 'Note well! The fear of the Lord is wisdom,
and departing from wickedness is understanding'" (v. 28).
Gone is the element of the unknown and unsearchable.

Wisdom now means religious devotion, pure and simple. As such it rests in the hands of everyone who desires to please God. Wasted on this enthusiast is the language of digging for hidden treasure, enchanting rumor, wisdom's place, a divine establishing, and heavenly heights. In short, the world of the imagination has vanished, and in its place stands a closed realm of accommodation, a readiness to rest contentedly, oblivious to the wonders awaiting intellectually curious seekers.

Whoever equated wisdom and piety would have felt ill at ease in Deuteronomic circles, if the following sentiment is normative: "Hidden things belong to the Lord our God, but revealed things belong to us and to our descendants into the distant future, to observe all the words of this Torah" (29:28). Here, however, the tension between the hidden and the revealed remains. Nevertheless, Israelites are thought to possess a priceless treasure, the words of divine instruction. With it in hand, they need not worry about what belongs exclusively to their God's realm. Indeed, they must not surrender to the human impulse to earn divine favor the old-fashioned way, demonstrating ardor by searching far and near for something that already resides in their minds and on their tongues (30:11–14). This prosaic text soars loftily when venturing into imagined discourse. Because the commandment is neither too awe-inspiring nor too distant, one need not ask, "Who will ascend to heaven and retrieve it?" Likewise, the divine word is not in foreign lands beyond the sea, however much you have heard stories about exceptional intellects among foreigners. A gracious God has given you everything you need to obtain life, and that treasure is not

far away but very near. Such an attitude rules out idle speculation about the hidden things, by their very nature unknown.

What a world removed from that of Qoheleth! In his
view, a remote deity placed something of dubious value in
the human mind (3:11), but at the same time the creator
fixed it so that none could discover that mysterious gift and
use it to advantage. Linguistic ambiguity interacts with semantic clarity in this famous crux. The creator takes back
with one hand what is given with the other. Every created
thing is either beautiful or appropriate in its time, and God
has put either a temporal sense or an awareness of life's enigmas in the mind, but God has also made humans incapable
of discovering divine activity from beginning to end, by
which is meant either from infancy to mortality or *A* to *Z*.[3]
Moreover, Qoheleth insists, the pursuit of wisdom inevitably fails, for it is remote and exceedingly deep so that none
can find it (7:23). Rational exploration only empowered him
to discover human perversion of facts through clever and
devious scheming.

The admiring author of the first epilogue to Ecclesiastes
described his mentor's intellectual journey: "Besides being a
sage and teaching the people knowledge, Qoheleth listened,
searched out, and arranged numerous sayings; he sought to
find pleasant expressions and faithfully wrote reliable
words" (12:9–10). The person assessing Qoheleth's educational achievement has breathed little of the skeptical air in

---

[3] The ambiguity derives from the word *h'lm*, which can be pointed in one way to
indicate a temporal reference and in another way to suggest hiddenness. In my judgment, the latter reading fits the context better than the former, although some critics
find no difficulty with a temporal meaning here. Another attractive solution requires
an emendation of the crucial word from *h'lm* to *h'ml*, yielding "burden-some task."

which the instructor lived. Nor is there the faintest hint of the ennui expressed by Qoheleth's foreign soul mate, Agur. Some readers understand his initial observation as something other than a declaration of atheism, but the ensuing confession of ignorance leaves room for no doubt (Prov. 30:1–4).[4] The simple statement "I have not learned wisdom nor do I know the holy one" speaks volumes, and this word is attributed to a representative of much vaunted foreign wisdom. Sarcasm prevails here, both in the rhetorical questions that deny human acquisition of secret knowledge and in the poignant barb "Surely you know." Here modesty has given way to poking fun at others who seem totally unaware of wisdom's hiddenness.

Humility with respect to intellectual prowess has engendered something entirely unexpected in the teaching of Ben Sira: a warning against pondering hard questions (3:17–24). Affinities with Deut. 29:28 (29, Eng) exist, but the Hellenistic environment in which Ben Sira lived gives force to the caveat against speculative reason. If by the clause "that which has been assigned to you" Ben Sira means to imply the revealed Torah, the kinship with Deut. 29:28 is even greater.[5] The larger issue remains; what kind of speculation did Ben Sira discourage? At least three answers commend themselves, and each depends on one's analysis of the intended audience. First, Ben Sira may have cautioned against an activity that has become associated with apocalyptic literature, specifically the exploration of hidden times of di-

---

[4] On this poignant expression of despair, see my article "Clanging Symbols," 51–64 in *Justice and the Holy*, eds. Douglas A. Knight and Peter J. Paris (Philadelphia: Fortress Press, 1989) and the references therein to an alternative view by Paul Franklin.

[5] Similar restriction of intellectual curiosity occurs in Egyptian wisdom.

vine action. Specialists who "knew the times" consulted previously hidden texts, boasted of receiving new revelations, and predicted coming events—with limited success. Their confidence in the revelatory power of dreams rested firmly on one branch of biblical tradition in Genesis and occasionally elsewhere, but Ben Sira's sober suspicion of dreams also has strong prophetic warrant, particularly in Jeremiah.

A second explanation for Ben Sira's restriction of scholarly curiosity takes its cue from the popularity of Greek philosophy in his day, especially Stoic teachers.[6] In this view, he advises against speculation about the nature of the creation and the activities of all the elements, in short, theogony and cosmogony. This reading of the text appears somewhat forced in the face of Ben Sira's own extensive remarks about the universe when discussing moral theory. In the realm of theodicy, as well as the related problem of free will, popular Hellenistic philosophy has greatly influenced Ben Sira's thoughts. The claim that theodicy for Ben Sira was essentially an anthropological issue rather than a theological problem depends on an implausible separating of the dual issues of free will and theodicy.[7]

The third understanding of Ben Sira's warning against exploring the unknown points to esotericism in certain social groups of the ancient world. Scribal elitism in Babylonia finds expression in colophons restricting some texts to select

---

[6] Martin Hengel, *Judaism and Hellenism*, vols. I–II (Philadelphia: Fortress Press, 1974), demonstrates the widespread impact of Greek thought on Jewish literature, although one suspects that some of this Hellenistic thought is quite superficial. Ben Sira definitely fell under such influence, as I discuss in *Sirach* (NIB, vol. V; Nashville: Abingdon Press, 1997).

[7] On this problem, see my article, "The Problem of Theodicy in Sirach."

readers.[8] Within prophetic groups in Israel a kind of esotericism surfaces, giving rise to a colophon in Hos. 14:9 about the truly wise reader who will grasp the (hidden) meaning. This sense of elitism surfaces in scribal texts from Egypt and Mesopotamia, becomes very much at home in Sirach and Qumran, and inspires apocalyptic writers like the author of 2 Esdras to distinguish between the twenty-four revealed Scriptures and those seventy sacred texts reserved for the wise (14:45–47). The high praise heaped on these hidden books—"in them is the spring of understanding, the fountain of wisdom, and the river of knowledge"—suggests the emotive power of this belief in an esoteric body of knowledge.

Ben Sira's allusion to things too difficult for his hearers recalls a remark in Ps. 139:6 ("Such knowledge is too wonderful for me; it is so exalted, I cannot fathom it"). The psalmist here celebrates the Lord's full knowledge of human subjects, a result of searching, and imagines that any attempt to escape divine surveillance would result in failure. The possible hiding places—heaven, Sheol, the sea, darkness—are deemed as present to this awesome Lord, whose intimate knowledge began at the moment of the psalmist's birth and will extend to the length of his allotted days on earth. The psalmist alludes to the belief that the Lord kept a scroll on which were inscribed the names of the faithful.[9] In a sim-

---

[8] Given the limited number of individuals possessing the ability to read cuneiform, these colophons represent an elite group within the elite. John Baines discerns the same distinction within Egyptian scribes, some of whom he calls the core elite, as opposed to the sub-elite ("Literacy and Ancient Egyptian Society," 574).

[9] Shalom M. Paul, "Heavenly Tablets and the Book of Life," *JANESCU* 5 (1973) 345–53.

ilar vein the author of Psalm 131 eschews pride and denies having been preoccupied with major issues and things beyond mortal ken ("things too wonderful for me," v. 1). This psalm of only three verses closes with a powerful image for calm, that of a weaned child with its mother.

In 2 Esdras the angel Uriel raises a voice for suppressing intellectual curiosity about supramundane affairs, while an insistent Ezra pushes for answers to earthly matters that might offer clues about deeper mysteries. Uriel's point hinges on an obvious failure among men and women to understand things pertaining to daily existence, from which he concludes that heavenly mysteries would naturally tax the brain excessively. The two disputants cannot agree about the domain of Ezra's queries, for he insists that they probe terrestrial matters like fire, wind, and past events. The angel's impossible questions concern the weight of fire, measure of the wind, and recovering a bygone day (4:5), all very much earth-centered and yet unanswerable. To illustrate the poverty of creaturely knowledge, Uriel raises the ante: "What if I had asked how many dwellings are in the heart of the sea . . . which are the exits of hell or entrances to paradise?" and prompts Ezra to utter a despairing complaint that it would have been better not to have been born than to live in a state of ignorance about the reason for suffering. The essential difference between this stifling of intellectual pursuit and Ben Sira's cautionary advice quickly leaps to the fore: this discouragement comes from a representative of the heavenly realm rather than from a teacher of flesh and blood.

The angel's challenge to Ezra on a second occasion calls

attention to the corollary of limited knowledge, namely an inability to solve impossible tasks like anticipating future population, recovering scattered raindrops, making withered flowers bloom again ... and showing a picture of a voice (5:36–37). Here we see full-blown apocalypticism probing the imponderables while discouraging such questioning, just one of many anomalies in this genre.[10]

The preceding survey of different attitudes toward the intellectual potential of ancient Israelite sages covers a wide spectrum of literature and diverse historical periods. To some extent one can assign optimistic views to earlier sages during the heady days of the monarchy, perhaps in the prosperous reign of Hezekiah (possibly even that of Uzziah). Historical events in the disastrous sixth century and their consequences generated a sober understanding of reality, one chastened by restrictions of various kinds. This awareness of limited horizons expresses itself in the dialogues within the Book of Job and in Qoheleth's reflections on the conditions of finitude. The subsequent resurgence of a hierocratic ruling class with the high priest Simon as its chief representative encouraged renewed optimism, this time carefully guarded by setting limits defined by religious tradition. Ben Sira breathed this liberating air, although making sure that dominant winds blew from only one direction. The remarkable growth of personal piety in this period of limited freedom and economic hardship has a parallel in an-

---

[10] On apocalyptic as more than a literary genre, see John J. Collins, *The Apocalyptic Imagination* (New York: Crossroad, 1984), "Early Jewish Apocalypticism," *ABD*, vol. 1, 282–88, and James C. VanderKam, *Enoch and the Growth of an Apocalyptic Tradition* (CBQMS 16; Washington: The Catholic Biblical Association of America, 1984).

cient Egypt.[11] The crisis associated with the Middle Kingdom gave rise to a strong sense of personal piety characterized by humility and submission. That religious attitude
eventually elevated the principle of fate above all else, particularly during the Ptolemaic period when *Papyrus Insinger*
and the *Instruction of Ankhsheshonqy* were written.

SOCIAL CONTEXT

Reconstructing the social context underlying ancient texts
is notoriously difficult, even when their dates of origin can
be ascertained with arguable plausibility.[12] Authors do not
necessarily describe their own historical setting, and frequently they create imaginary worlds for esthetic, ethical,
and apologetic purposes. Nevertheless, many texts provide
clues enabling readers to reconstruct the social worlds their
authors inhabit, at least to some degree. That observation
applies best to Sirach and Qoheleth, less so to Job and
Proverbs.

To whom did Ben Sira address his cautionary advice? His
sporadic use of the customary expression for addressee, "my
son," may be a literary conceit deriving from the Book of

[11] Jan Assmann, "Weisheit, Loyalismus und Frommigkeit," 11–72 in *Studien zu altägyptischen Lebenslehren*, eds. E. Hornung and Othemar Keel (OBO 28; Freiburg/Göt-
tingen: Vandenhoeck & Ruprecht, 1979).

[12] See the volume of essays edited by Ronald E. Clements (*The World of Ancient
Israel*). The key words in regard to establishing dates for ancient texts is "arguable
plausibility," for all such attempts employ circular reasoning, to some degree, and
depend on a reconstruction of developments in language and thought that may, or
may not, correspond with actual reality.

Proverbs, although some units appear to have been intended exclusively for students preparing for a career as professional scribes. Other sections of the book seem to have a broader clientele in mind;[13] a similar ambiguity characterizes the Book of Proverbs, where its anthological nature readily explains such differences in audience. The primary audience in the older proverbial collections consisted of children within a family setting, and later instructions were directed exclusively to young boys. The teachers included both fathers and mothers, although the male voice dominates. No woman joins Ben Sira in giving advice to young men, and a definite bias against daughters pervades his thinking.[14] The initial epilogue to Ecclesiastes identifies Qoheleth's hearers as the general populace rather than students preparing for a career as specialists in wisdom. Except for the second epilogue, this book lacks the usual expression "my son," even when indicating by other means that its hearers were males ("Enjoy life with the woman you love. . . ." 9:9; "Rejoice, young man, in your youth. . . ." 11:9).

In all this literature, a feminine voice clamors for attention, both directly and indirectly. In Prov. 31:1–9 a Queen Mother dishes out useful counsel to her son, Lemuel, the heir apparent if not reigning king, but this material is attrib-

---

[13] Oda Wischmeyer, *Die Kultur des Buches Jesus Sirach* (BZNW 77; Berlin and New York: Walter de Gruyter, 1995), provides a comprehensive analysis of the society in which Ben Sira carried out his teaching.

[14] Warren C. Trenchard, *Ben Sira's View of Women* (BJS 38; Chico, CA: Scholars Press, 1982), exaggerates the degree of misogynism in Ben Sira's teaching. Claudia V. Camp, "Understanding a Patriarchy: Women in Second Century Jerusalem through the Eyes of Ben Sira," 1–40 in *"Women Like This." Early Wisdom and Its Literature*, ed. Amy Jill Levine (Atlanta: Scholars Press, 1991) provides a more nuanced view.

uted to a foreigner.[15] Similarly, persuasive speech is placed
in the mouth of personified Folly, the foreign woman par
excellence, as well as that of her counterpart, personified
Wisdom. In addition, the masculine discourse never quite
escapes the presence of feminine consciousness, for re-
pressed fear and suppressed desire shape the conversation at
numerous points. The only truly missing voice is that of the
boys themselves, a situation that also occurs in Egyptian and
Mesopotamian wisdom literature, with the single exception
of the conclusion to the *Instruction of Anii.* Here the son,
Khonshotep, enters into lively dialogue with this father
about the rigors of living up to expectations and sees his
argument collapse before paternal authority.

Recent feminist interpretations of the Book of Proverbs
claim to recover a much greater feminine presence in dialogue than the facts warrant.[16] For example, they understand
the narrator in Prov. 7:6–27 as a mother warning her son
against the hazards of the strange woman. Moreover, they
think the association of mother with father in a few texts
within Prov. 1–9 calls into question the usual assumption
that the dominant voice in this collection is paternal. In
their view, mothers carried the brunt of education in a
child's formative years, hence the advice in these chapters
may derive from both mother and father. This effort to attribute more texts to feminine authors extends to the poem
in Eccles. 3:2–8, the well-known "time for everything."
Such readings have more heuristic value than intrinsic plau-

---

[15] This text stands alone among ancient Instructions in that its putative source is a
woman, somewhat surprising when one considers the fact that the teacher par excellence is given a feminine persona.

[16] Athalya Brenner, ed. *A Feminist Companion to Wisdom Literature,* and *On Gendering Texts: Female and Male Voices in the Hebrew Bible.*

sibility, and the frequent dependence on dubious interpretations of narratives about intelligent women renders suspect these efforts to recover women's voice. These interpreters fail to recognize that the adjective *ḥākām* in the oft-cited texts has nothing to do with a professional group of sages. The astute woman of Tekoa and the prudent mother in Abel, like Esther, Judith, and so many more Israelite women, did not belong to a class of sages. The family context implied in older proverbial collections suggests that a mother's instruction may indeed be embedded in some of these proverbial sayings, but this possibility has not yet been studied sufficiently.

One feature of the instructions in Prov. 1–9 suggests that the boys receiving teaching belonged to a low socioeconomic group. The frequency and fervor of the subject of laziness, missing from Egyptian Instructions with their targeted audience of prospective courtiers, arose from the very real danger of lapsing into poverty brought on by indolence.[17] The temptation to engage in highway robbery for fun and profit also points to young people with minimal financial resources and lacking sufficient patience to wait for an inheritance,[18] which would in all likelihood consist of a small plot of land and a few domestic animals. Ben Sira offers his hearers the prospect of upward mobility, within limits imposed by a priestly ruling class. A hierarchy consisting of ruler, priests, judges, physicians, scribes, and ordinary citizens existed in Ben Sira's world; the sages therefore en-

---

[17] Roger N. Whybray, *Wealth and Poverty in the Book of Proverbs* (JSOT SS 99; Sheffield: JSOT Press, 1990).

[18] Newsom, "Woman and the Discourse of Patriarchal Wisdom: A Study of Proverbs 1–9."

joyed some degree of honor and a modest standard of living just above peasants and holders of small tracts of land.

Their status did not protect sages from the allurements of the Hellenistic civilization, although it did minimize their vulnerability. By nature open to foreign ideas, they readily endorsed new concepts and practices. Ben Sira expects his listeners to attend Greek banquets and to enter into all aspects of this social ritual, such as serving as chief host, pronouncing an invocation to the gods, supervising the entertainment, and enjoying the reward of a wreath for effective service. Ben Sira adapts the Hellenistic notion of "friendship," uses Stoic teachings about the nature of free will in the context of divine justice, employs the language of Stoicism in ascribing everything to God, and selects freely from Greek epithets for the deity. He defends physicians and their medicines in the same manner some Greek writers did, even though submitting such radical views to traditional Hebraic ideas as well.[19] Ben Sira looked on Egyptian teachings with equal openness, both in describing the advantages of sages as opposed to rival professions and in endorsing some ideas that exist elsewhere only in *Papyrus Insinger*.[20] His praise of famous men has encomiastic features although the deeds he recalls are thoroughly traditional.[21]

[19] Lutz Schrader, *Leiden und Gerechtigkeit. Studien zu Theologie und Textgeschichte des Sirachsbuches* (BET 27; Frankfurt am Main: Peter Lang, 1994), applies traditional literary criticism to Sirach, finding evidence, he thinks, of late redaction. He does not discover *extensive* Hellenistic influence.

[20] Jack T. Sanders, *Ben Sira and Demotic Wisdom* (SBLMS 28; Chico, CA: Scholars Press, 1983), argues that Ben Sira actually knew and used *Papyrus Insinger*.

[21] Burton L. Mack, *Wisdom and the Hebrew Epic* (Chicago and London: The University of Chicago Press, 1985), and Thomas R. Lee, *Studies in the form of Sirach 44–50* (SBLDS 75; Atlanta: Scholars Press, 1986) view these chapters as an encomium (although Mack emphasizes Ben Sira's adaptation of this form), but their interpretation

Now if Ben Sira targeted a small group of students for professional assignments as scribes and ethical instructors, where did he carry out his responsibilities as mentor? On the basis of the reference to "my house of learning" (presumably *bet midraŝî* or *bet mûsarî*—the Hebrew of 51:23 has not been preserved and one must guess at the exact reading), commentators understand Ben Sira as a professional educator, although one cannot rule out the use of symbolic language in this familiar verse.[22] Astonishingly, writing plays virtually no role in the teaching of *Sirach*—or in biblical wisdom generally—and learning consists in listening to knowledgeable people talk. Nowhere does Ben Sira tell students to read written texts, although he advises them to keep an accurate record of business transactions in writing. The figure of Zenon, an official of the Ptolemaic empire in the third century, comes to mind. The vast archive of papyri that have survived indicates an obsessive accountant who seems to have kept a written record of every business transaction of his life.

Perhaps Ben Sira concurred in Plato's opinion that, like a painting, written words are forever mute even when addressed directly by a seeker desperate to grasp their import. Listening was the primary mode of learning for Ben Sira and Qoheleth, and having listened attentively they put their finished thoughts into written form. The elegant prologue to *Sirach*, composed in Alexandria by his grandson, asserts that

---

has been challenged by Chris A. Rollston, "The Non-Encomiastic Features of Ben Sira 44–50," M. A. Thesis, Emmanuel School of Religion, Johnson City, Tennessee, 1992.

[22] Fox, "The Social Location of the Book of Proverbs," 236 ("The passage [in which *bet midraŝ* occurs] concludes the book and recommends it to the reader. Through it, one may gain wisdom 'without money' ").

Ben Sira studied sacred texts, specifically the Torah, the Prophets, and the other writings. Numerous allusions in *Sirach* to biblical content confirm a familiarity with Jewish sacred literature, but such acquaintance could easily have come from participation in worship and from oral tradition.[23]

What prompted Ben Sira to stifle natural curiosity among bright thinkers? The larger context leaves little doubt that his concern was to encourage humility. Intellectual pride may not have been altogether missing from Hebraic literature, but the emerging ego in Hellenistic texts touched even conservative authors such as Ben Sira, who openly expresses the desire to be recognized by *name* as an author.[24] Contrary to much postmodern criticism, the notion of authorship is not a modern concept, but was very much at home in the Greek environment of the second century B.C.E. In Ben Sira, competing impulses rest uneasily: a zealous wish to fulfill divine commandments through ethical conduct and a hope to bequeath something of equal worth to the sacred tradition of his day. Religious duty lay at the heart of his teachings, and prayer crowned both intellectual achievement and works of righteousness. This discouragement of intellectual pursuit does not declare war against Hellenism; no such declaration of war exists in *Sirach*, despite sporadic skirmishes.[25] Traditional piety asserts itself here, one steeped in

[23] Literate individuals in antiquity read aloud (cf. Augustine's remark in *Confessions* 6, III, 3 that Saint Ambrose read in silence because he was never alone, possibly also to discourage others from interrupting his thoughts). Learned persons also read texts aloud in certain communal gatherings, the illiterate benefiting from their erudition.

[24] This desire to be known as an author is new to wisdom literature; on the place of the ego, see Peter Höffken, "Das Ego des Weisen," *TZ* 4 (1985) 121–35.

[25] Rudolf Smend, *Die Weisheit des Jesus Sirach* (Berlin: G. Reimer, 1906) 23, thinks that Ben Sira declared war against Hellenism, but Schrader, *Leiden und Gerechtigkeit*, 117, considers that view no longer tenable. I discuss the extensive influence of Hellenism on Ben Sira in *Sirach*.

a Deuteronomic view about the sufficiency of Torah for all of Israel's needs.

Ancient Mesopotamian mythic tradition found a place for tablets of destiny, powerful determiners of orderly existence in the hands of the gods. Stories about the pursuit of these secrets have survived the ravages of time.[26] In addition, Sumerian wisdom and its later manifestation in Akkadian and Babylonian texts was essentially magic, a premium being placed on human manipulation of the gods through knowledge and ritual. Naturally, this situation encouraged esotericism, the guarding of exclusive information for the benefit of a select group. To some extent, similar circumstances existed in ancient Egypt, where magical incantations flourished within a society deeply interested in the state of the dead.[27] Israelite literature certainly has residues of magical thinking, but these have been subjected to a dominant worldview inimical to magic. For this reason, the search for the unknown, and the effort to discourage such pursuits, had nothing to do with the wish to attain magical sources of power.

Perhaps something far more seductive than magic attracted Israel's sages and drew them into unaccustomed speculation. Several hints within poetic flourishes describing Wisdom as a feminine personification suggest a near equivalence of knowledge and the sacred. In some unspecified and unspecifiable sense, true wisdom participates in transcendence. To achieve wisdom therefore brings one into

[26] Foster, *From Distant Days*, incorporates this idea in the title of his translation of these texts. The story titled *Anzu, the Bird Who Stole Destiny*, recounts an attempt to use the tablet of destiny for personal benefit.

[27] Raymond O. Faulkner, *The Ancient Egyptian Book of the Dead* (New York: Macmillan Publishing Company, 1972).

direct contact with God. Jewish mystics coined the phrase "garments of Torah," an objective genitive describing the Torah as God's visible garment.[28] In this revelation of divine will the individual beholds God's outer clothing, an accommodation to human finitude akin to Yahweh's sheltering of Moses' eyes from looking on divine radiance, according to the sacred legend recorded in Exod. 33:17–23 and 34:1–7. A different view of the matter occurs in Exod. 34:27–35, where Moses talks with God face to face and emerges with an extraordinary radiance of countenance. Such self-disclosure assures divine presence at all times, rendering every attempt to search for hidden transcendence as ridiculous as a person carrying a torch and searching for the sun in the desert at midday.[29]

If a link once existed between knowledge and the sacred, why has it become severed in our time? As stated earlier, our thoughts and actions are subject to countless controls, all products of time and place: deliberate controls that have been formulated into written laws; norms, seldom committed to paper, that order our lives; latent controls that occupy the realm of the unconscious and shape conduct for both good and ill; cognitive controls resulting from rational observation and careful reflection; coercive or seductive controls wielded by powerful individuals or groups, often through monopolizing visual imagery, information, and products. The language we use shapes discourse and prior thoughts; our myths become the script from which we play

---

[28] Michael Fishbane, *The Garments of Torah: Essays in Biblical Hermeneutics* (Bloomington & Indianapolis: Indiana University Press, 1989).

[29] Seyyed Hossein Nasr, *Knowledge and the Sacred* (Albany: State University of New York Press, 1989) 152, uses this image.

out the drama of our daily existence and the ultimate truths before which we bow. The groups to which we belong, and those rejecting us or rejected by us, influence our ideas and behavior, as does our desire to be accepted and to avoid isolation. The level of access to desired goods and the anticipation of compensation for activity or punishment for behavior shape what we do and say.

Besides these influential forces that determine our thoughts and action, others exercise increasingly weighty control over our lives, particularly ethnicity and gender. At considerable risk of oversimplifying a vastly complex issue, one could say that Enlightenment European tendencies to think in terms of polarities, the careful juxtaposing of either/or possibilities, are currently under attack from Asians, who think of both/and, yin implying yang, and from African-Americans stressing concrete entities rather than universal absolutes.[30] Feminists, both male and female, add another important dimension, the relational, to cognitive thought. Familiarizing ourselves with competing ideologies both enriches and impoverishes, opening up fresh possibilities while heightening our interior Tower of Babel, the conflict resulting from the accumulative voices of our experience.

What does all this talk about controls have to say about Ben Sira's advice to be content with revealed knowledge? Precisely this: he believed in both freedom of the will and in divine determinism. Cognizant of the Greek ideal in his day, he counseled students to explore the vast unknown, to

---

[30] *Theological Education* 32 (1995) 1–98. This entire issue explores new understandings of theological scholarship.

make maximum use of their intelligence in the service of ethics. Believing in the adequacy of Israel's sacred tradition for ascertaining the divine will in matters having to do with ethics and religion, Ben Sira refused to relinquish this precious legacy—even at the price of respect in the Hellenistic world. Nevertheless, he recognized the necessity of reaching new understandings of the Torah, which opened the way for ever-new and unexpected interpretations. In this interaction of competing worldviews he seems to have discovered a happy combination, the marriage of human intellectual inquiry and divine disclosure.

CONCLUSION

From this vantage point, how does the aphorism about the divine inclination to conceal things and the royal predilection to search things out fare? It actually amounts to an understatement on both counts, for the biblical God conceals more than things and royal subjects accompany the king in the intellectual search. A significant tradition within the Bible broadens the intentional concealing to include transcendence, in some ways an astonishing view in light of the overwhelming emphasis elsewhere on divine disclosure. The revelatory one simultaneously hides, in effect each unveiling being accompanied by a veiling.[31] Every spoken word gives rise to more words, every answer to more questions. Even Job's final confession that immediate sight has

---

[31] Samuel Terrien, *The Elusive Presence* (New York: Harper & Row Publishers, 1978), and Samuel E. Balentine, *The Hiddenness of God.*

replaced the experience of the community ensues in additional ambiguity with respect to his own response to that unveiling. The prophetic concession "Truly you are a God who hides" (Isa. 45:15a) captures this insight in all its pathos and mystery. This hiding means that no revelation is final and absolute, but that the essence of deity mandates a concealing of ultimate reality.

Similarly, the search for the unknown, wider by far than royal sport, occupies the human mind from birth to death. The disclosure from above and search from below eventuate in a celebration of a union between knowledge and the sacred, a *hieros gamos*. This desire for oneness, more powerful than the wish to reunite severed genders in the myth of Androgenes—according to which Zeus hurls a lightning bolt at the less-than-agile Androgenes, separating Zeus's hapless victim into male and female—invigorates the intellectual task, giving its language a liveliness and playfulness that enables thinkers to live in the face of mute words bearing witness to the silence of eternity.

Conclusion

In the ancient Near East education preceded literacy and arose as an effort to create an orderly society characterized by a kind of utilitarian morality. The primary teachers in this community were parents, and the home provided a natural setting for their instruction. Indirectly, the entire adult population contributed to moral training, for parents used communal insights, often formulated in maxims, to persuade their children that the teachings had wider sanctions than that of the individual household. Although such education occurred at home, it was eventually complemented by special guilds which sought to perpetuate a monopoly on certain skills. Over time, guilds associated with temples and the royal court became dominant, opening up their training to a few outsiders as the need for more scribes and clerks increased.

Literacy grew out of a system of accounting that developed symbols with commonly acknowledged values. A system of signs with phonetic values made literary communication possible, but this form of writing had limited clientele. The discovery of an alphabet led to considerably wider communication, although no positive correlation exists between the simplicity of writing and literacy. Few people could read and write in Egypt and in Mesopotamia, and extensive training was required for those core-elite scribes. In Israel a rural population and agricultural demands discouraged formal schooling, and few inducements to learning existed here or in neighboring states. That situation did not change until a combination of factors came together quite recently: the invention of the printing press, the Protestant insistence on reading the Bible, the Industrial Revolution, which created a need for trained workers, the invention of eyeglasses, urban living, available materials for writing, and increased philanthropy.

Those most interested in education were sages, and their central concerns were knowledge and religion. These two themes intersect from beginning to end, although personal piety waxed and waned. Magic was central to the wise in Egypt and Mesopotamia, less so to biblical sages. Teaching was both direct and indirect, hortative and hypothetical. Teachers used instructions, with both positive and negative sanctions, and proverbial sayings, along with deeply philosophical reflections and personal observation. Their literature contains a high degree of self-promotion, and with the possible exception of grim reality with respect to divine injustice and the suffering of the innocent, it describes an ideal world rather than the one they actually occupied.

Formal settings for education existed in Egypt and in Mesopotamia, normally in temples or at the royal court. Biblical evidence for schools is meager, and epigraphic data change the situation only slightly. Although formal schools probably existed in Judah from the eighth century on, the small quantity of scribes needed for carrying on the official affairs of state and commerce, as well as writing everyday documents, could have been trained by a couple of scribal guilds. The demands of correspondence in foreign languages may have necessitated governmental schools.

Students learned by observation, that is, empirically. By examining nature and human society, they drew conclusions and formed analogies between different realms. In their view, the deity planted the secrets of living within an orderly universe and left it to humans to discover these formulas for living. Furthermore, they boasted that a special figure, neither fully divine nor human, mediated divine knowledge to them. In a rare moment, one sage even has the deity appear in a tempest, and like a teacher asked impossible questions. For these sages, both piety and fate were quite real.

Because of the numerous vocational options in Egypt and Mesopotamia, students were often reluctant learners. The military offered more excitement and better pay, women of the night posed an alluring alternative to study, and many other vocations allowed one to be in the open air. The scribes describe this inner conflict in considerable detail, only once letting a student's voice be heard. Teachers responded to students' resistance with harsh beatings and with idealized glorification of the scribe's profession.

In the literature preserved by sages, the dominant voice is that of a parent, usually the father. A father/teacher addresses a son/student in an endless series of imperatives, exhortations, and threats. That voice does begin to crack, for within the ranks some individuals challenge revered tradition and undercut the very institution. The biblical Job and Qoheleth demonstrate the extent to which biblical wisdom exercised self-criticism.

The vocabulary for educational achievement centers on verbs of seeing and hearing, the sage being known in Egypt as "the hearer." Several texts within biblical wisdom contain clusters of verbs describing the intellectual process, and this phenomenon suggests that sages were by no means epistemologically naive. Curiously, the verb "to write" rarely occurs in this literature, and sages placed emphasis on discourse rather than on reading texts and learning from them.

Nevertheless, in the ancient Near East a few texts gradually gained such popularity that they came to be used by students as they learned to read and write. Such canonical texts dealt with mythic topics in a sublime way and demonstrated the literary craft at its best. By copying them, students gained the requisite skills and broadened their intellectual horizons at the same time. Some biblical texts may have functioned like this, particularly Job and Qoheleth.

Given the many years of training required to become a competent scribe in the ancient world, one could hardly object if this accomplished individual took all the credit for such effort. For some reason, however, certain scribes insisted that they could not have attained such knowledge apart from divine assistance. Perhaps their familiarity with effective surprises, which strike researchers when they least expect them, gave rise to this humble acknowledgment. Clearly, the pious strain of thought that emerged in Egypt during the Middle Kingdom and eventuated in fatalism opened the door for such humility.

As the emerging fatalism implies, students also came up

against closed doors, the restraint of reason. Regardless of how valiantly they assaulted them, the doors remained securely shut. The sages encountered mystery, as well as certain areas deemed "off limits." The combination of unknowable and unknown was vexing, but it did not drive scholars into madness—perhaps because they found themselves involved in a love affair with knowledge itself. In their minds, this intellectual pursuit was nothing short of sacred.

ABBREVIATIONS

AB	Anchor Bible
ABD	Anchor Bible Dictionary
ABRL	Anchor Bible Reference Library
AnBib	Analecta Biblica
ANET	*Ancient Near Eastern Texts Relating to the Old Testament*, James B. Pritchard, ed., 3rd ed. Princeton, NJ: Princeton University, 1969
BEATAJ	Beiträge zur Erforschung des Alten Testaments und des Antiken Judentums
BET	Beiträge zur biblischen Exegese und Theologie
BETL	Bibliotheca Ephemeridum Theologicarum Lovaniensium
Bib	*Biblica*
BJS	Brown Judaic Studies
BT	The Babylonian Talmud
BZAW	Beihefte zur Zeitschrift für die alttestamentliche Wissenschaft
BZNW	Beihefte zur Zeitschrift für die Neuentestamentliche Wissenschaft
CB	Century Bible
CBC	Cambridge Bible for Schools and Colleges
CBOTS	Coniectanea Biblica Old Testament Series

CBQMS	Catholic Biblical Quarterly Monograph Series
ET	English Translation
FthSt	Freiburger Theologische Studien
HUCA	*Hebrew Union College Annual*
IRT	Issues in Religion and Theology
JANESCU	*Journal of the Ancient Near Eastern Society of Columbia University*
JAOS	*Journal of American Oriental Society*
JBL	*Journal of Biblical Literature*
JEA	*Journal of Egyptian Archaeology*
JNES	*Journal of Near Eastern Studies*
JSOT	*Journal for the Study of the Old Testament*
JSOT SS	Journal for the Study of the Old Testament Supplement Series
MHUC	Monograph of Hebrew Union College
MT	Masoretic Text
NCB	New Century Bible
NIB	New Interpreter's Bible
OBO	Orbis Biblicis et Orientalis
RSR	*Religious Studies Review*
SBLDS	Society of Biblical Literature Dissertation Series
SBLMS	Society of Biblical Literature Monograph Series
TS	*Theological Studies*
TUMS	Trinity University Monograph Series
TZ	*Theologische Zeitschrift*
UF	*Ugarit-Forschungen*
VT	*Vetus Testamentum*
VTS	Vetus Testamentum Supplement
WMANT	Wissenschaftliche Monographien zum Alten und Neuen Testament
YHWH	The Tetragrammaton, or sacred name of Israel's God (often pronounced Yahweh)
ZAS	*Zeitschrift für Ägyptische Sprache und Altertumskunde*
ZAW	*Zeitschrift für die altestamentliche Wissenschaft*
ZDMG	*Zeitschrift der deutschen morgenländischen Gesellschaft*

SELECTED BIBLIOGRAPHY

Baines, John. "Literacy and Ancient Egyptian Society," *Man* 18 (1983) 572–99.

Blenkinsopp, Joseph. *Wisdom and Law in the Old Testament. The Ordering of Life in Israel and Early Judaism.* Oxford: Oxford University Press, 1995.

Bolle, Sara Denning. *Wisdom in Akkadian Literature: Expression, Instruction, Dialogue.* Leiden: Ex Oriente Lux, 1992.

Brown, William P. *Character in Crisis. A Fresh Approach to the Wisdom Literature of the Old Testament.* Grand Rapids: William B. Eerdmans Publishing Company, 1996.

Brunner, Hellmut. *Altägyptische Erziehung.* Wiesbaden: Otto Harrassowitz, 1957.

——. *Die Weisheitsbücher der Ägypter: Lehren für das Leben.* Zurich: Artemis, 1988.

Crenshaw, James L. "Education in Ancient Israel," *JBL* 104 (1985) 601–15.

——. *Old Testament Wisdom.* Atlanta and London: John Knox Press & SCM, 1981.

——. ed. *Studies in Ancient Israelite Wisdom.* New York: Ktav, 1976.

——. *Urgent Advice and Probing Questions: Collected Writings on Old Testament Wisdom.* Macon: Mercer University Press, 1995.

Davies, Graham I. "Were there schools in ancient Israel?" *Wisdom in*

Ancient Israel, eds. John Day, Robert P. Gordon, and H.G.M. Williamson. Cambridge: University Press, 1995, 199–211.

Demsky, Aaron. "Education in the Biblical Period," *Encyclopedia Judaica*, vol. VI, cols. 382–98, Jerusalem, 1971.

———. "Literacy," *The Oxford Encyclopedia of Archaeology in the Near East*, ed. Eric M. Meyers. New York and Oxford: Oxford University Press, 1997, vol. III, 362–69.

———. "On the Extent of Literacy in Ancient Israel," *Biblical Archaeology Today: Proceedings of the International Congress on Biblical Archaeology, Jerusalem, April 1984*, ed. Janet Amitai. Jerusalem, 349–53.

Daedalus. Spring, 1975. *Wisdom, Revelation, and Doubt. Perspectives on the First Millennium B.C.*

Dürr, Lorenz. *Das Erziehungswesen*. Mitteilungen der Vorasiatesägyptischen Gesellschaft 36/2. Leipzig: J. C. Hinrich, 1932.

Foster, Benjamin R. *From Distant Days: Myths, Tales, and Poetry of Ancient Mesopotamia*. Bethesda, MD: CDL Press, 1995.

Fox, Michael V. "The Pedagogy of Proverbs 2," *JBL* 113 (1994) 233–43.

———. *Qohelet and his Contradictions*. JSOT SS 71. Sheffield: Almond Press, 1989.

Gadd, Cyril J. *Teachers and Students in the Oldest Schools*. London: University of London, 1956.

Gammie, John G. and Perdue, Leo G., eds. *The Sage in Israel and the Ancient Near East*. Winona Lake: Eisenbrauns, 1990.

Goldin, Judah. *Studies in Midrash and Related Literature*, eds. Barry L. Eichler and Jeffrey H. Tigay. Philadelphia, New York and Jerusalem: The Jewish Publication Society, 5748=1988.

Golka, Friedemann W. *The Leopard's Spots: Biblical and African Wisdom in Proverbs*. Edinburgh: T. & T. Clark, 1994.

Haran, Menahem. "On the Diffusion of Literacy and Schools in Ancient Israel," *VTS XL. Congress Volume, Jerusalem, 1986*. Leiden: E. J. Brill, 1988, 81–95.

Harris, William V. *Ancient Literacy*. Cambridge and London: Harvard University Press, 1989.

Heaton, E. W. "Memory and Encounter: An Educational Ideal," *Of Prophets' Vision and the Wisdom of Sages. Essays in Honor of R. Norman Whybray on his Seventieth Birthday*, eds. Heather A. McKay and David J. A. Clines. JSOT SS 162. Sheffield: Sheffield Academic Press, 179–91.

———. *The School Tradition of the Old Testament*. Oxford: Oxford University Press, 1994.

Hermisson, Hans-Jürgen. *Studien zur israelitischen Spruchweisheit*. WMANT 28. Neukirchen-Vluyn: Neukirchener, 1968.

Jamieson-Drake, David W. *Scribes and Schools in Monarchic-Judah. A Socio-Archaeological Approach*. Sheffield: JSOT Press, 1991.

Kaplony-Heckel, Ursula. "Schüler und Schulwesen in der Ägyptischen Spätzeit," *Studien zur altägyptischen Kultur* 1 (1974) 227–46.

Klostermann, August. "Schulwesen in Alten Israel," *Th. Zahn Festschrift*. Leipzig: A. Deichert (A. Böhme), 1908.

Kraeling, Carl H. and Robert M. Adams, eds. *City Invincible. A Symposium on Urbanization and Cultural Development in the Ancient Near East*. Chicago: University of Chicago Press, 1960.

Kramer, Samuel Noah. *The Sumerians*. Chicago and London: University of Chicago Press, 1963.

Lambert, W. G. *Babylonian Wisdom Literature*. Oxford: Clarendon Press, 1960.

Landsberger, Benno. "Scribal Concepts of Education," *City Invincible*, 94–123.

Lang, Bernhard. "Schule und Unterricht im Alten Israel," *La Sagesse de l'Ancien Testament*, ed. Maurice Gilbert, BETL 51. Gembloux: Duculot, 1979 (Revised, 1990) 186–201.

Lemaire, André. *Les écoles et la formation de la Bible dans l'ancien Israël*. OBO 39. Fribourg: Editions Universitaires; Göttingen: Vandenhoeck & Ruprecht, 1981.

———. "Writing and Writing Materials," *ABD*, vol. VI, 999–1008.

Lichtheim, Miriam. *Ancient Egyptian Literature*, vols. I–III. Berkeley: University of California Press, 1973–80.

———. *Late Egyptian Wisdom Literature in the International Context. A Study of Demotic Instructions*. OBO 52. Freiburg and Göttingen: Universitätsverlag and Vandenhoeck & Ruprecht, 1983.

———. *Maat in Egyptian Autobiographies and Related Studies*. OBO 120. Freiburg and Göttingen: Universitätsverlag and Vandenhoeck & Ruprecht, 1992.

Mendelson, Alan. *Secular Education in Philo of Alexandria*. MHUC. Cincinnati: Hebrew Union College Press, 1982.

Millard, Alan. "An Assessment of the Evidence for Writing in Ancient Israel," *Biblical Archaeology Today*, 301–11.

Murphy, Roland E. *The Tree of Life. An Exploration of Biblical Wisdom Literature*. New York et al.: Doubleday, 1990.

Niditch, Susan. *Oral World and Written Word. Ancient Israelite Literature*. Louisville: Westminster John Knox Press, 1996.

Otto, Eberhard. "Bildung und Ausbildung in Alten Ägypten," *ZÄS* 8 (1956) 41–48.

Pearce, Laurie E. "The Scribes and Scholars of Ancient Mesopotamia." *Civilizations of the Ancient Near East*, vol. IV, ed. Jack M. Sasson. New York: Charles Scribner's Sons, 1995, 2265–2278.

Perdue, Leo G. *Wisdom and Creation. The Theology of Wisdom Literature*. Nashville: Abingdon Press, 1994.

Perdue, Leo G., Bernard Brandon Scott, and William Johnston Wiseman, eds. *In Search of Wisdom. Essays in Memory of John G. Gammie*. Louisville: Westminster John Knox Press, 1993.

Puech, Emile. "Les écoles dans l'israël préexilique: Donées épigraphiques," *VTS Congress Volume, Jerusalem, 1996*, 189–203.

Rad, Gerhard von. *Wisdom in Israel*. Nashville: Abingdon Press, 1972.

Shupak, Nili. *Where can Wisdom be found? The Sage's Language in the Bible and in Ancient Egyptian Literature*. OBO 130. Fribourg and Göttingen: University Press and Vandenhoeck & Ruprecht, 1993.

Sjoberg, A. W. "The Old Babylonian Edubba," *Sumerological Studies in Honor of Thorkild Jacobsen on His Seventieth Birthday*, ed. S. Lieberman. AS 20. Chicago: University of Chicago Press, 1975, 159–79.

Weeks, Stuart. *Early Israelite Wisdom*. Oxford Theological Monographs. New York and Oxford: Clarendon/Oxford University Press, 1994.

Wente, Edward. "The Scribes of Ancient Egypt," *Civilizations of the Ancient Near East*, vol. IV, 2211–2222.

Westermann, Claus. *Roots of Wisdom. The Oldest Proverbs of Israel and Other Peoples*. Louisville: Westminster John Knox Press, 1995.

Whybray, Roger N. *The Intellectual Tradition in the Old Testament*. BZAW 135. Berlin and New York: Walter de Gruyter, 1974.

INDEX OF AUTHORS

Adams, Robert M., 15
Albertz, Rainer, 63, 192
Alster, Bendt, 54
Amenemope, 221
Aristotle, 45, 48, 115
Arzt, Max, 5, 11
Assmann, Jan, 266
Astell, Ann W., 165

Baines, John, 18, 30, 32, 40–3, 263
Balentine, Samuel E., 172, 182
Barclay, William, 3, 11
Barré, Michael L., 112
Baurain, Cl., 31
Ben Yohai, Simeon, 9
Bergler, Siegfried, 69
Black, Jeremy A., 89
Blenkinsopp, Joe, 4, 61
Bolle, Sara Denning, 51–2, 150,
    155, 202
Bonner, Stanley F., 44
Bonnet, C., 31
Boström, Lennart, 180, 197, 227
Botterweck, G. Johannes, 216
Bream, H. N., 168
Brenner, Athalya, 190–1, 268
Brown, William P., 1
Brueggemann, Walter, 2, 87

Bruner, Jerome S., 27, 152, 184
Brunner, Hellmut, 5, 22
Bryce, Glendon E., 95, 173
Buccellati, Giorgio, 51, 151, 236
Bühlmann, Walter, 177

Camp, Claudia, V., 267
Carlston, Charles E., 169
Carpenter, Eugene E., ix
Clements, Ronald E., 182, 266
Clifford, Richard J., 66
Collins, John J., 66, 176, 265
Crenshaw, James L., 2, 5, 51, 58,
    63–4, 66, 69, 75, 89, 97, 103,
    112, 130, 156, 173, 178, 182–4,
    189, 192, 200–1, 213, 215, 219,
    231, 236, 241–3, 249, 252, 261–2,
    272
Crossan, John Dominic, 156
Crüsemann, Franz, 61, 63, 124, 192

Davies, Graham I., 5, 34, 88, 97,
    104–5, 110–1
Day, John, 5
Day, Peggy L., 162
Demsky, A., 5
Di Lella, Alexander A., 171
Diodorus, 45, 48

Drazin, Nathan, 4
Dürr, Lorenz, 4–5

Eichler, Barry L., 3
Enheduanna, 17
Epicurus, 51, 205
Euripides, 47

Falk, Marcia, 165
Falkewitz, Robert Seth, 155
Faulkner, Raymond O., 273
Fensham, F. C., 189
Fewell, Danna Nolan, 235
Fiddes, Paul, 172
Fishbane, Michael, 274
Fontaine, Carol R., 191
Foster, Benjamin R., 17, 56, 273
Fox, Michael V., 55, 61, 96, 108–9,
    165, 225, 228, 241–4, 271
Franklin, Paul, 261
Freedman, David N., 89
Frymer-Kensky, Tikvah, 18, 179

Gadd, C. J., 15, 19–20
Gamaliel the Elder, 8
Gammie, John G., 16, 178, 242
Gardiner, Sir Alan, 145
Garelli, Paul, 141
Gilbert, Maurice, 5
Gitin, Seymour, 212
Goldin, Judah, 3, 9–10, 156–7, 175,
    179
Golka, Friedemann, W., 5, 86, 93,
    187–8
Good, Edwin M., 222
Gordis, Robert, 178
Gordon, Robert P., 5
Goshen-Gottstein, M. H., 140
Gracian, Baltasar, 7
Greenberg, Moshe, 182, 194–5
Gunn, David Miller, 235
Gutiérrez, Gustavo, 224

Hadley, Judith M., 69
Hanson, Paul D., 140
Haran, Menahem, 36, 96, 101–2
Harris, Rikvah, 16
Harris, William V., 43–4, 47, 168,
    179

Hayes, John H., 58
Heaton, E. W., 5, 90
Heim, R. D., 168
Hengel, Martin, 262
Herford, R. Travers, 175
Hermisson, Hans-Jürgen, 5, 177
Herodas, 48
Herodotus, 41, 47
Hildebrandt, Ted, 231, 255
Hillel, 9
Hipparchus, 46
Höffken, Peter, 272
Hoffman, Yair, 222
Hornung, E., 266
Humphreys, W. Lee, 96

Jamieson-Drake, David W., 5,
    110–1
Jeremias, Jörg, 192
Jerome, 6
Jongeling, K., 22
Josephus, 6
Joshua, Rabbi, 239

Kahn, Jack H., 225
Kalugila, Leonidas, 173, 189, 226
Kaplony-Heckel, Ursula, 25
Keel, Othemar, 266
Klostermann, August, 4
Knight, Douglas A., 183, 261
Koch, Klaus, 183
Kolarcik, Michael, 193
Kraeling, Carl H., 15
Kramer, Samuel Noah, 15, 116–7,
    148, 199
Krings, V., 31

Lambert, Wilfrid G., 56, 119, 153
Lang, Bernhard W., 5, 69, 182
Laqueur, R., 118
Lasine, Stuart, 256
Lee, Thomas R., 270
Leemhuis, F., 22
Leeuwen, Raymond C. van, 231
Lemaire, André, 5, 89, 100–1, 103
Levenson, Jon D., 65, 140
Levine, Amy Jill, 267
Lichtheim, Miriam, 7, 53, 145–7,

149–50, 160–1, 164, 166, 176, 181, 200, 231
Lindenberger, James M., 55, 166–8, 172, 201, 233
Link-Salinger, Ruth, 248
Lohfink, Norbert, 189, 212
Long, Burke O., 75

Machinist, Peter, 211
Mack, Burton L., 180, 270
Mack-Fisher, Loren R., 86, 178
Mazar, Amihai, 31, 38
McBride, S. Dean, 140
McKane, William, 54
Mendelson, Alan, 11, 14
Mendenhall, George, 168
Merikare, 85
Miles, Jack, 189–90
Millard, Alan R., 31, 37
Miller, Patrick D., Jr., 140
Moore, C. A., 168
Morris, Nathan, 4
Müller, D., 226
Müller, Hans-Peter, 240
Murphy, Roland E., 69

Nasr, Seyyed Hossein, 181, 185, 274
Neusner, Jacob, 140
Newsom, Carol, 161–2, 193, 222, 269
Niditch, Susan, 99
Nöldeke, T. H., 172

Ogden, Graham, 227
Oppenheim, A. Leo, 141
Otto, Eberhard, 22

Pardee, Dennis, 32
Paris, Peter J., 183, 261
Parker, Simon B., 99
Paterson, John, 3
Paul, Shalom M., 263
Pearce, Laurie E., 15
Perdue, Leo G., 16, 64, 153, 178
Perlitt, Lothar, 192
Person, Raymond F., 233
Pfeiffer, Egon, 227
Phaleas of Chalcedon, 48

Pherecydes, 46
Philo, 11–14
Plato, 29, 45, 48
Pritchard, James B., 54
Puech, Emile, 101

Rad, Gerhard von, 51, 87, 111, 178, 200
Rainey, Anson F., 86
Rankin, Orvid S., 239
Ray, J. D., 85
Reese, James M., 174
Reinick, G. T., 22
Ringgren, Helmer, 216
Rollston, Chris A., 271

Sanders, Jack T., 170, 270
Sappho, 45
Sasson, Jack M., 15, 235
Schmandt-Besserat, Denise, 30
Schmid, Hans Heinrich, 146
Schmidt, W. H., 233
Schotroff, Willi, 61, 124
Schrader, Lutz, 270, 272
Scott, Bernard B., 64
Scott, R.B.Y., 239
Selms, A. van, 92
Seow, Choon-Leong, 124
Sheppard, Gerald T., 226
Shupak, Nili, 24, 93, 109, 191, 205
Simpson, William Kelly, 147
Skehan, Patrick W., 171
Smend, Rudolf, 272
Snaith, John G., 171
Socrates, 29
Sokoloff, Michael, 212
Stegemann, Wolfgang, 61, 124
Steiert, Franz-Josef, 240
Steussy, Marti, 235
Swift, Fletcher H., 4

Tait, W. J., 89
Terrien, Samuel, 179, 276
Tigay, Jeffrey H., 3
Trenchard, Warren C., 267
Trible, Phyllis, 235
Tsevat, Matitiahu, 216

Ulrich, Eugene, 252

VanderKam, James C., 176, 265
Vanstiphout, Herman, 22, 30
Velde, H. Te, 22

Washington, Harold C., 24, 95
Weeks, Stuart, 5, 102, 106, 200
Weinfeld, Moshe, 183, 234, 252
Wente, Edward F., 18
Westermann, Claus, 61, 180, 187–8,
    240
Wheeler, Barbara, 141–2
Whybray, R. Norman, 5, 61, 178,
    197, 230–1, 269

Williams, James G., 158
Williams, Ronald J., 22, 55
Williamson, H.G.M., 5
Willis, John T., 215
Winston, David, 174, 248
Wischmeyer, Oda, 267
Wiseman, William J., 64
Wolff, Hans Walther, 154
Wolters, A., 232

Zeno, 8
Zevit, Ziony, 212
Zimmerli, Walther, 178
Zuckerman, Bruce, 223

INDEX OF SUBJECTS

Abecedaries, 33–4, 62, 101–3
Agricultural economy, 39, 280
Alphabet, 9, 30, 33, 37, 39, 86, 90, 100–1, 106, 280
Aphorisms, *see* sayings
Apocalyptic speculation, 252, 261–5
Authorship, 62

Ben Sira, *see* Sirach

Canaanite wisdom, 85–6, 161
Clan-wisdom, 62
Controls, 184, 274
Court wisdom, 62
Creation, 64–6, 120, 128–30
Creator, 2, 57, 61, 66, 71, 82, 128–9, 244, 250, 260
Creed, 124–7

Daughter, *vii*, 17
Debate formula, 74
Deir-el-Medinah, 24
Deuteronomy, 35, 39–40, 230, 233–4, 252, 259, 273
Dialogue, 20, 51, 55–6, 60, 150–1, 225

Ecclesiastes, *see* Qoheleth
Egyptian wisdom, 26, 64, 67, 75, 109, 198, 261, 268
Elitism, 16, 40, 43, 63, 68–9, 171–2, 178, 262–3
Eloquence, 2, 177–8, 230
Encyclia, 11–14
Entertainment, 34, 74–5
Epistemology, *viii*, 73, 242–3, 246, 249–50
Eroticism, 70, 179–80, 202, 244
Ethical wills, 3
Examinations, 48, 73
Expository teaching, 27

Family, 24, 86–7, 93, 180, 189
Fate and Fortune, 160, 242
Father, 1, 3, 10, 16, 19, 147, 150, 153–4, 156–7, 159, 161–3, 170, 187–9, 199–200, 268, 281
Fear of the Lord, 66–7, 223, 227
Female sages, 190–1, 269
Feminine voice, 267–9
Folly, personified, 124, 131, 180, 196–7, 245, 268
Foreign woman, 4, 78, 131, 268

Gezer calendar, 94, 105–6
Greek banquets, 270

Hearing, 126, 150, 153–5, 174, 213, 244, 271, 282
Heated person, the (hot-tempered), 24, 72, 109, 191
Hellenization, 235, 246, 248, 252, 261–2, 270, 272, 275
Hezekiah, 107, 232, 265
History, 41
Humility, 72, 185, 261, 266, 282
Hypothetical instruction, 27, 280

Imaginary speech, 194–9, 201–2, 259
Inscriptions, 30–1, 38, 42, 46, 62, 89, 100–8
Instructions, 23, 25, 27, 42, 52–4, 56, 58–9, 61–2, 95, 123–5, 132, 136, 163–4, 188, 199, 201, 209, 221, 230, 253, 256, 268–9

Job, Book of, *ix*, 27, 37, 55–6, 61–3, 66, 74, 76, 88, 111, 125–8, 130–1, 133–4, 159, 162, 172, 183, 192, 207, 210, 214, 216–7, 222–5, 234, 237, 239–40, 245, 247, 249–50, 258, 265–6, 276–7, 282

Learning process, 115–30, 167, 211–2
Letters, 32, 46, 74, 101–4
Libraries, 21, 47, 89
Limitation of knowledge, 24–5, 42, 62
Lists (onomastica), 25, 42, 62
Literacy, *vii*, 18, 20–1, 36, 39–49, 63, 279–80
Literature, forms of, 22, 43, 52

Magic, 12, 21–2, 26, 30, 32, 42, 76, 110, 153, 273, 280
Mesopotamian wisdom, 26, 58, 64, 109–10, 240, 268
Misogynism, 267
Moral formation (character), 1, 23, 71–3
Mother, 1, 10, 144, 189, 268–9

Myth, 27, 33, 42, 56–7, 65–6, 68, 221, 246, 273

Numerical sayings, 137

Orality, 40, 86, 88–9, 93, 153, 155, 236
Ostraca, 37–8, 90, 101, 104, 232

Papyrus, 22, 30, 37, 45, 48, 89, 236
Paradox, 167–8, 175, 184–5
Passions, mastery of, 13, 24, 52, 73, 152, 158, 164–5, 191
Pedagogy, 90, 94, 118–9, 130–8
Philanthropy, 44, 49
Philo, 11–14
Physicians, 17–18, 269–70
Pictorial reliefs, 41
Prayer, 9, 17–18, 24, 33, 61, 182, 185, 272
Principle of order (*Ma'at*), 24, 57, 59, 70, 109, 145, 196–7
Proverbs, Book of, *ix*, 4, 54–5, 58, 62, 74, 86, 90, 95, 97, 130–3, 162, 172, 206, 210, 226, 229–33, 244–5, 252, 266–9
Punishment, corporal, 81, 117, 147–9, 165–7, 170, 203, 208, 281

Qoheleth (Ecclesiastes), *ix*, 27, 54–7, 62–5, 72–3, 88, 111, 130, 136, 160–2, 165, 170, 172, 183, 191–3, 202, 210, 212–3, 215, 222, 225–8, 237, 241–6, 249–50, 260–1, 265–7, 282

Rhetorical strategies, 130–1, 133–7
Riddle, 52, 55, 58–9, 116, 138, 155–6

Sacred, 181, 255, 272–4, 283
Sayings, 9, 25, 27, 52–6, 58, 62, 64, 67, 86, 132, 157–8, 174, 209, 230–3, 240, 250–1, 253, 255–6, 279–80
Schools, *viii*, 15, 19, 23, 40, 44, 61–2, 74, 85–113, 188, 221, 229–32, 234, 280–1
Scribes, *viii*, 15, 19–24, 29–31,

35–6, 38–43, 77, 85–8, 98–9,
107–8, 111–2, 142, 146–9, 151,
221, 235–7, 269, 271, 279, 281–2
Seal impression (bullae), 38
Seeking and finding, 214–5, 245
Seven Sages, 20, 155, 175–6
Shame, 79, 165–6, 198, 257
Silence, 14, 24, 72
Sirach (Ben Sira), *viii–ix*, 18, 54–5,
57, 61–2, 70–2, 76–7, 86, 98, 109,
112, 123, 126–8, 130, 162, 166,
169–82, 192, 202, 207, 210, 213,
217–9, 222, 228–30, 237, 246–50,
261–7, 269–72, 275–6
Skepticism, 2, 14, 24, 119, 146,
207, 242, 260–1
Social setting, 21, 62, 124, 266–76
Solomon, 40, 76, 107, 110, 131,
176, 203, 248, 251, 256–7
Son, *vii*, 17, 23, 42, 47, 81, 144,
147–8, 150, 153–4, 156–7, 161–3,
165–6, 169, 187–8, 199–200, 268,
281
Stages of life, 6–7, 164
Statements of truth, *see* sayings
Stoics, 8, 248, 262, 270
Symbol, 26, 29–30

Tablets of Destiny, 20, 57
Teachers, 9–11, 15, 19, 24, 27, 44,
48, 72, 87, 89, 106, 108, 117–20,
122, 130, 133, 135–7, 145–6,
148–9, 161–2, 188, 200–1, 205–8,
221, 243, 279, 281
Theodicy, 53, 55–7, 65, 110, 223–4,
262, 280
Torah, 8–9, 71, 162, 175, 228–9,
261, 272–4, 276

Veiling, divine, 256–8, 275–7
Virtues, four cardinal, 129

Wisdom, personified, 65, 69–70,
74, 109, 115, 118, 128–9, 131,
171–3, 180, 196–7, 217, 244–8,
268, 273
Wisdom of Solomon, *ix*, 14, 55, 64,
70, 77, 129, 167, 179, 182, 192,
203, 248–9, 251
Women, instruction of, 168–9, 179,
267
Wooden tablets, 37, 45

Zenon, 48, 271

INDEX OF SCRIPTURAL REFERENCES
AND OTHER TEXTS

HEBREW BIBLE AND APOCRYPHA

Genesis	234, 262
12:6	206
12:8	107
26:8	190
26:22	107
Exodus	
32:15–16	35
33:17–23	274
34:1	35
34:1–7	274
34:27–28	35
34:27–35	274
Numbers	
6:24–26	38
Deuteronomy	233–4, 252
5:22	35
6:4–9	9
6:9	39
12–26	230
29:29 (MT 28)	218, 251, 259, 261
30:1–14	129–30
30:11–14	183, 252, 259
31:12–13	6
Judges	
5:28	190
7:1	206
14	58
Ruth	234–5
2 Samuel	
6:16	190
13:13	202
15:1–6	193
16:15–17:23	77
1 Kings	
4:29–34 (Heb. 5:9–14)	75
10:8	107
2 Kings	
9:30	190

10:1–6	6
18–20	107
1 Chronicles	234
5:13	207
25:8	209
27:32	6
Ezra	112
Nehemiah	
8:7–8	6
Esther	269
Job	
4:8	134
4:12–17	135
4:17	128
5:9	216
5:9–16	61
5:27	134
6:5–6	135
7:8–10	135
8:8	216
8:8–10	133, 207
9:5	107
9:5–10	61
9:10	216
10:6	214
11:7	216
11:12	136
12:7–9	136
12:20	134
12:25	134
13:1–2	134
13:26	210
15:5	207
15:7	134
15:10	134
19:23	210
19:26	36
20:3	135
28	57, 217, 242, 245, 247, 250, 258
28:23	217

28:27	217, 258
28:28	247, 250, 258
31	76
32:15	107
33:14–18	135
33:33	208
34:24	216
35:11	206
36:26	216
38:16	216
42:5–6	223
42:6	224
Psalms	65
14:1	192
19	257
37	55
49	55
53:1	192
73	55, 126, 128
94:12	207
119:99	99
119:108	207
131	264
131:1	264
139	215
139:1–4	214
139:6	263
139:23–24	214
145:3	216
Proverbs	
1	181
1–9	4, 179, 189, 196, 268–9
1:1–7	153
1:6	59
1:6–19	132
1:8	153
1:10–19	161
1:11–14	193
1:20–33	196
2:1–6	251
2:6	181
2:16	78–9

3:3	98, 210	20:25	195
3:5	251	21:9	191
3:11–12	208	21:19	191
3:19	197	22:17	154
4:1	154	22:17–24:22	96, 109,
4:3–4	137		154, 188
4:3–9	199	22:17–21	94–6
4:5	97	22:29	96
4:7	97	23:22	96
4:13	173, 214	23:23	97
5:1	154	23:29–35	194
5:7	154	24:29	194
5:7–14	232	25:1	77, 107
5:11–14	197	25:2	56, 172,
5:12–14	187		251, 255
5:13	208	25:2–29:17	108
5:20	79	25:2–29:27	108
6:6–11	133, 190	25:3	216, 255
6:20–35	123, 132	25:4–7	256
6:24	79	25:14	121
7–9	54	25:24	191
7:3	98, 210	25:27	216
7:4	202	26:4–5	122
7:5	79	26:14	121
7:6–23	189	27:8	121
7:6–27	268	27:15	121, 191
7:22–23	122	28:26	207
7:24	154	28:28	251
7:24–27	189	30:1–4	129, 261
8	196, 244	30:1–14	183,
8–9	181		231, 250
8:22–31	197	30:7–9	61
9	197, 244	30:8–9	195
9:13–18	132	30:15–16	122, 194
9:17	124, 197	30:18–19	120
10:1–22:16	108	30:18–20	190
13:24	81	30:20	194
14:10	177	30:29–31	137
14:12	136	31:1–9	189,
14:13	177		231, 267
16:1	80	31:10–31	190
16:32	191	31:27	232
17:3	121	31:29	195
17:16	97		
18:15	215		
18:23	122	Qoheleth	
19:21	80	(= Ecclesiastes)	
20:14	194	3:2–8	190, 268
20:24	251	3:6	215

3:11	57, 215, 245, 260	32:33	207
4:6	137	Lamentations	
7	245, 250	1	102
7:6	121	2	102
7:23	213, 260		
7:24	213	Ezekiel	68–9,
7:25	212		198
7:27	212		
7:28	212, 245	Daniel	240
8:1	156, 213	1–6	235
8:17	215	1:3–20	99
9:9	267		
11:1	79	Hosea	198
11:5	160	14:9	263
11:9	267		
12:1–7	82	Amos	201, 233
12:9–10	213, 260	3:3–8	94
12:10	177, 210	3:7	218
12:13–14	227	4:6–11	94
Song of Songs	202	Jonah	235
Isaiah	37, 65, 196, 201	Habakkuk	37, 235
1:2	4	2:2	36
8:3	4		
8:16	36	Zechariah	233
10:19	36		
28:6	206	Judith	235, 269
28:9ff	4		
28:9–13	90–2	Wisdom of Solomon	
28:23–29	93, 206	1:16–2:20	192
28:26	94, 206	1:16–2:24	162
29:12	36	3:14	167
36–38	107	6:17–20	174
38:9	107	7	248
40:4	171	7:7	181
40:28	216	7:17–22	14–15
45:15	277		
50:4–11	92	Sirach (= Ben Sira)	
55:1–2	97–8	1	181
		1:2–3	59
		1:26	182
Jeremiah	68, 99, 235, 262	3:2	199
		3:17–24	218, 261
23:29	69	3:20	198
31	183	3:21	219
31:33	210	3:21–23	251
32:12	36	3:23	219

5:3	215	51:23–25	98
6:18–37	170	51:28	98
6:22	171		
6:24	171	1 Esdras	
6:27	173, 213	3–4	235
6:33–37	174	3:1–4:41	75
7:22–23	121		
8:6–9	174	2 Esdras	235, 264
8:9	175	4:5	264
9:10	121	5:36–37	265
10:30	178	14:45–47	263
11:3	121		
11:19	195		
12:12	170	NEW TESTAMENT	
13:3	122		
13:26	170	Matthew	
14:20–27	182	7:7	173
15:2	179		
20:4	167	Mark	
20:12	137	3:31–35	167
20:16	195		
21:15	176	Luke	
22:10	195	12:13–21	195
22:16–17	177		
23:18	194	1 Corinthians	
24	181	3:1–3	200
27:2	121		
27:6	177		
29:26–28	194	DEAD SEA SCROLLS	
30:1	81, 170		
30:20	167	11QPsa	207
33:3	153		
33:17	178		
34:1	123	OTHER JEWISH AND	
37:13–14	251	CHRISTIAN TEXTS	
37:14	178, 207		
38:22	191		
38:34	18, 182	Aboth (*Sayings of Fathers*)	
39:1–3	59	II	8–9
39:32	210		
40:28	80	Aboth de Rabbi Nathan	
42:7	211	5	6–7
44:5	211		
45:11	211	Epistle of Aristeas	75
48:10	211		
51:13–30	182	Gezer calendar	94
51:17	207		
51:23	*viii*, 171,	Makkot, B.T.	
	271	102, 11	175

Pirke Aboth   175, 201
  5:13   7
  5:18   7
  5:21   10

Sayings of Ahiqar, The   55, 77,
                                166–8,
                                203, 231
  Saying 4   81
  Saying 34   233
  Saying 50   163
  Saying 76   163
  Saying 109   201

Teachings of Silvanus, The   160

**TEXTS FROM EGYPT,
MESOPOTAMIA, AND
RAS SHAMRA**

Admonitions of Ipuwer, The   55

Ankhsheshonqy   53–4,
                                62, 146,
                                164, 266
  19:10   79
  26:24   80

Atrakhasis   221

Babylonian Theodicy, The   56, 150,
                                156,
                                224, 240

Book of Amduat   68

Book of the Dead   55

Book of Gates   68

Book of the Heavenly Cow   68

Book of Kemit   221

*Colloquy between a
  Monitor and a Scribe*   148, 198

*Complaints of
  Khakheperresonb, The*   176

Counsels of a Pessimist   54

Counsels of Sube'awilum   161

Counsels of Wisdom   54,
                                154–5

Counsels to a Prince   54

*Dialogue between a
  Master and his Slave, A*   56, 75,
                                156

*Disputation between
Enkimansi and
Girnishag, The*   148, 198

*Dispute of a Man with
  his Ba*   55, 60,
                                150

Enuma elish   221

Gilgamesh Epic   221

Harper's Songs, The   55

Instruction of Amenemope   109,
                                188, 231
  3:9–10   153
  19:14–17   80
  22:17–24:22   54
  31:1–10   54

Instruction of Anii   67, 78,
                                144–5,
                                150–3,
                                157–61,
                                181,
                                185,
                                188,
                                199–200,
                                253, 268

Instruction of Khety   77, 173,
                                221

Instruction of Suruppak	54, 188	10	163
		16	164
I Will Praise the Lord of		17:19	79
Wisdom	56, 76,	24	160
	223, 240	32:7	160
Old Man and the Young		*Papyrus Lansing*	81, 147,
Girl, The	83		149,
			158, 165
Papyrus Anastasi	131		
I	73	*Papyrus Sallier*	
IV	146	I, 6:9–7:9	146
IV, 9:4–10:1	147		
V	146	*Protests of the Eloquent*	
V, 8:1–9:1	147	*Peasant, The*	55, 159
V, 9:2–10:2	147		
		Ptahhotep	82,
Papyrus Chester Beatty IV	179–80		153–4,
			167,
Papyrus Insinger	53–4,		188, 198
	58, 146,		
	159–60,	*Schooldays*	148, 198
	164–9,		
	181,	*Scribe and His Perverse*	
	185,	*Son, A*	147, 199
	199,		
	253,	*Sumerian Man and His*	
	266, 270	*God, The*	56